Teachers United

Teachers United

The Rise of New York State United Teachers

Dennis Gaffney

State University
of New York
Press

Published by
STATE UNIVERSITY OF NEW YORK PRESS
ALBANY

For information, address
State University of New York Press
194 Washington Avenue, Suite 305, Albany, NY 12210-2384

Production, Susan Geraghty
Marketing, Fran Keneston

Except for quotes taken from secondary sources, any writing in direct quotes
was recorded by me and was edited as little as possible for clarity and gram-
mar. In cases where people recalled conversations to me, the text was para-
phrased, and it appears in dialogue form without quotations. All the photos
used in this book were provided by NYSUT, except those that were gracious-
ly provided by Lynn Costello, Frances Brown, and Bob Allen.

Library of Congress Cataloging-in-Publication Data

Gaffney, Dennis, 1959–
    Teachers united : the rise of New York State united teachers / Dennis Gaffney.
        p. cm.
    Includes bibliographical references and index.
    ISBN 978-0-7914-7191-3 (hardcover : alk. paper)
    1. Teachers' unions—New York (State)—New York. 2. Teachers—New York (State)—
New York. I. Title.

LB2844.53.U62N74 2007
331.881'13711009747—dc22
                                                            2006032874

10   9   8   7   6   5   4   3   2   1

For my parents,
Walter and Anne Gaffney,
and my brother Walter,
all teachers.

CONTENTS

Acknowledgments   ix

Introduction   1

PART I. BEGINNINGS

1 Radical Roots: The Rise of the United Federation
   of Teachers   7

2 Teacher Militancy in the 1960s   29

3 Entering the Political Fray: The Jerabek Attack   49

PART II. GROWING UP: THE MERGER

4 Planting the Seeds of Unity   67

5 Merger Negotiations Begin   77

6 The Concord Convention: From Two Enemies,
   One Union   97

7 A National Merger?   115

8 Coming Apart   135

PART III. MATURITY

9 Wielding Political Power 155

10 Educational Reform 181

11 International Solidarity 203

Conclusion 215

Appendix 219
    Teacher Groups and Their Acronyms 219
    NYSUT Officers, 2006 220
    Former NYSUT Officers 223
    NYSUT Board of Directors, 1973–2005 226

Notes 231

Selected Bibliography 251

Index 257

ACKNOWLEDGMENTS

I imagine that writing a book is akin to taking an around-the-world trip on a sailing ship: the obstacles are formidable, the trip takes longer than expected, and you can't complete the journey without a competent crew. I wouldn't trade my crew for any other.

I'd like to begin by recognizing those who began this project prior to my involvement, including Tom Hobart Jr., who has diligently pursued the gathering of NYSUT's history for nearly two decades. I'd also like to thank Dorothy Fennell, who produced an oral history of NYSUT that created a treasure trove that I visited repeatedly. I'd also like to recognize Claudia Shacter-deChabert, whose thesis paper, "A History of the New York State United Teachers: The Merger Story," provided a rich map and resource for the middle chapters of this book. I am grateful, too, for the librarians who guided me in my primary research, especially Thomas Dickson, Assistant Archivist at the Archives & Records Center at the United Federation of Teachers; Richard Strassberg and Patrizia Sione at the Kheel Center for Labor-Management Documentation and Archives, part of the Catherwood Library at Cornell University, where NYSUT's historical records are stored; and Dan Golodner, AFT Archivist at the Walter P. Reuther Library at Wayne State University.

I want to give special thanks to Joan Cassidy, NYSUT's research librarian, who often pointed me to essential resources before I knew I needed them. I couldn't have had a more competent librarian as my guide. She was my de facto personal research assistant, and she never made me feel that I was a nuisance, although I'm sure I was. I was also lucky to have Bob Carillo as my point person at NYSUT, who was always friendly, capable, and efficient in steering this book to port. The union is lucky to have him—and so was I. Tony Bifaro also stepped in at key times to keep the ship on course. And for all they did to make the sailing smooth, thanks to so many who were helpful at NYSUT, including Betsy Sandberg, Ian Hughes, Maureen Casey, Brian O'Shaughnessy, Ben Frisbie, Joan Nauman, Ellen Haskell, Paula Boughtwood, and Kathleen Graham.

For fear of leaving many teachers and other unionists out, I'd like to acknowledge those who opened up their lives and shared their memories, including Antonia Cortese, Paul Cole, Walter Dunn, Herb Magidson, Jean Lux, Bob Allen, George Altomare, Lynn Costello, John DeGregorio, Vito DeLeonardis, Sylvia Matousek, Doug Matousek, Ken Deedy, Dick Rowley, Alan Lubin, Carol Slotkin, Kathleen Donahue, Nat LaCour, Rachel Moyer, Chuck Santelli, Fred Nauman, Eric Chenoweth, Karen Anderson, Fernando Leiva, Camila Leiva, Dan McKillip, Eadie Shanker, Robert Paliwodzinski, Elaine Sanders, Frances Brown, Monserrat Banda Arteaga and the other Mexican teacher unionists, and Walter Tice. Unfortunately, for the sake of brevity and readability, many who made key contributions to NYSUT are underrepresented on these pages. One short book cannot accommodate so many contributions. My apologies.

Special thanks to my readers and writing advisors as well, who helped me turn what often felt like a mound of chaos into an ordered narrative. My friends David Pettie, Peter Blaustein, David Luberoff, Alain Jehlen, and Caroline Chauncey not only provided guidance on the page, they provided support and encouragement that kept the ship from getting stuck in the doldrums. My friend and neighbor Christopher Ringwald provided assistance at numerous major and minor junctures along the way, and he freely shared his many book-writing talents to make my first trip easier. Dan Golodner, Paul Grondahl and Rick Kahlenberg also gave me sound advice on my preliminary manuscript that improved this book. I learned lifelong writing lessons from each of them. I'd also like to thank Bill Zinsser, a teacher who cared enough to put me on the path to writing well.

Everyone who reads this book also should be grateful to my editor, Kate Cohen, who deftly turned a lengthy manuscript into a compact book. She put far more than polish on the story and the prose, employing enviable writing skills. Thanks as well to the people at the State University of New York Press. Editors Lisa Chesnel and James Peltz helped provide this important story with a safe port from which to sail. Finally, it was my wife, Kathy Ray, who encouraged me in this project, listened to my struggles, and helped me solve numerous storytelling problems. She also worked as a meticulous editor. Both she and my daughter, Sophia, also reminded me to laugh and live during the hard stretches of this book. Thank goodness.

INTRODUCTION

My brother was a public school teacher in New York City, my father taught at a community college, and I'm an adjunct professor at the University at Albany, so when I began writing this book I assumed that I understood what teachers and their unions do. Teachers taught, I thought; unions negotiated salaries and benefits.

But the more I researched the history of the New York State United Teachers (NYSUT), the more I realized how uneducated I was. My first surprise was to discover the condition of the teaching profession in the 1950s, before New York's teachers had unionized. Although they viewed themselves as professionals, they were little more than hired hands. They were told how to teach, and the books they used and the size of their classes were considered none of their business. They were not even allowed a lunch break—they had lunch duty. They were paid with a pinch of prestige and a jigger of pity; one salary comparison of the day placed their incomes below those of car washers, which made moonlighting and summer jobs unwritten requirements of the job. Teachers were a disorganized bunch—over one hundred teacher organizations tripped over each other in New York City alone—and they were powerless.

My next surprise was to learn what New York teachers had risked to become a union. I assumed that miners and steelworkers in some distant past had risked their lives and their livelihoods to unionize, but not teachers. I was wrong again. On November 7, 1960, New York City teachers went out on strike, igniting what would become a nationwide teachers' movement, one of labor's greatest successes of the last half-century. As the day approached, school administrators had told those who walked picket lines that they would be fired. Older teachers, many with over a quarter of a century behind them in the classroom, were warned that they would lose every penny in their pensions if they walked. Still, a few thousand teachers took to the streets. "If that's not courage," asked one teacher, "what is?"

I also imagined that a united teachers' union evolved naturally, but in fact NYSUT was hardly inevitable. In 1972, New York City unionists

1

and upstate teachers were divided by nearly all the things that can divide people. New York City teachers looked down on Upstate Hicks; upstate teachers looked down on City Slickers. Unionized urban teachers thought of nonunionized suburban and rural ones as naïve; nonunionized ones thought of unionized ones as stooges. Such prejudices were inflamed by the two national teachers' organizations—the National Education Association and the American Federation of Teachers—that had spent a half-century trying to destroy each other. But against such odds, the state's two bickering teachers groups, led by Tom Hobart and Albert Shanker, the greatest educational activist of the last fifty years, managed to join together to become one union allied with organized labor.

I also assumed that New York teachers had always been political players. But before teachers formed NYSUT, state politicians often politely ignored teachers. And most teachers disdained politics; they believed their job began and ended in the classroom. But when state legislators, led by an assemblyman named Charles Jerabek, assaulted teachers in the early 1970s, teachers learned that what goes on in the halls of schools is often decided in the halls of power. Teachers entered the political fray—and New York's politicians now court teachers, knowing that a NYSUT endorsement will win them funds, legitimacy, and something even more important: the support of a small nation of men and women who vote and make phone calls, knock on doors, and write letters for the people and causes they believe in. Since NYSUT was formed in 1972, two U.S. senators and two New York governors— all underdogs at the time they were endorsed by teachers—have publicly credited the union with their victories.

Political power, like economic power, is often seen as corrupting. But the measure of power is what is done with it. Through their union, teachers have lifted themselves out of poverty and entered the middle class. Through their union, teachers have demanded more of themselves, creating substantive training programs and higher professional standards for teachers. And through their union, teachers have reformed education in New York, helping the state's children achieve standards as high as any. NYSUT's members have even taken their ideals abroad, fighting for labor, human rights, and democracy in places like Poland, South Africa, and Mexico.

This book is a history, but it's also a collective biography of the many people in a union and how they have faced many challenges—to win dignity, earn a decent living, improve the education of our children, and to help improve the daily lives of workers all over the world. Along the way, the people in NYSUT have created something else: a community.

"The union is like an extended family," says Walter Dunn, a long-time NYSUT activist and a former vice president of the union. "We've been through all the same battles together. There's a kinship. The union movement calls each other brothers and sisters. We use the word *solidarity*, and it's not just a term. It's a feeling people have of being connected with each other." I've learned much in writing this book, and I've found NYSUT's story hopeful and inspiring. I hope you do, too, because, as any teacher will tell you, there's so much more to learn and do.

PART I

Beginnings

CHAPTER 1

Radical Roots:
The Rise of the
United Federation of Teachers

On most mornings in the fall of 1960, Fred Nauman, a thirty-year-old New York City science teacher, would rise before dawn to commute from his home in Brooklyn's Kensington neighborhood to Junior High School 73, in Bedford-Stuyvesant. He usually arrived well before the 8:40 a.m. bell to ready science experiments for his students, and he had hoped that the morning of November 7, 1960, a Monday, would unfold like all these others.

But as the day approached, it became clear that it wouldn't.

Over the weekend, he and his fellow teachers had phoned one another, and in each call, Nauman expressed his disbelief: How had this happened? Why hadn't the conflict between teachers and the New York City Board of Education, over salaries and the recognition of their new teachers' union, been resolved? Would he and other teachers really have to *strike*?

On that Monday morning, Nauman gobbled down his bagel and gulped his coffee, and was out before his wife, Judie, had awakened. She had not been pleased the year before, when Fred had left his $6,000-a-year job repairing office machines at IBM to become a $4,800-a-year public school teacher. Family finances had become even tighter three months before, when the couple moved to a larger, more expensive apartment and Judie had stopped working as an executive secretary at the Associated Press to stay home with Steven, the couple's first child. On November 7, Steven was just over a month old.

Judie worried that if Fred walked the picket line that day, he'd be fired. It wasn't an idle worry. In the weeks prior, New York City Superintendent Dr. John J. Theobald had repeatedly stated that he would enforce the Condon-Wadlin Act, the New York State antilabor legislation, which made it illegal for public employees, including public school teachers, to strike. If Theobald enforced the law, any striking teachers would be fired. If rehired, Nauman would have to wait three years before receiving a pay raise. Still, Nauman was set on walking a picket line. Teachers needed to raise their pitiable salaries, and a strike just might deliver that.

His gray Dodge sedan pulled up to JHS 73 by 6 a.m. He and the other strikers around the city established their picket lines hours before schools opened. That way, teachers who refused to strike couldn't slip into the school without having to cross the line. Nauman counted only ten other teachers, all men and most of them younger than thirty, walking the picket line with him, a small percentage of the sixty teachers in JHS 73. As he walked that cold morning, he was anxious to know what was happening across the city and how it would all turn out. How many of the other fifty thousand teachers at the city's public schools were walking picket lines? Would teachers, divided for so long in New York City, act in unity on this one day? Or would today be the day he lost his job?[1]

Nauman and the city's other public school teachers would not have had to choose whether to strike that November day in 1960 if it weren't for the meeting of a few young men seven years earlier. Two were teachers who had met on the first day of school in 1953. They weren't introduced by other teachers, or by teacher unionists—unless you place their mothers, both working-class seamstresses, into those two categories.

Mamie Shanker and Pauline Altomare worked together at a sewing factory called J. & J. Clothing at the corner of Prince Street and University Place in lower Manhattan. The factory employed two hundred people, mostly women, who cut and sewed men's coats and jackets. Pauline Altomare was full of spunk, a natural leader who was chosen by her peers at J. & J. Clothing as shop chairlady, the equivalent of a shop steward, for the Amalgamated Clothing Workers Union.[2] Pauline was a neighbor of Mamie Shanker's in Astoria, Queens, a working-class neighborhood then largely inhabited by Italian-Americans, along with a mixture of second-generation Americans of Irish, German, Greek, Polish, and Jewish ancestry. Mamie was a Jewish immigrant from czarist Russia, who had come to America before World War I. At first, she worked in sweatshops, putting in upwards of seventy hours a week at her sewing machine for meager wages and no benefits.[3] At one point, Mamie worked briefly at the Triangle Shirtwaist Factory, which later became infamous for the March 25, 1911, fire that killed 146 workers, most of them Jewish and Italian teenage girls trapped in the inferno by locked exits or killed when they fell from a fire escape that failed.[4]

During her years in the trade, Mamie discovered that unions were willing to defend workers from unsafe conditions, as well as fight to whittle down exhausting weekly hours and increase paltry wages. She joined both the Amalgamated Clothing Workers Union and the International Ladies Garment Workers Union, and in Mamie's home, unions were revered just below God, a hierarchy that would guide her only son, Al, all his life.[5]

One day in the spring of 1953, Mrs. Altomare and her son George picked up Mrs. Shanker from work in their twenty-year-old Chevy. George, then a graduate student at City College in Harlem, mentioned to Mrs. Shanker that he was planning to teach in the fall. You know, my boy is going to be teaching, too, my boy Albert, Mrs. Shanker replied in her thick Russian accent—Vere are you going to be teaching? Astoria Junior High School, George said. That's vere mine boy Albert's going to be teaching, Mrs. Shanker replied. Vy don't you get together?[6]

On Monday, the day classes started that fall, George, just twenty-two years old, sought out Al, as he was known, at the faculty meeting in the auditorium at Astoria Junior High School, a cookie-cutter public school built of red brick that stood five stories high. Shanker, then twenty-five, was tall, lanky, and academically inclined. He fell into teaching because he was having trouble completing his doctorate in philosophy at Columbia University, and he had begun to feel guilty that he hadn't earned a dime since he married three years earlier.[7] Altomare and Shanker began eating their brown bag lunches together in an empty classroom on the second floor with a few other teachers who would later become union activists, including Delores Tedesco, Dick Thaler, and John Stam. Another was Dan Sanders, a social studies teacher, who would become a close confidante of Shanker's and a statewide teacher leader.[8]

The lunchtime colleagues shared their experiences in the classroom. None of them were paid well—that was no surprise. Shanker and Altomare started at about $50 a week, about a quarter of what their mothers were making at the clothing factory.[9] Many junior high school teachers in the system were full-time substitutes, and were paid even less than regular teachers and received no benefits.[10] Sanders, who

was a full-time substitute, was once out for a month with the mumps—
and he received no salary during his illness.[11] Two years after these
teachers came together, the *New York Times* would print an editorial
titled "Teach or Wash Cars." It asked why anyone would bother to
teach in the New York City schools for an average salary of $66 a week
when they could make more—$72.35 a week—washing cars.[12]

Work conditions matched the pay. A junior high school teacher
might teach two hundred or more students in five periods, an average
of forty students in each class. Teachers had no prep periods and were
often assigned to oversee students during lunch. The newcomers at
Astoria Junior High complained about these conditions during their
lunchtime gatherings, but perhaps their most colorful complaints were
about Abe Greenberg, the school's assistant principal. Greenberg used
to look out through his office window with binoculars to spy on teachers during the day. Were you sitting down? Greenberg believed teachers should be standing up. Were the students standing up? Greenberg
believed they should be sitting down. One day early in the semester,
Shanker told his peers that the assistant principal had appeared in his
classroom doorway. The new teacher thought the administrator had
come to help him. He motioned the assistant principal to come in, but
Greenberg stayed just where he was. "Mr. Shanker," Greenberg finally
said, "I see a lot of paper on the floor in the third aisle. It's very
unsightly and very *unprofessional*."[13]

The school bureaucrat's behavior might have been merely an
unpleasant footnote in all their lives, had he not been the catalyst that
roused Sanders, Shanker, and Altomare to leave their school in Astoria one day and travel to a small two-room union office in lower Manhattan. It was a trip that would bring the men to teacher unionism in
New York City, and over time, launch a teachers' revolution.

The office that the men visited was rented by the Teachers Guild, the
New York City union that was affiliated with the American Federation
of Teachers (AFT). The office was located at Broadway and Fifth
Avenue, across the street from the historic Flatiron Building. The guild
office, though, had little distinction. It was a fourth-floor walk-up
located above a cut-rate barbershop, and had but two rooms with loft
ceilings. In the first room, guild staff and volunteers made phone calls,
wrote, and did other office work. In the second, which was more open,
wooden chairs were pulled out for guild delegate assembly meetings or
other gatherings. The office was grimy and untidy, and in the early

morning or late at night, little visitors could be heard scurrying along the wood floors. They were rats.

When the teachers from Astoria Junior High School entered the guild's office they were stepping into a thirty-seven-year-old stream of teacher labor unionism in New York City. The guild was descended from the Teachers Union (TU), the small band of New York City teachers who formed the city's first teachers' union in 1916. That same year, teachers in the TU joined with those from other urban areas, including Chicago, Gary, Oklahoma City, Scranton, and Washington, D.C., to form the AFT, a small national teachers union that was founded with fewer than three thousand members. The AFT was affiliated with the American Federation of Labor (AFL), a federation of skilled workers that had been organized and was led at the time by the craggy-faced cigar maker Samuel Gompers.

By forming a union, teachers made a dramatic break from their usual habit of joining associations, such as the National Education Association (NEA), which had dominated the New York State and national education landscape for many decades. Teachers in the NEA considered themselves professionals, like doctors and lawyers, and they yearned to share the same social status. By joining a union, New York City teachers were abandoning this pretension and admitting they were like other workers who had to negotiate and sometimes tussle with their bosses to win better wages, rights, and respect. An appeal found in *The American Teacher*, a TU publication, in February 1916, argued for this revised self-image.

> Teachers with few exceptions are not organized. Teachers with few exceptions are regarded as being nerveless and without backbone. Their pay is miserable. Their hours are seemingly short, but their work is exhausting. In spite of all this teachers have failed to learn the lesson learned by labor everywhere—namely the necessity of Organization. Teachers have refused to recognize that they are workers—highly skilled workers it is true—but workers nevertheless. They have failed to see the identity of their interests with the interests of all labor; and so the idea of union has been repugnant to them. . . .
>
> You owe it to yourselves, Fellow Teachers, to assert your manhood and womanhood, to Organize for your protection, to be able to fight with dignity and force for proper conditions, for proper salaries, for a share in the control of the schools, for a voice in the formulation of school courses of study.

Or would you rather, hat in hand, wait in some politician's ante-room preparatory to licking his boots, and there beseech him to help you.

Which method do you prefer, Fellow Teacher? It is for you to choose![14]

Teachers devoted themselves to the TU, but those who did so were a small minority of New York City teachers. At the onset of the Depression, just 1,200 of the 30,000 teachers in the city belonged to the union. In the Depression of the 1930s, teachers, along with other workers, became more radical, and the TU became dominated by Communist Party members. Seeing this, many of the TU founders broke off to form a new union in 1935, and that new union became the Teachers Guild. In 1940, the AFT revoked the TU's charter and granted a new charter to the guild. By 1953, many of the guild's original members were in their fifties and sixties and had been fighting for teachers' rights for decades. Many, including Charlie Cogen, guild president at the time, and Rebecca Simonson, Cogen's predecessor, had been among those who had broken off from the TU.

Cogen, born in 1903 on Manhattan's Lower East Side, was typical of the group's members. Like almost everyone who belonged to the guild, and like many teachers in the city, he was Jewish. Cogen also came from a union background. His father, a Russian immigrant and a union garment worker, would often bring his young son to listen to speakers at labor rallies. The guild president was also typical in that he was well educated. He came up through the city's public schools, earned his bachelor's degree at Cornell University, and taught in New York City public schools before getting his law degree at Fordham University. Unable to find sufficient work as a lawyer during the Depression, he was forced to take a $4.50-a-day teacher-in-training job at Grover Cleveland High School in Queens. He later became one of the original faculty of the prestigious Bronx High School of Science, and, eventually, chairman of the social studies department at Bay Ridge High School in Brooklyn. Along the way, Cogen earned a master's degree in economics from Columbia University.

Cogen and the other guild leaders—who all volunteered their time—were the cream of the teaching profession. Sanders was shocked by the quality of the people he met; almost everyone in the guild had a doctorate in something.[15] Shanker compared the guild to a debating society and described a typical guild executive board meeting as "an exhilarating intellectual experience."[16]

"You'd go to a Guild meeting and listen to some very brilliant people expound on the state of the world," Shanker said. "After three hours you'd leave edified with nothing done."[17]

But during their first visit to the guild's office, Shanker, Sanders, and Altomare didn't meet these well-educated guild leaders. Instead, they met another man, who was neither Jewish nor from New York City. He was a blonde midwesterner who liked to wear bow ties, and he would serve as mentor to the spirited young men from Astoria. He had arrived in New York City only a few months earlier to work as an organizer for the union—its only employee other than the secretary. His name was David Selden.

David Selden had grown up in Michigan and talked far more slowly than the typical New Yorker. What impressed Altomare upon first meeting the man was not how well he spoke, but how well he listened. He had the look of a square-jawed cowboy, and seemed to have a streak of wisdom and wit that reminded Altomare of another midwesterner, the sage comedian from the pre–World War II era, Will Rogers.

Selden was a Socialist. He had come to New York City to do a job that most labor organizers of the day considered a Sisyphean task: organizing teachers. But unionizing teachers was Selden's mission. Previously, he had been based in Poughkeepsie, New York, as the AFT's "Eastern organizer," directing all organizing drives east of Lincoln, Nebraska.[18] His turf was later narrowed to New York, Pennsylvania, and New Jersey, and his job put him on the road almost constantly, organizing new AFT chapters and bolstering established ones. Often it seemed that as soon as he had set up one chapter, another would dissolve.

After Selden took a job as the guild's sole paid organizer in the spring of 1953, he learned fast that organizing New York City teachers wouldn't be any easier. Each morning, some eight hundred thousand New York City students—a group whose size alone would have rivaled the populations of Cincinnati or Kansas City—made their way to school. More than forty thousand teachers taught those students in six hundred elementary schools, one hundred junior high schools, and ninety high schools. When Selden arrived in New York City, the vast majority of those teachers didn't belong to any teachers' group, much less to the guild.

The midwesterner must have been relieved when Shanker, Sanders, and Altomare walked into his office. When he was done listening to them, Selden "grabbed hold of us," Altomare remembered later, and got them to work.[19] Sanders, who had written for the campus newspaper at City College and had been a stringer for the *New York Times* covering college sports, was recruited to write for the *Guild Bulletin*, the union's newspaper. All three were put to work organizing their school, Astoria JHS. The teachers relished the task. Shanker, the most intellectual in the crew, used logic to persuade teachers to join the guild. Altomare convinced teachers to join by citing the small and large indignities that teachers had to suffer. Sanders won new members with an infectious congeniality; people were buoyed by his presence and seemed eager to join the club that would have him as a member.

The men also used another tactic. On weekends, Sanders and his wife, Elaine, used to invite "the Guildies" from PS 126 to their apartment for weekend get-togethers.[20] Each Friday, Shanker would mix whiskey sours for after-school parties at his apartment on 29th Street in Astoria, located about a mile from the junior high. The rules were unwritten, but understood: if you hadn't joined the union, you wouldn't get an invitation to the parties. Teachers would ask, Can I come? Sure, they'd be told, but you have to give nine dollars—half a year's membership—to join the guild.[21] The method might not have been ideologically pure, but it was effective. "After the whiskey sours," Altomare said years later, "we didn't need Shanker's logic."[22]

In less than two school years, the majority of teachers at Astoria Junior High had joined the guild, a success rate that dwarfed that in any other school in the city. Shanker, with a smile, would later compare the concentration of guild activity in the Queens junior high school to the concentration of "dissidents who met under the czar in Siberia" before the Russian Revolution.[23]

After two years at the guild, though, Selden had made little headway. New York City was a hotbed of American radicalism, yet its teachers, like those elsewhere, were averse to joining a union. The staunchest antiunionists were the school system's older generation of teachers, who were largely Irish-American women. These were the teachers who declined invitations to join the guild with the phrase, "We are professionals." Shanker would sometimes discuss this attitude with his mother. "Teachers are so smart, they're stupid," Mamie Shanker would tell her son. "They don't realize that they have to have a union."[24]

But Selden was also surprised to bump into opposition among many younger Jewish teachers, the most recent wave of educators to roll into the city's public school system. These were the sons and daughters of Eastern European and Russian Jews who had immigrated to New York City in the late nineteenth and early twentieth centuries. Many of these families had settled in the Lower East Side and worked in the clothing industry. They were unabashedly liberal, even radical, and almost always pro-union. The rub, though, was this: they expected their sons and daughters to climb the social ladder and become professionals, who didn't need unions. Selden found Jewish teachers almost always sympathetic to unions; they just wouldn't join one. My parents, one said, would drop dead if I ever joined a union.

Other times, teachers rebuffed Selden by explaining that they already belonged to a teachers' group. And they did. In the 1950s and earlier, teachers paid from 50 cents to a few dollars to join one of the city's roughly one hundred teacher groups. Teachers in Manhattan met on one side of the East River; teachers from Brooklyn met on the other. Queens teachers didn't take subways to the Bronx, and Manhattan teachers weren't inclined to make a ferry crossing, which left the Staten Island educators with their own teachers' group. High school teachers, who believed they should be better paid than elementary and junior high teachers, had formed their own organization. English teachers met separately from math teachers, who met separately from science teachers.

How else could teachers divide themselves? Religiously, of course. Catholic teachers had their group; Jewish teachers had theirs. As if to prove their point, Orthodox Jewish teachers broke from non-Orthodox Jewish ones. It wasn't long before Shanker, making fun of all the splinter teacher groups in the city, was referring to the Female Health Education Teachers of Bensonhurst.[25] It was a joke, but barely.

It was as if teachers had used that old political tactic—divide and conquer—against themselves. New York City's Board of Education took full advantage of the divisions. Fred M. Hechinger, education editor of the *New York Times*, summed up the status of New York City teachers this way: "The huge education bureaucracy has made [teachers] voiceless pawns in a machine."[26] Each year, the board would invite dozens of the teachers' groups to appear before them to make their case. All were aware that they were competitors. If science teachers convinced the board to purchase more beakers, English teachers might be allotted fewer Shakespeare texts. If high school teachers convinced the board they deserved a raise, elementary teachers might have to forego one. Each year, the board listened politely—and then did what it pleased. What the board meted out was more often crumbs from the tin than pieces from the pie.

Selden dreamed of building the guild membership until it was the dominant teachers' group in the city. A few times a week he would visit schools and discuss pressing educational issues with teachers over brown-bag lunches, and at the end of the hour, a few teachers might sign membership cards for the guild. But the pace of guild growth was glacial. In two years on the job, the guild's membership had risen from about 1,800 members to about 2,000.[27]

Riding on a subway to one such school meeting, Selden calculated that at this rate it would take about twenty-five years to herd the majority of New York City teachers into the Guild. His worst-case estimate was a century—or never. For a missionary, even a patient one, this was a dismal prognosis. Selden applied for a teaching job in Westchester County, the suburban district just north of New York City, and considered quitting his New York City job. Instead, he decided to stay and make recruitment more light-hearted. He began scheduling Guild meetings at night rather than just after school, which allowed for more leisurely get-togethers, including a monthly beer-and-peanuts party. At gatherings, Selden entertained new members by playing labor songs on his cheap banjo while Altomare played his guitar, strumming songs such as "Teacher's Blues." "Oh unions are for workers but a teacher has prestige," went that song. "He can feed his kids on that old noblesse oblige." Guild get-togethers were becoming fun.[28]

The organizer also believed that the guild needed to do a better job at setting itself apart from other teacher groups. In the in-house paper "Big Guild, Little Guild," Selden and his union friend Ely Trachtenberg suggested that the union should sell itself like a candidate for public office in order to become the dominant teachers' group in the city. The first thing it needed to do was to stop taking positions that repelled members, such as opposing prayer in the public schools. Instead, the paper called for the guild to focus on bread-and-butter issues such as salaries, benefits, and working conditions.

Selden also saw another key issue that the guild could promote to separate itself from competitors: collective bargaining. Establishing the right to bargain collectively would mean that a single united union would represent them at the bargaining table, where administrators would be required to bargain with them "in good faith." Private employees had gained the legal right to bargain collectively in 1935 under the National Labor Relations Act, known as the Wagner Act because Senator Robert F. Wagner of New York had introduced it. The

law was often referred to as the "Magna Carta of Labor." It gave workers more power in their relationship with their employers and it also
brought order to the relations between management and employees
during a time of strikes and violence and near-revolt by the masses.
Under the Wagner Act, unionism in the private sector flourished. But
the act specifically excluded public employees from the rights of collective bargaining—and in the 1950s nearly all public employees,
including teachers, still didn't have these rights.

In the spring of 1956, Selden and the more militant guild members were able to convince the organization's delegate assembly to make
collective bargaining the group's first priority. From then on, almost
every piece of guild literature stated that collective bargaining was the
cure for teacher ailments. Was your salary too low? A collective bargaining agreement with the board would increase it. Your principal was
a despot? The guild would find ways to restrain him when it won collective bargaining rights. Selden and the others dreamed that if the
guild became the most dominant teachers' group in the city, it would
eventually win the right to represent all city teachers when collective
bargaining was won.[29]

Selden's plan also included another crucial idea: that bold actions
by the guild would bring in members. The older Guild leaders maintained that membership had to grow more before the group could take
more decisive action, a traditional organizing approach. But Selden
and his young recruits believed, on the contrary, that bold teacher
action would bring in members. Evolution was proving too slow. They
wanted a revolution.

Buoyed by his successes organizing at Astoria Junior High School, and
eager to add members to the guild, Altomare took an appointment in
1956 to teach history at Franklin K. Lane High School in Woodhaven
in Queens. In doing so, he was becoming what was called a "union col-
onizer," intending to recruit a new group of workers: high school
teachers. But in his first year at Lane he recruited only eight new guild
members.[30] The problem was that most high school teachers who
joined a teachers' group joined the High School Teachers Association
(HSTA), which along with the guild and the TU was one of three
major teachers' groups in the city. HSTA had one issue: it demanded
that high school teachers receive more pay since their job required
more education than elementary and junior high school teachers. The
demand went back to 1947, when the city's Board of Education, in an

effort to attract more elementary school teachers, raised their salaries to those of high school teachers. The leveling of salaries embittered high school teachers, who left the guild and joined the HSTA in the late 1940s and early 1950s.[31] High school teachers avoided the guild because the union had long supported the single salary schedule for all teachers on the grounds that elementary teachers were worth as much as their high school equivalents. "Equal salary for equal work," was the guild's slogan.

Altomare soon realized that he wasn't going to convince many high school teachers to join the guild. But he and the other young guild recruits had another idea: Why not merge the Guild, which consisted of maybe two thousand teachers, with the HSTA, which had maybe three or four thousand members? In 1957, Altomare broached the idea with HSTA leaders. They told him they would only merge if the guild supported the policy of paying high school teachers more, something that Altomare knew wouldn't work because guild leaders opposed it.[32]

While Altomare was thinking merger, HSTA upstarts took a bold action that would change teacher politics in the city forever. In January 1959, eight hundred teachers who taught at evening high schools resigned en masse to protest their pitiful wages. In labor parlance, it was a wildcat strike because it was initiated not by union leaders, but by the rank-and-file. The young guild activists were amazed. Teachers rarely talked strike, much less launched one. The Teachers Union had never struck; neither had the guild. The AFT had opposed strikes since its inception in 1916, as had the NEA. High school teachers were taking the kind of bold action that insurgents at the guild had only dreamed of.

Hoping to find a bridge to these militant high school teachers, Shanker, Altomare, and Selden would drive to the nightly picket lines at Jamaica High School in Queens, offering donuts and coffee to the shivering strikers.[33] Selden called his station wagon and Shanker's Volkswagen minibus "Guild Coffeemobiles."[34] On these trips, they met some of the young members of the HSTA: Roger Parente, the HSTA secretary who taught at Theodore Roosevelt High School in the Bronx; John Bailey, one of the strike's leaders; and Samuel Hochberg, HSTA vice president.

Selden, Shanker, and Altomare returned from those picket lines and suggested a radical move to the guild leadership: support the evening high school teachers and their strike. The older guild leaders hesitated. To support it would increase the likelihood of its success, and thereby give the HSTA the upper hand in the ongoing organizing battles. But Selden and his friend Trachtenberg pushed another argument they had developed in "Big Guild, Little Guild." It was that teachers needed to support all their fellow teachers, because as one teachers' group gained muscle, all teachers would gain strength. Selden put it succinctly: What if they won the strike without your support?[35] Guild leadership reluctantly endorsed the action. Guild phones and mimeograph machines were used to publicize a strike rally at city hall, and Guild members even walked picket lines with the high school teachers. A solidarity, fragile but genuine, slowly grew between the young men of the competing teacher groups.[36]

The HSTA strike, the first one by teachers in New York City history, was an unequivocal success. After a few weeks, the Board of Education raised the daily wages for evening high school workers, who taught the equivalent of four courses each night, from $12 to $21, beyond what even the strike organizers had hoped.[37] The strike was a lesson of what a daring act could win teachers—and the potential of teacher unity. On the picket line, Altomare and Bailey made a pact: We will meet with each other until a merger is forged.

Shortly thereafter, the young guild leaders—Selden, Shanker, and Alice Marsh, a teacher at Joan of Arc Junior High School in Manhattan who would later become a legislative representative for New York City teachers[38]—met with the three HSTA activists, Parente, Hochberg, and Bailey, at Altomare's apartment in Astoria. The young teachers swore to keep the meetings secret from their leaders. Secret meetings might have been undemocratic, but both sides knew that the leaders of either group might kill the delicate negotiations if they knew of them, something they didn't want to risk.

Inspired by the high school strike, Selden wanted the guild to organize its own one-day strike to win a salary increase for all teachers. It was the kind of bold action he believed would attract new members. But the guild's senior membership feared that if it failed, the move could destroy their group. Rebecca Simonson, the guild's well-respected former president, challenged the young activists to bring out five thousand teachers for a mass meeting to show that there was support for the action. Selden and the other young activists knew that five thousand teachers had not come together anywhere, any time, for any purpose. So they counter-bargained: two thousand teachers. They compromised: bring out three thousand teachers and the guild's leaders would endorse the strike.[39]

Attracting three thousand teachers to one meeting was a Herculean task. To make matters worse, HSTA's senior leaders refused to support the guild's action. Guild organizers scheduled a rally at the St. Nicholas Arena on West 66th Street, which was often used for sporting events. The guild activists pulled every organizing tactic they knew, but fearing that the crowd would still fall short of three thousand, Altomare gave the custodian of St. Nicholas a few bucks to remove about five hundred chairs from the arena.[41]

On the night of the rally, St. Nicholas Arena, minus the five hundred chairs, was nearly filled with teachers. In a voice vote, the crowd approved the Guild's one-day action for April 15, 1959. It marked the first time that a teachers' organization in New York City had openly called for a strike. The evening before the stoppage, guild president Cogen went on TV to exhort teachers to "stick to their guns." While the guild president was being interviewed, an aide passed him a note saying that New York City's superintendent of schools, Dr. John J. Theobald, wanted to meet with union leaders for last-minute negotiations.[42] Cogen came on the eleven o'clock news later that night and called off the strike; teachers had been promised considerable raises. The next day, the guild printed bulletins hailing the victory. What seemed like a flood of new members—upwards of eight hundred teachers—joined the Guild.[43]

The young guild members continued to push for a merger with HSTA, convinced that unity would bring teachers even better results. They suggested a compromise on the salary issue. Allow a salary differential, they proposed, but apply it to anyone, even elementary school teachers, who completed a master's degree. Parente, Hochberg, and Bailey were intrigued by the offer, but when they took the idea to the more conservative HSTA leadership, they rejected it.

The guild negotiators' next move was to suggest that Parente, Hochberg, and Bailey abandon the HSTA and form a new group of high school teachers that supported teacher unity. In the fall of 1959, Bailey and Altomare scraped some of their own money together to put an ad in the *New York World Telegram & Sun*'s education page, which was read by thousands of teachers daily. It announced the formation of The Committee for Action Through Unity, or CATU (pronounced *kay'-too*), a group of high school teachers who supported teacher unity and better pay for all teachers with supplemental education. The response to the ad was phenomenal. Within days, CATU had 1,200 new members, almost half the size of the guild.[44] The effort to create a willing partner to merge with would have been an unambiguous success if not for a few powerful teachers who were outraged by the plan: the guild's Old Guard.

President Cogen called the guild's executive board to order. Guild leaders immediately attacked the young rebels for secretly negotiating a potential merger with the high school teachers without the approval of the guild's leadership or members. They also criticized them for establishing CATU, which they saw as a potential rival to the guild. Jules Kolodny, an elder statesman in the guild, motioned to censure Selden and Altomare. Shanker, by then an organizer and a board member, and a good friend to both Selden and Altomare, stood up to confront the board. He told them that thousands of teachers had signed up with CATU, signaling the desire for teacher unity. Well, what are you going to do about it? the combative Shanker asked. The old-timers pulled back on the censure of Selden or Altomare.[45] Cogen, a voice of reason, knew that to destroy the bridge that had been built to the high school teachers would leave the guild the marginal group that it had been for over two decades. The guild's board initiated formal merger talks with CATU.

Through the fall of 1959 and into early 1960, CATU and the guild leadership hammered out an agreement. But what to call the new group? "Teachers Union" was taken. They avoided the word *association*; it smacked of the NEA. The name United Federation of Teachers (UFT) was suggested. President Cogen complained that the words *united* and *federation* were redundant, but the name stuck.[46]

On March 16, 1960, at the old Astor Hotel, 500 guild delegates overwhelmingly voted for the merger, and with the 1,500 sign-ups from CATU, the UFT boasted a membership of roughly 5,000. New York City teachers had finally come together. Now it was time to act.

Almost cocky, UFT leaders presented the Board of Education with a list of demands. These included: an across-the-board raise, including a $1,000 bonus for all teachers who had received additional education; duty-free lunch periods; ten days a year paid sick leave for full-time substitutes; and an automatic deduction of union dues from pay checks. The Board of Education and Superintendent Theobald balked at these requests, especially the UFT's key demand: that the union represent all of New York City's teachers in collective bargaining. The board's hesitance was understandable. At the time, few public employees anywhere in the country bargained collectively. Besides, how could the board agree to bargain with one group of teachers if teachers couldn't choose one group to represent themselves?

"I do not bargain with members of my own family," was Dr. Theobald's response to the demands. The UFT called a strike for May 17, 1960, Teachers' Recognition Day, when parents would traditionally walk though the city's schools pinning flowers onto the blouses and jackets of teachers. At the last minute, Superintendent Theobald agreed to the bulk of the demands, and the action was put off.

But in June, representatives from all city teachers groups except the UFT were invited to the board offices at 110 Livingston Street. These teacher groups, which had opposed collective bargaining, came from the meeting advocating "divisional bargaining," which was separate bargaining for elementary, junior high, and high school teachers. UFT leaders assumed the board was up to an old trick: dividing teachers in order to conquer them. All summer, Theobald ignored pleas from UFT leaders that the superintendent follow through on his promises.

The UFT's collective bargaining committee voted to launch a strike on November 7, the day before the Kennedy-Nixon election. They figured that the authorities, Democrats in New York City, wouldn't dare invoke the Condon-Wadlin Act lest it alienate Democratic voters.

The UFT's executive board and delegate assembly approved the strike on October 4 and 5, but no other teachers' group in the city endorsed the measure, seeing it for what it was: a power play by the UFT to become the dominant teachers' group in the city. Superintendent Theobald, as well as the Board of Education and James E. Allen Jr., the state education commissioner, also warned that any teacher who went on strike would jeopardize "that teacher's state certificate and his rights to teach in any school district in New York State."[47] Many old-timers were told they would lose their teachers' pension if they walked that day. Nervous school officials forbade teachers to meet on school grounds to discuss a strike. Instead, guild teacher leaders met at churches, synagogues—even at a funeral parlor.

In the days prior to the strike date, Shanker remembers a guild meeting where some of the old-time leaders, aware of Theobald's threats and the skepticism about the strike from the city's labor unionists, spoke of calling off the strike. Look, Shanker told them, we have no choice but to go out. With Condon-Wadlin, a strike is going to be illegal next year and every year. If we're going to allow that to stop us, then forget about the union. We're finished. There's no argument that anybody can come up with to call this strike off that allows us to continue to have a union or any chance of building one. I admit this is risky. But the other way is a certain death warrant.

After Shanker's speech, old-time guild firebrands such as Si Beagle and David Wittes defended the strike, and all rumblings about calling it off ceased. The last editorial before the November 7 strike day in the UFT's paper, *The United Teacher*, said: "This is a strike for our dignity, our self-respect. We will smash once and for all the concept that teachers are educated fools."[48]

As the Monday strike day approached, the tiny UFT headquarters on East 23rd Street was jammed with volunteers who manned phones, turned out mimeographed flyers, and painted signs. "It was all thunder and lightning, do or die," Jeannette DiLorenzo, a teacher at JHS 142 in Red Hook in Brooklyn, recalled. "Even the old were young again."[49]

Since the UFT office was closed from Saturday night to Monday morning, UFT organizers moved their headquarters to Selden's and Shanker's apartments during the weekend. Each apartment had two phone lines. In one call after another, the men told the teacher troops not to believe what would be reported on the radio the next morning since the Board of Education would likely underestimate the number of teachers out. Altomare also suggested a technique to keep administrators from knowing who stayed out: drop paper clips into the school's time clocks.

At about 3 a.m. on Sunday night, Selden and Altomare, their preparations over, walked over to Shanker's to get some more wine, which they had been sipping while they worked. The three men knew that not all—or even most—of New York's teachers would walk out. What they hoped was that enough teachers would strike to cause havoc in the schools. Striking with such meager forces was like putting your head in a lion's mouth and hoping it didn't bite. The men hoped the lion—Mayor Robert F. Wagner Jr., son of Senator Wagner, architect of the Wagner Act—was sympathetic to their dreams. On the walk over to Shanker's house, Altomare asked Selden a question he hadn't dared consider: What happens if teachers cave in?

Win or lose this strike, said Selden, we'll have created a teachers' union movement that won't fail. As the sun came up on that freezing

New York morning, Altomare headed to the guild office to wait for news of the strike. Despite the wine, the hour, and his lack of sleep, Altomare never in his life felt more awake.[50]

On the morning of November 7, all over the city, teachers strung placards over their shoulders and joined picket lines. "Better Salaries, Better Schools" said one sign; "United We Stand" said another. One parent on the line wore a sign: "Parents Want Justice for Teachers." A news clip about the strike was titled "Reading, Writing—and Pickets." The newscaster said, "When problems hit the nation's biggest city, they're usually big—such as the first strike of school teachers in New York City's history."[51]

At JHS 73 in Brooklyn, Fred Nauman and his fellow teachers got out early to walk their picket line; it was cold enough to see their breath. The picketers passed a transistor radio around, spinning back and forth between local news channels. Would the strike be a success? It was a question on the mind of nearly every public school teacher in the city.

At Public School 165 on the Upper West Side, a teacher named Ray Frankel walked the picket line with just four of her colleagues. Some of the other teachers appeared in the school's windows to watch the picketers, and a few started crying. "Stop crying and come out," she yelled at them.[52] As each hour passed, the radio reported higher and higher estimates of strikers. One thousand teachers . . . two thousand teachers . . . with each announcement, the dread that Nauman had felt slowly began to lift. Three thousand teachers . . . four thousand teachers . . .

At Public School 100 in Queens, Nat Levine, bowing to the vote not to strike by his UFT colleagues at the school, showed up for work. But by lunchtime he could no longer stomach the choice he had made. He grabbed a piece of chalk and wrote a message on the board for himself, but also for his students who would enter the classroom in the afternoon: "To thine own self be true."

Outside JHS 142 in Red Hook in Brooklyn, Jeanette and John DiLorenzo and about eighty other teachers picketed, joined by longshoremen and merchant seamen from the nearby piers. Later that morning, Jeanette drove around to check out other public schools in south Brooklyn, and at many of the elementary schools, not a single teacher was walking. By the time they circled back to JHS 142, half of the striking teachers had deserted their picket line, and by day's end

Jeanette was hoping "to find a way to get back in that building with some kind of dignity."[53]

DiLorenzo's observations were accurate: the turnout from elementary school teachers had been dismal. Most of the strikers came from the more militant staff at the junior highs. By the end of the day, the board had conceded that 4,600 teachers had gone out. Later newspaper accounts would report that 5,600 teachers had walked picket lines and that another 2,000 teachers called in sick. Whatever the exact numbers were, Nauman was exhilarated come the end of the day: thousands of other teachers had risked their jobs as well.

That night, the teachers once again returned to the St. Nicholas Arena, and from the cheers that rose up from within, a passerby might have thought that a raucous crowd had gathered for a professional wrestling match. As the meeting was breaking up, Selden was told that he had a phone call. "Okay, listen," the caller said. "Vill you take mediation?"

"Who is this?" Selden asked.

"Dubinsky. I vant to meet with you."[54] It was David Dubinsky, the legendary president of the International Ladies Garment Workers Union (ILGWU), the union that Mamie Shanker and Pauline Altomare belonged to. Dubinsky was well connected to the Democratic Party, and he didn't want the strike to embarrass the mayor or disrupt the election. That night, Cogen, Hochberg, Kolodny, and Selden met in Dubinsky's Manhattan apartment, and by the end of the evening, a compromise had been worked out. The mayor would appoint a special labor committee consisting of three labor unionists, all of whom were sympathetic to the cause and to collective bargaining, to investigate the teachers' demands. Dubinsky was one of the panelists. The second was Harry Van Arsdale, the tough leader of the International Brotherhood of Electrical Workers and the president of the New York City Central Trades and Labor Council. The third was Jacob Potofsky, president of the Amalgamated Clothing Workers Union, the other union that Mamie belonged to. Mayor Wagner—and the city's top labor leaders—had supported the feeble strike by teachers; the UFT leaders called off the strike.

Superintendent Theobald announced that the Board of Education would not enforce the Condon-Wadlin Act and reversed his command to fire strikers. The labor committee that was established recommended that the board make concessions on pay and working conditions to teachers and that a collective bargaining election be held before the end of the school year. In June 1960, the Board of Education polled New York City teachers whether they wanted collective bargaining. Despite the opposition to collective bargaining by the NEA, which had set itself up as an alternative to the UFT, 27,367 teachers voted "yes" to 9,003 who voted "no." In October 1961 the Board of Education directed the City Labor Department to hold a collective bargaining election to decide which group would represent teachers.

The UFT had two rivals. One was the TU, but a more serious threat came from the NEA, which came into New York City with organizers and established the Teachers Bargaining Organization (TBO), an alliance of many of the scattered teachers' groups in the city. Money flowed in from NEA headquarters, and the association's organizers sent teachers antiunion leaflets headed, "Do You Want Hoffa and Bossism?"[55] NEA leaders were confident they would win the election in part, one NEA organizer would later say, because "teachers as professionals would never vote for a union."[56]

Meanwhile, organized labor, including the United Auto Workers, mobilized behind the UFT, providing $250,000 to the union over a half-year period before the vote.[57] In the *New York Times*, an ad supporting the UFT was endorsed by political giants such as Eleanor Roosevelt, A. Philip Randolph, president of the Brotherhood of Sleeping Car Porters, and Herbert Lehman, the former New York governor. On each of the ten days that teachers had to return their ballots, a hundred UFT volunteers phoned teachers to urge them to "vote for the organization that won the right to vote."[58] On December 16, 1961, the votes of 33,000 teachers, 77 percent of the city's teachers, were counted. The UFT won overwhelmingly, receiving 20,045 votes to 9,770 cast for the TBO, and only 2,575 for the TU. The UFT would now speak for all of New York City's teachers.

But negotiations between the UFT and the Board of Education broke down almost immediately when the board dragged its feet over money, offering little. "What other means are there besides a strike," asked an exasperated Cogen. "We've tried everything else—like gentle persuasion. . . . This is time to stop talking and get a little action." Teachers, though, were still reluctant to strike, and voted to support one on April 11, 1962, by a margin of only 313 votes—2,544 to 2,231. Once the day arrived, though, teachers heeded the call—about twenty-two thousand of them walked picket lines, seven thousand of whom weren't even members of the UFT. Teachers held signs that read that they were tired of being treated as "low-paid babysitters."[59]

The board was stunned by the teacher response; in that 1962 strike, a full one-half of the city's teachers didn't report to their classrooms, crippling the city's nine hundred public schools. The president of the Board of Education called the stoppage "reckless, irresponsible . . . immoral, and illegal," and the board convinced a state Supreme Court justice to invoke the Condon-Wadlin Act and issue an antipicketing order.[60] The afternoon of the strike seven thousand teachers surrounded City Hall, packing Murray Street and overflowing onto Broadway.

Charlie Cogen, the UFT's five-foot-tall leader, scrambled onto a sedan to address the crowd. "This is the greatest day in the history of education in the City of New York," he said. The crowd of teachers broke into a chant of "Stay out, stay out," and cheered their gray-haired leader, a veteran of the Teachers Guild who had taught in the 1930s for $4.50 a day. A few days later, a *New York Times* reporter called the strike a "revolt by teachers—a revolt against the status accorded them, a revolt against the conditions under which they worked."

The court injunction ended the strike, but the Board of Education made concessions. In the negotiations that followed, teachers secured a $1,000 across-the-board raise—the largest pay raise in New York City school history—and established new salary differentials for teachers who had different levels of experience. The contract also guaranteed teachers a free lunch period. For many teachers who had worked during their lunch hour their entire careers, it was like manna from heaven.

A few days after the strike ended, *New York Post* reader Monroe Lockman wrote: "As a union truck driver, I support the teachers' strike. Perhaps someday, if they fight hard enough, they may earn almost as much as I do."[61] The most important gain, though, was not more money, or even better work conditions, but more power. UFT leaders had won the right to bargain collectively, which meant that the Board of Education would have to negotiate with the UFT, which represented all teachers in the city. Now, every contract negotiation, said Al Shanker, "opens up afresh opportunities for direct teacher participation in the revitalization of our schools."[62]

With this success, New York City's teachers had ushered in a new era in the history of the American labor movement. The 1880s saw the consolidation of the craft unions and the founding of the American

Federation of Labor. The 1930s saw the creation of the great industrial unions and the Congress of Industrial Organizations. The 1960s, with teachers at the forefront, would see the unionization of government employees. In January 1961, President John F. Kennedy would sign Order 10988, giving legitimacy to union organizing among public employees. New York City teachers had led the way, becoming the first teachers in any major city to win the right to bargain collectively.

Teachers all over the country watched this three-year transformation of their New York City colleagues. They saw the city's teachers, once dismissed as disorganized and impotent, become a powerful, unified force. The word of their success spread from New York City like a fire, igniting rebellion and organizing efforts in elementary schools, high schools, and universities all over the state. Teachers no longer pleaded for respect, decent wages, and fair working conditions; they saw they could demand them—and win.

For New York teachers, the 1960s had arrived.

CHAPTER 2

Teacher Militancy in the 1960s

In 1957, Robert Allen began his first year as a sixth grade teacher at the Laurel Street Elementary School in Rome, New York, a small city in central New York. The fit, clean-cut young man had started teaching just three days after he left the Army, and from the day he made the switch, he couldn't help comparing life in the schools to life in the military.

The military was a man's world. But the teachers in his elementary school were mostly women, which was the norm, and perhaps one reason the public schools paid far less than the Army. Allen earned $3,800 his first year as a teacher. Feeling a little homesick for the military, he signed up for a second job as a lieutenant in a tank company at the Rome Armory, which required that he work just fifteen days during the summer and four evenings a month over the rest of the year. It paid $4,000 a year.

It took the twenty-six-year-old a little longer to discern how differently his superiors in the two jobs treated him. In the military, ranks were clear, indicated by the stripes sewn onto men's sleeves. Yet Allen found that military men almost always approached each other with respect, handed up and down the chain of command, especially to those who did their job well.

But in the schools, Allen found that administrators bestowed upon teachers what he called a "grandmothers-and-apple-pie" kind of respect. Each year, administrators would hold a Teacher Recognition Day, and the mayor would parade around the school to hand out white flowers that the teachers would pin to their lapels. To Allen, the recognition felt more like a paternalistic pat on the head, especially since the rest of the year, administrators talked to him and other teachers with a "phony politeness."[1]

Worse yet, it seemed teachers accepted the attitude. Hell, he thought, lowly privates talked back more to their superior officers than teachers did to their principals. In the fall of his first year, he attended a meeting of the Rome Teachers Association, which was a local of the

New York State Teachers Association (NYSTA). NYSTA was affiliated with the National Education Association (NEA) and represented teachers almost everywhere in the state outside of New York City. The president of the Rome association, the junior high librarian, made introductory remarks and then opened the meeting up to the audience.

The first teacher stood and asked the librarian a question. But instead of answering, the president looked to the man sitting next to her on the stage, Rome's superintendent. He answered. With the next question, she again turned to the superintendent. It was the kind of deference that teachers, almost always women, were expected to give their administrators, almost always men. As the president deferred again and again, Allen simmered. This was supposed to be the Rome *Teachers* Association, not the Rome *Administrators* Association. Afterward, he and a few of the other young teachers confronted their president.

I thought this was *our* group, he said. I mean, who runs things around here?[2]

Instead of answering the question, the president started to cry. The truth was that administrators, not teachers, ran Rome's teachers' group, ran NYSTA, and ran the NEA. Since well before the oldest teachers in the system could remember, NYSTA's most powerful official was not its president, but its executive secretary, usually a former school administrator. Teachers often chose administrators as their local presidents as well. By choosing administrators to run their associations, teachers were mimicking the power relations in their own schools, which were like those in factories. The principal was the boss, and he usually treated teachers like wage employees, and nonunionized ones at that, who had little say in the operation of a school.

Teachers all over New York shared Allen's distaste for the way schools were run. In Buffalo in the early 1960s, Tom Hobart, a shop teacher who would later become president of NYSTA, went to his first meeting of the Buffalo Teachers Federation, the local NYSTA affiliate. At the meeting, teachers stood up and complained about how administrators dominated the BTF and they proposed a new bylaw that would require that all BTF committees contain a majority of teachers. Only four teachers, including Hobart, voted for the motion; the rest in attendance, whether teacher or administrator, voted to preserve the status quo. The BTF leadership then moved to have the four teachers who had supported the failed motion known to the administrators at their schools. That motion passed handily.[3]

In 1964, in the North Syracuse Central School District, a newly hired teacher named Sylvia Matousek bristled at the way pregnant teachers were treated there. As soon as a woman became pregnant, she was required to tell the superintendent. "The big joke was that you'd call the superintendent at two o'clock in the morning," Matousek remembered later, "and say, 'Oh, well, I think I just got pregnant.'" As soon as a woman's pregnancy began to show, she was asked to leave, and it was not a leave of absence. School administrators weren't required to rehire teachers after they left to have their children.[4]

In his second year of teaching, Robert Allen became active in the Rome Teachers Association. Each spring, when the district was drawing up its budget for next year, he and a few other teacher activists would appear before the school board. Each year, the teachers would ask for an improvement of their paltry salaries, and perhaps a few other changes. Allen was always struck by how quiet the board members were during the presentation; they never interrupted and rarely asked a question. Once in a while, a board member would jot down a note, but most of the time they just let the teachers' brief presentation run its course.

Thank you very much, the board president would say. We'll get back to you. And each year the board and the administrators would do as they pleased. Such was the wearisome dance that was repeated between teachers and administrators each year not just in Rome, but in Rochester, Ramapo, Roosevelt, Richmondville, and in every school district around the state.

Allen and other reform-minded teachers across the state referred to the annual negotiating process not as collective *bargaining* but as collective *begging*. But even that phrase was a misnomer, for teachers largely went through the bargaining process not as a collective, but as individuals. Starting salaries and even benefits were different for each teacher in a school.

"If they liked you, you got an extra day off," Allen remembered. "If they didn't like you, it was 'No, I'm sorry. We can't do that.'"[5] A teacher in one classroom didn't know what a teacher in the next classroom earned, much less what similar teachers earned in the next district. Teachers were divided and powerless and Allen knew it. "We didn't want to keep going to the school board with our goddamn hat in hand," Allen said. "We didn't want to be put off by anybody who wanted to put us off and could put us off. [We wanted] respect as professionals."[6]

Teachers in New York City earned that respect in the early 1960s. They had gone from badly paid, little respected, and politically dismissed to a political powerhouse. And they had done so by striking. That first citywide teachers strike had led to the establishment of one union—the United Federation of Teachers—that had the legal right to sit down and bargain with the Board of Education. As a result of that success, the American Federation of Teachers (AFT), the national teachers union to which the UFT belonged, experienced a major resurgence. Its membership had hovered at between 40,000 and 50,000 for years. In New York City alone, the UFT increased its membership from 15,000, the prestrike level, to 44,000. Over 5,000 teachers in Cleveland joined the AFT, as did nearly 10,000 teachers in Detroit and 11,000 more in Philadelphia.[7] Fueled by its New York City local, the AFT would grow to 175,000 members in 1968.

The UFT's success also caught the attention of teachers in NYSTA chapters in the growing suburban communities of Long Island, in upstate cities like Rochester and Rome, and in hundreds of rural districts. These teachers did not have a militant philosophy, or television cameras that recorded their angry words and rebellious actions. Yet they pushed persistently for change in their schools and slowly, steadily, change came.

At first, Allen and other activist teachers from outside New York City didn't believe in striking for what they wanted—that was not the NEA way. Instead, they lobbied state legislators to overturn the Condon-Wadlin Act. That antilabor law was drafted largely as a reaction to the Buffalo teachers' strike of 1947, one of the first major walkouts by educators in the country. At the time, teachers in Buffalo, who were part of NYSTA, were hurting; a typical example was that of Millard Scott, who was trying to support his wife and three children on a salary that in 1947 was lower than it had been in 1932, though the cost of living had tripled.[8]

In 1947, teachers asked for a $500 cost-of-living bonus and a minimum salary range from $2,400 to $3,600 to make up for wages that had been stunted by both the Depression of the 1930s and by World War II. On February 2, 1947, Buffalo teachers vowed to strike. That decision infuriated many state legislators, including William F. Condon, a Republican representative from upstate, who offered a bill on February 12 that punished striking teachers. Raymond Ast, the president of the Buffalo Teachers Federation, described the bill as "a shotgun aimed at our heads."[9] Teachers took to the streets in subzero weather anyway, closing down the entire system. Almost everyone condemned the strike. On February 25, the *New York Times* ran an editorial that described the strike as both immoral and illegal. Even Dr. Arvis Eldred, executive secretary and leader of NYSTA, which the local Buffalo teachers belonged to, condemned it. Buffalo Mayor Bernard J. Dowd beseeched State Education Commissioner Francis Spaulding to order teachers back to work and on March 1, he did.

One of the few places that teachers got support was from organized labor. Teamster drivers bringing coal to the city's schools, necessary to prevent pipes from freezing, refused to cross teachers' picket lines. On a Sunday night, March 2, Mayor Dowd promised annual pay raises of $300 to $625. The teachers returned to their classes.

In response to the strike, New York legislators approved the Condon-Wadlin Act of 1947, considered one of the most antilabor bills ever passed in New York. During a strike of public employees, the law punished not unions, but the individuals who walked the picket lines. The law required the automatic dismissal of any public employee who went on strike. Those fired could be rehired, but only on the condition that they forego pay increases for three years and remain on probation for five years. The law spread like a contagion: Ohio, Michigan, and Texas also passed bills that same year that were modeled after the New York legislation.[10]

Public employees hated Condon-Wadlin for its harsh penalties against strikers, but the bill was also disliked because it didn't grant public employees, including teachers, the right to bargain collectively, a right that could have led to more negotiated settlements that would have precluded the need for strikes. In the mid-1960s, NYSTA had to fight school district by school district to win the right to bargain with administrators. On Long Island and in Westchester, in nearly one hundred New York communities, such as Hempstead, Wantagh, New Rochelle, and Mt. Vernon, teachers signed contracts in which school boards agreed to bargain with them. Yet the agreements were piecemeal and scattered and dependent on the goodwill of each school board.[11]

To expedite the process, NYSTA's leaders mobilized to fight for a state law that would grant their association collective bargaining powers. Each spring, Allen and other NYSTA leaders would drive to Albany to lobby state senators and assemblymen to replace the Condon-Wadlin Act with the Rose-Dominick Bill, sponsored by Assemblywoman Dorothy Rose and Senator D. Clinton Dominick III. The bill was designed to give upstate and Long Island teachers the same negotiating rights that teachers in New York City had won. However, NYSTA's leadership avoided the phrase "collective bargaining" because it was a union term, and these upstate teachers wanted nothing to do with unions. They instead used the euphemism "professional negotiations." NYSTA's leaders not only saw teachers as better than the working class, they saw them as a special case among all government workers. That's why the Rose-Dominick Bill was written just for teachers and not for other government employees.

Each year, Allen would meet with state legislators to promote the bill. They would listen politely as he explained that the legislation would give teachers real respect, and they would tell him how much they respected teachers and how much they supported the Rose-Dominick Bill. But each year, the bill would founder. After a few years, Allen realized that the legislators were yessing him, paying the kind of phony respect to teachers that the Rome school board had paid him. Each year's failure meant that each spring the young teacher had to sit once again before his school board and beg for better salaries and improved work conditions. And each year, the board members would listen, smile, thank him, and send him on his way.

What finally won upstate teachers the collective bargaining powers they so desired was not persistent lobbying, but a paralyzing strike in New York City. Organized labor—from which NYSTA teachers so badly wanted to distinguish themselves—would finally kill the Condon-Wadlin Act and win teachers a seat at the bargaining table.

The 1960s and early 1970s were a militant time not just for teachers, but for all American workers, and the unrest rivaled that of almost any other period in American history. Each year after 1963, the number of strikes rose across the country, peaking in 1970, and remaining at that level until the mid-1970s. If there was a capital for the unrest, it was New York City. In 1966 alone, New York City workers struck in the construction, airline, newspaper, cemetery, and taxi trades. But the most disruptive strike was that by the transit workers in New York City. They had been unionized since the 1930s, when private companies ran most of the buses and subways, and they had held onto the right to unionize once the transportation network was taken over by New York City. Still, they were poorly paid. At 5 a.m. on January 1, 1966, just hours after New York City Mayor John Lindsay took office, 35,000 bus and subway employees stopped working. The thirteen-day strike affected six million commuters.[12] The mayor tried to relieve the logjam by staggering rush hours, using commuter trains, and encouraging carpools, but nothing worked. One editorial in the *New York Times* suggested that the city had not been so disabled since the Civil War draft riots. To get the city operating again, Mayor Lindsay eventually acquiesced to the demands of the transit workers, improving pay, working conditions, and pensions.

Under the Condon-Wadlin Act, the striking transit workers were supposed to lose their jobs, be fined, and not receive any pay increases. But the state legislature, not wanting to force stiff punishment on transit workers after they had settled, gave them amnesty in 1966, and in doing so, buried the law for good.

New York Governor Nelson Rockefeller appointed a panel chaired by professor George Taylor of the Wharton School of Business to figure out how to replace Condon-Wadlin with a new law "protecting the public against the disruption of vital public services by illegal strikes, while at the same time protecting the rights of public employees."[13] In just nine weeks, the panel released its report, and its recommendations became the core of the Public Employees Fair Employment Act, which Rockefeller signed into law just three weeks later.

While the new law maintained the ban against public employee strikes, it softened the penalties against striking to make them more enforceable. But it also set up a formal process to help resolve disputes before they escalated into a strike. The law granted all public employees, including public school teachers, the right to unionize and engage in collective bargaining. The state Public Employment Relations Board (PERB) was created to administer the law and act as a referee in disputes. If employees reached an impasse in negotiations with management, the law provided for mediation and arbitration. The landmark legislation became known as the Taylor Law.

When Bob Allen read the report he was thrilled, because he knew it would forever change the status of upstate teachers. Now Allen's board of education couldn't just listen quietly and then dismiss him; they would have to bargain in good faith with teachers. Compared to the victory of New York City's teachers, born from strikes, this was a quiet revolution. But that was just fine by Allen, a moderate man in what was then a moderate organization.

Allen may have understood the importance of the Taylor Law, but it was not clear that NYSTA's leaders did. After the law passed, NYSTA organized a weeklong training program to discuss how teachers should respond to the law. The Rome teacher was shocked to discover that a NYSTA board member from his region of the state nominated not a teacher, but a high school principal to attend the training. Allen was livid. How blind could NYSTA's leaders be? The point of the Taylor Law was not to empower *administrators* to negotiate with administrators. The point was to empower public *employees*, which in the case of the schools, were *teachers*. Didn't they get it? He typed an angry letter expressing his frustration to Gladys Newell, NYSTA's president. Not only was it unwise and unfair to have administrators represent teachers, he wrote her, it violated the Taylor Law. You're not thinking this through, he wrote. Get some legal advice. You can't stack this with administrators. Administrators are going to be involved, but they're going to be involved *on the other side*.

A few weeks later, Dean Streiff, the director of field services for NYSTA, called Allen. Mrs. Newell asked me to call you back, he said. You know, we've been thinking about this, and you're probably right. So we want to invite you to come down and spend the week with us to discuss the Taylor Law.[14] Allen attended the training session with about fifty or so other teachers and administrators at Sterling Forest, a modern conference center in Tuxedo, New York. Day after day, lawyers educated teachers about the new powers that the Taylor Law had provided them. At the end of the session, Streiff offered eight teachers who represented different regions of the state one-year positions as organizers. They were all men; one of them was Allen.

Now a NYSTA teacher organizer, Allen was part traveling salesman and part missionary, hired to preach the gospel of the Taylor Law to teachers in ten counties, which included the cities of Utica, Rochester, Syracuse, Binghamton, and Rome. Almost every morning, the former military man would put on his suit and tie and drive his Ford Fairlane to meet with teachers, a commute that might take two hours each way. What Allen discovered was that most teachers were confused about what the Taylor Law meant—mostly because they couldn't quite grasp that they were labor. Teachers knew that they were salaried; they knew they were hired and fired by principals or by other administrators; they knew they weren't employers. But it was a leap for them to consider themselves employees, because for years NYSTA had been telling them—and they had been telling themselves—that they were professionals.

Allen's job was to teach teachers that they belonged in the employee half of the equation; the Taylor Law spelled that out clearly.

And though the law permitted them to organize like a union and bargain like a union, Allen and the other organizers never uttered the word. Instead of talking about unionizing, Allen informed teachers of their new "rights and responsibilities" under the Taylor Law or told them how they might "bargain contracts under the auspices of the Taylor Law." The first thing he had teachers in local associations do was petition each school board to win recognition as a "bargaining unit." Most upstate teachers were so ignorant of unions that they didn't know that *bargaining unit* as well as *mediation*, *fact-finding*, or *arbitration* were all union terms. Allen also had to work hard to educate teachers, so accustomed to subservience, that they were equal in power to their administrators during contract negotiations.

If the board wants to meet in the boardroom, tell them they have to make room for you at the table, Allen told local teacher leaders. If you have one meeting in the district office, have the next one in the high school faculty room. You put your ashes in the same ashtray they put their ashes in.

After those first visits to teachers, Allen would always give the same send-off. In five minutes, I'm going to walk out in the parking lot, he told them, jump in my car, and drive out of here. Tomorrow morning, I'm not going to be here—but you are. If you don't want to change things here, you don't have to. You're going to bargain the contract, not me. He did this to make it clear that the Taylor Law had handed power not to him or NYSTA bureaucrats, but to those who stepped up to battle in each school district, in each contract: teachers.[15]

As the Taylor Law changed schools, it also changed NYSTA. Allen noticed that after the law was passed, men began displacing women within the association. "The Taylor Law seemed to light a fire under men," Allen said. Few women applied for NYSTA's staff positions and women quickly began disappearing from leadership in local schools and other elected positions, where they had once been common. Was it that the Taylor Law had put teachers in a more adversarial position during negotiations, one that women at the time were less comfortable with than men? Was it that men wanted the increased power the Taylor Law granted teachers in each school and in the association? Or was it that Taylor meant that NYSTA was becoming more like a labor union, an institution with a long history of male chauvinism? All Allen was sure of was that he rarely saw a woman applicant for a staff position in one of the field offices.

As Allen and his peers moved ahead upstate, he read in the *Rome Daily Sentinel* about teachers from New York City—although to him they seemed to come from a different country. While he and many upstate teachers had welcomed the Taylor Law, teachers in New York City had attacked it. Allen and upstate leaders praised the powers to negotiate that the new law had granted them; New York City teachers denounced the punishments that still existed in the law against strikes and strikers. The Taylor Law had set a fine of up to $10,000 for every day a public employee union struck. A striking union could also be forced to collect its own dues from members for eighteen months instead of having the employer—a city, for example—collect them through payroll withholding. Government officials also had the right to file for a court injunction against any public union or individuals who struck illegally, and judges could jail unionists for ignoring an injunction.[16]

On May 23, 1967, three months before the Taylor Law went into effect, eighteen thousand unionized New York City workers, representing approximately two hundred thousand municipal workers, packed Madison Square Garden in the heart of Manhattan for a rally protesting the law. In attendance were members of the Transport Workers' Union, the UFT, and District Council 37 of the American Federation of State, County, and Municipal Employees (AFSCME). The crowd cheered when a declaration was read describing the Taylor Law as the "illegitimate offspring of a diseased bipartisanship." Workers pledged to "stand together in defense of one another until this evil law and its promoters are left in the dust of history."[17] But the union protests did little to stop the law, which went into effect on September 1, 1967.

The week after its passage, the UFT became the first union to strike under the new law as teachers refused to show up for the opening day of school. The union called it a "mass resignation" to avoid the penalties the law included against strikers. The strike lasted two weeks, with 47,000 of the 59,000 teachers in New York City staying out, an unprecedented show of teacher unity. Teachers emerged from the strike with a twenty-six-month contract that gave them a 20 percent increase in pay and benefits, gains that dwarfed those by every other major group of municipal employees at the time. The union also won the right to remove disruptive students and gained funding to lower class size in high-needs schools.

Still, there was a price to pay. The UFT was fined $150,000 for leading what everyone knew was a strike. Al Shanker, who had been chosen president of the New York City teachers' union in 1964, was found in contempt for defying the court order aimed at stopping the walkout. He had arranged to be taken into custody a few minutes after 6 p.m. on December 20, 1967, just after he addressed 1,800 UFT members in an emotional two-hour meeting. He was taken by car to the jail at 434 West 37th Street. A photograph of the good-bye kiss he gave his wife Eadie showed up in the next day's *New York Times*. Many of the teachers who saw the photo were distraught, but also proud. Tough, working-class leaders such as Mike Quill, the transit union leader, were the kind who usually went to jail for defying the powers-that-be. But now one of their own, a former public school teacher, was willing to lead them into battle, and to be taken prisoner. Shanker belied the stereotype of the rarified teacher who avoided the rough-and-tumble of politics. He was powerful, threatening, brilliant, vision-ary, tough, committed, controversial, and tireless. As Shanker was taken to jail, hundreds of teachers went so far as to sing for their leader, and the song they sang was "For He's a Jolly Good Fellow."

After he emerged from jail, a newscaster asked him what he thought he'd proven by his stay in prison. "I wasn't trying to prove any-thing," Shanker responded. "I didn't ask them to send me here. I think what has been proven is that teachers are not going to give up their fight for professional dignity, and they're not going to give up the fight for good schools, and if this is the price that we have to pay for it peri-odically then that price is gonna be paid."[18]

In many ways, Shanker was an unlikely leader. As a child, Albert had severe eczema, and his hands sometimes had to be tied to prevent him from scratching the sores. He reached his adult height of 6'3" by the age of twelve, and was always physically awkward. He was unable to see without thick glasses and his long face wasn't the kind you'd find on a movie billboard.

In some ways, though, his early experiences prepared him for the leader he would become. Growing up, he saw firsthand the importance of unions. His father, who had been a rabbinical student in Poland, delivered newspapers seven days a week, delivering the day's first editions at 2 a.m. "He'd get back at seven in the morning, totally exhausted," Shanker remembered. "Then at ten o'clock the afternoon papers would come out, and he'd start all over. . . . Imagine in the snow and heat all those pounds and pounds of paper in a pushcart, climbing five or six flights of stairs to deliver a two-cent newspaper. He worked like a beast."[19]

Al saw the gains his mother won through her membership with the Amalgamated Clothing Workers Union and the International Ladies Garment Workers Union. The unions whittled away her seventy-hour workweek and won her benefits and even a pension. Just below unions in his family were the public schools, a devotion that Shanker would carry on his entire life. "When I grew up," he later told Edwin Newman, the NBC correspondent, "my parents would never attack the teachers of public schools. . . . They came from overseas. To them the public school system represented something that they could give their children, something that they and their grandparents never had."[20] His mother spoke reverentially of teachers, and spoke of them in the same breath as doctors and lawyers.

As a Jewish child growing up in the 1930s in Ravenswood, a largely Irish section of Queens, Shanker was persecuted for being Jewish, a prejudice that undoubtedly contributed to his lifelong identification with the underprivileged. Just after his eighth birthday, a gang of boys surrounded Shanker in a vacant lot. Christ killer, they taunted him, we're going to hang you. They dragged him to a tree and one of the boys wrapped a rope around his neck. Others lifted him up in the air and then let him drop. His feet dangled. The noose tightened. The gang fled. He desperately grabbed at the rope to loosen it so he could breathe. By the time a passing woman cut the rope, he was barely conscious.[21]

"I could never play with the kids," he would say almost sixty years later. "There was always this 'Jew boy' and 'Christ killer' stuff. If I tried to go out and play, I'd get beat up."

Aware of the rise of Hitler in Nazi Germany, he understood the connection between the prejudice he felt personally and what happened to Jews elsewhere. In the years after the attack, the boy would sometimes sit on the footbridge of the Queensborough Bridge and gaze into the East River and wonder why so many people hated Jews so much.

"I was very interested in politics because politics had something to do with why some kids were beating me up," he later explained. When his parents marched for Franklin Delano Roosevelt for president in the 1930s, their son marched with them.

One of the boy's first social successes came with the Boy Scouts, where he was recognized for his strong mind and his leadership abilities. Here, he launched his first political rebellion. Tired of the amount of time the troop spent engaged in military drills, he drafted a petition that called for less marching and more camping and hiking. His scoutmaster agreed, and when he was drafted, he chose the fourteen-year-old as acting scoutmaster. Shanker quickly revealed his talents for organizing: he boosted the troop's enrollment from seventeen to eighty-five and added a Cub Scout chapter. For the rest of his life, he treasured his weathered copy of the *Boy Scout Handbook*.[22]

His successes continued at Stuyvesant High School, where, instead of gangs, he found bright, ambitious students. He received 100s on his math and chemistry Regents. He also headed the debating team. A former classmate of his in the high school, which was heavily Jewish, later observed: "Shanker got involved with the debating club and defended the Arabs. He'd win all the time."[23] No one was surprised when he listed "lawyer" in his high school yearbook as his expected profession.

In the late 1940s, he attended the University of Illinois, in Champagne-Urbana, where he learned that anti-Semitism wasn't confined to the streets of New York City. While looking for a place to live, he saw ads with restrictions like "No Jews or Negroes Wanted" or "White Anglo-Saxon Protestants Only." Some restaurants near the college refused to serve African Americans. Shanker joined an interracial group at a local Unitarian church that engaged in sit-ins and court action to end the segregation at these restaurants and in theaters, too. Still, the Unitarian students made an issue of his Jewish heritage when he decided to run for office.[24]

He found refuge as the chairman of a campus socialist study group and a member of the Young People's Socialist League. It was there that he first walked the picket line for the civil rights of African Americans, a cause he believed in and would fight for his entire life.[25]

When Shanker abandoned his PhD in philosophy at Columbia University, became a teacher, and threw himself into the work of the Teachers Guild, he became a favorite of the older generation of union intellectuals such as Cogen, David Wittes, a guild accountant, and Jules Kolodny, a lawyer. Shanker was rare among labor leaders in that he was a voracious reader. Sandra Feldman, Shanker's assistant for many years before she became UFT president, remembers that he carried at least one bag full of books whenever he traveled abroad. "He was a teacher," Feldman said, "but he was also a learner."[26]

The labor leader also had amazing recall of what he read. Fred Nauman, the Brooklyn science teacher involved in the 1960 New York City teachers' strike, later worked as an assistant for Shanker. Nauman noticed that the teacher leader spoke in almost perfect outlines when he gave his ad-libbed speeches. Nauman would sometimes look up passages that Shanker quoted in his talks without notes and found them close to verbatim.[27]

But what impressed so many teachers most about Shanker was his pugnacity. It was as if, unable to protect himself as a child, he had vowed as an adult to defend himself and teachers to the end. He spoke with a passion and directness that was more akin to a traditional labor leader than someone who had been on an academic track. When James B. Donovan, president of the Board of Education in New York City during the early 1960s, referred to teachers as donkeys, Shanker upped the ante, calling Donovan an "ass" that teachers "had no confidence in."[28] Shanker was not afraid to rail against the powers-that-be; he was not afraid of the news cameras; and he was not afraid to recommend a strike if he thought that was what teachers needed to do.

In 1968, Bob Allen—and teachers all over the country—watched as Shanker, then thirty-nine, led a series of three strikes that would cause chaos in the city for half a year and make him a national symbol of teacher militancy. The strikes revealed the power of the UFT and Shanker's ability to stand strong for teachers, even when the fight turned ugly and divisive.

At its simplest, the conflict was between the rights of teachers and those of largely minority communities in the city who were given local control of their schools as part of a decentralization experiment. The strikes were triggered by events in the Brooklyn school district that included the neighborhoods of Ocean Hill and Brownsville, both areas dominated by Puerto Ricans and African Americans. The dispute between the UFT and the Ocean Hill–Brownsville governing board began to simmer when the Board of Education allowed that local board, which was controlled by black community leaders, to select black and Puerto Rican principals outside of civil service lists, which were dominated by white examination-qualified applicants and preferred by the UFT.

The conflict erupted when the Brooklyn board sent letters to nineteen UFT teachers, including Fred Nauman, telling them they had been reassigned to other schools. Rhody McCoy, the superintendent of the Ocean Hill-Brownsville district, said he ordered the teachers' transfers because they had opposed the minority community's attempt to control the schools. The board wanted to replace the teachers—who were all white, with one exception—with black teachers who were more in tune with their district's educational philosophy. The union felt that the firings violated the due process clause they had fought so hard to win through negotiations with New York City's Board of Education. To Shanker and others, the rights of teachers were being threatened by local school boards and administrators who wanted the freedom to hire and fire whomever they pleased.

"We cannot allow this to happen," Shanker wrote to parents in early September 1968, "and we must be sure that this situation does not occur when the whole city school system is decentralized. Teachers cannot work in such conditions. If a teacher is not good, he should be dismissed, but he must have a fair trial. Teachers, like any other job-holder, must be assured of job security and union rights, whether the Board of Education is central or local."[29]

The UFT decided to strike on September 9, 1968. It was the first of three strikes that disrupted the schools until mid-November. More than a million children lost nearly two months of school because of the strikes, which pitted the white middle and working classes, including teachers, against much of the city's African American community. The public had a hard time understanding the issue of "due process" and saw the union's strikes as an attempt to fight the decentralization of the city's schools, which in part, it was. The press was hostile too. The *New York Herald Tribune* called the UFT "The United Federation of Teamsters." An editorial in the *Daily News* described the strike as "an example of greed plus a public-be-damned attitude."

Some unions opposed the strike, as did some UFT members, such as John J. O'Neil, a UFT vice president. The New York City chapter of the American Civil Liberties Union also condemned the teachers. The battle broke apart one of the strongest political alliances in the city, that between the Jewish and the African American communities. Shanker wouldn't back down, McCoy wouldn't back down, and the rhetoric became nastier as the two sides dug in. On a radio program, a black teacher read an anti-Semitic poem written by a student. Demonstrators spat at teachers, and newspaper editors pilloried the UFT as racist and regressive. A man threatened Shanker and his son Adam one day when they were out walking in Prospect Park.

Through it all, Shanker defended his teachers in newspapers, and when reporters turned against the teacher strikers, he appeared on television and radio talk shows to get his message out unfiltered. For the mostly Jewish teachers, Shanker's militancy evoked some of the pre–World War II images of Jews, such as the Jewish prizefighters, gangsters, and tough labor unionists, who were not just comfortable defending themselves, but also attacking their enemies.

Midway through the strife, some anti-Semitic leaflets surfaced in the neighborhoods of Ocean Hill-Brownsville. Shanker claimed they were the work of the black teachers association and the union copied and distributed them "to show everybody the kind of thing we were fighting against."[30] To his followers, the move was more evidence of their leader's pugnaciousness; to his critics, it was a blatant attempt to exaggerate anti-Semitism among blacks—creating a further tension between the two groups—in order to win the public relations war. Shanker's decisions in this period would make him bitter enemies who would never forgive him for the animosity he flamed during the debacle.

After the last strike, which lasted five weeks, the union got its way. The nineteen dismissed teachers returned to their school; due process rights were not only defended, they were strengthened. But once again there was a price to pay, and the UFT lost the right to an automatic dues check-off and was hit with another serious fine. Shanker was again jailed for fifteen days. But in the UFT election that same year, teachers voted for Shanker by a margin of nine to one. The reputation he earned in those strikes was immortalized in Woody Allen's 1973 movie *Sleeper*. In the sci-fi comedy, Allen's character wakes up after two hundred years of suspended animation to discover that the civilized world had been completely destroyed. When Allen asks what happened, his doctor explains: "A man by the name of Albert Shanker got hold of a nuclear warhead."

That UFT strike in 1968 and a ten-day strike the same year by city sanitation workers prompted Governor Rockefeller to add harsher strike penalties to the Taylor Law. In 1969, New York lawmakers removed the cap on union fines and introduced new penalties against individual strikers, making them give up two days' pay for each day they stayed out on strike. But what Bob Allen noticed was the defiant attitude of New York City's teachers in 1967 and 1968, which would not remain within the city's borders. Rebellion was in the air, wafting north and west across the state, and teachers in small towns and suburban communities could not help but breathe it.

In the 1967–1968 school year, the first after the passage of the Taylor Law, upstate teachers had the upper hand in negotiations with school boards. One big advantage they had was NYSTA, which queried teachers in each district about their work conditions. How much do you make? How do salaries increase with experience? What benefits do you receive? Do you get sick days? How many? The researchers compiled the data, ranked the districts, and used the data as ammunition in negotiations. The association trained teachers or sometimes brought in labor lawyers to represent local teacher groups. School boards, though, at first used administrators or local lawyers with little experience in labor law. NYSTA won a few "lighthouse" contracts in places such as Ithaca and Utica, and these became models for many of the teachers in smaller districts.

Sometimes school administrators resisted the law. Tony Bifaro, who would later work as the assistant to NYSUT's president, was hired in 1967 to teach high school English in Brocton, a rural district in the western-most corner of the state. After the Taylor Law went into effect, the young teacher volunteered for the district's bargaining team. The next day his superintendent asked him to withdraw his name, saying it could jeopardize his tenure in the district. "I told him that that was a threat," said Bifaro, "and I wasn't going to accept that." The encounter only spurred the young teacher to get more involved in teacher politics.[31]

By 1970, over six hundred teacher contracts had been bargained collectively and more than 98 percent of all teachers in the state were covered by negotiated contracts. Ninety percent of the contracts included a grievance procedure, and nearly half of the contracts provided binding arbitration of grievances as a final step, which meant that no issue in those cases would ever be left unresolved.[32]

But each year, negotiations in New York State got tougher for teachers. Allen noticed that soon he was negotiating with labor lawyers the districts had hired. School boards began to take advantage of a loophole in the Taylor Law that said that if an impasse were reached, the school board would become the final arbiter of a contract. Knowing this, some school districts refused to negotiate in good faith, trying instead to bully teachers into an impasse. In response, NYSTA teachers began to take an action that was unimaginable only a few years earlier: they launched strikes.

In August 1970, two teachers from Lindenhurst, Stanley Rosengarten and Robert Bukowski, served a ten-day prison sentence for an eleven-day strike in May. They were the first teachers outside of New York City to serve jail terms for striking—and the first NYSTA teachers to do so. "The wrong people went to jail," said Manny Kafka,

NYSTA's president. "Those school board members who refused to negotiate a decent contract—or to provide for educational improvement—are the ones who should have gone behind bars."[33]

The conflict in Lindenhurst that summer set the stage for the 1970–1971 school year. Teachers struck in Springville, near Buffalo, in Niagara Falls, in northern Westchester County, and on Long Island. In the Bethlehem Central School District near Albany, a teachers' strike began fifteen minutes after pupils had arrived for classes. In Wappingers Falls, a court injunction was taken out to force teachers back to work, but teachers there voted narrowly to stay out anyway. In Ballston Spa, a suburb north of Albany, sheriff deputies were called in to create a corridor through teacher picket lines to allow pupils into the schools.[34] By the end of the school year, teachers in eleven school districts had struck. In the summer of 1971, Allen, who had risen to the position of assistant director of field services in NYSTA, noted in NYSTA's newspaper, the *Challenger*, that serious contract disputes existed in four hundred of the roughly one thousand school districts around the state.[35]

It had been only five years since the NEA, NYSTA's parent group, had reversed its antistrike stance and grudgingly acknowledged that "the Association realizes that teachers may have no choice but to resort to a withdrawal of services."[36] Teacher militancy among these nonunionized teachers had become common across New York State and across the country. Before the 1964–1965 school year, there had never been more than five teacher strikes in one year. Nationwide in 1970–1971, though, AFT locals had called 21 strikes. NEA-affiliated locals called 109.[37] As the two organizations became more and more alike, they battled over which group would lead teachers. Nowhere was the battle fiercer than in New York State.

As the two New York State organizations—the UFT-dominated Empire State Federation of Teachers and NYSTA—became more and more alike, the competition between them grew. In the late 1960s and early 1970s, Shanker and the New York City unionists launched an invasion into the rural and suburban districts that had been under NYSTA's control for well over one hundred years. The invasion of UFT organizers upstate and into Long Island threatened the very survival of NYSTA, and the organization's leaders responded with a fierce counter-attack, financed by the NEA. The two groups might have weakened, even destroyed, each other, if not for an attack launched against both groups, and all New York teachers, on April 1, 1971. The assault came from a conservative state legislature that would pass four laws that threatened all the gains that teachers had made in the previous ten years, and some gains, such as tenure, won even earlier. Teachers quickly learned that their most dangerous enemy was not local school boards or principals, but an unfriendly legislature that could turn back all their local successes with a single statewide vote. Suddenly, teachers were asking themselves a new question: Should we enter the statewide political fray, and if so, how?

CHAPTER 3

Entering the Political Fray:
The Jerabek Attack

The sun had set on Thursday, the first day of April 1971, and Lynn Costello, a high school social studies teacher from Blue Point, a small hamlet on the south shore of Long Island, was settling into his busy evening routine. He had taught his usual five classes—four in American history and one in government—to 9th and 10thgraders at the high school in East Islip. After school he coached track, running with the students to release some of the day's stress. He came home at last with eighty papers from his college-bound students, which meant that he spent much of the night hunched over a card table in his living room, hurriedly marking the papers to get them back to his students the next day.[1]

Keeping up with current events was essential to his teaching, so he watched the eleven o'clock news. The United States was still knee-deep in the Vietnam War and that day, the U.S. House of Representatives had voted to extend the military draft of young men. In Cleveland, fourteen men in Hell's Angels, the motorcycle gang, were indicted on first-degree murder. Absent from the news, though, was an event that would profoundly affect his life and the lives of all New York State teachers. Republican legislators spent much of the night cementing deals in order to get support for Republican Governor Nelson Rockefeller's state budget. They offered pet bills to the most conservative Republicans, who were reluctant to support the budget because it spent more and taxed more than they wished. The bills had been drawn up on Thursday, and were toasted with Dubonnet and martinis by Republican leaders attending a private party in the office of Senate Majority Leader Earl W. Brydges.[2]

Four of these bills were anti-teacher. One bill eliminated teacher sabbaticals for a year; another eliminated minimum salaries for teachers; a third required state college instructors to spend a minimum number of hours in the classroom each week; and a fourth weakened tenure.

One teacher later compared the four bills passed to nasty bee stings; another described them as a collective slap in the face; still another described the bills as an alarm that woke up a political giant that had been sleeping in the state for well over one hundred years: teachers.

At 10:20 a.m. on Friday, legislators friendly to teachers called the downtown Albany office of the New York State Teachers Association (NYSTA). "You won't believe what they're trying to do," one of them told NYSTA's leaders. The association's officers immediately scurried the one long block from their offices on Dove Street to the legislative chambers of the State Capitol just as the 10:30 a.m. session began. They buttonholed teacher-friendly assemblymen to see if the association's vehement opposition to the four bills might sway legislators. In the Senate, NYSTA officials fed questions about the bills through sympathetic legislators. "How can we ram these bills through without even holding hearings?" asked one legislator. "The leadership hasn't even *talked* to NYSTA about these bills," said another. At times, teacher leaders thought that their protests might kill the anti-teacher legislation. But each time, the Republican leadership intervened, calling recesses, party caucuses, conferences, and "at-ease" breaks, one after another. In these breaks, Republican leaders reminded legislators who wavered that a decision to renege on their vote for the budget would undermine the entire budget deal—as well as their pet projects. By 7:30 p.m. on Friday, Rockefeller's budget was secure. The Senate and the Assembly passed all four anti-teacher bills on a day New York's teachers would dub Sordid Friday.[3]

Lynn Costello and many of the other thirty thousand teachers on Long Island first learned of the bills from Long Island's major afternoon newspaper, *Newsday*. The front-page headline read: "GOPers Agree on Budget Cuts/Teacher Benefits Traded Away."

What upset Costello and other teachers most was that legislators had weakened the tenure law. The bill extended the probationary period for a teacher on tenure track from three years to five, meaning that a teacher would have to wait two more years before his or her job was protected from a potentially arbitrary firing. Tenure had been established in New York City in 1917 as a protection against firings by political hacks in the city, and was extended to all state teachers in 1945. Now, overnight, tenure had been drastically weakened. If legislators could pass such a bill with impunity, what might they do next—eliminate tenure all together? Without the due process protections of tenure, Costello and other teachers believed administrators would fire teachers for minor incidents or because of school politics. They could fire a teacher to bring in a friend or a nephew of the superintendent. They could fire experienced teachers who earned higher wages. They could fire "trouble-makers," such as union activists, and thereby destroy the union. As Costello and other teachers considered what legislators had done, they wondered: Who the hell was behind these bills?

Many of the laws passed on April 2 did not list the sponsoring legislator, obscuring the connection between pet bills and budget votes. But the sponsor of the four anti-teacher bills was clearly named on the list of bills that came out of the Rules Committee: "At Request of Mr. Jerabek," they said.[4]

Charles A. Jerabek represented the state's sixth assembly district in Suffolk County, which included the outermost half of Long Island, and he lived in Bay Shore, a hamlet in the town of Islip. Islip was one of the conservative bastions on Long Island, mixing older Republicans from the town's rural days with new ones who had fled New York City for suburbia in the 1950s and 1960s. Jerabek operated an industrial design company in Islip and had participated in Bay Shore politics for more than fifteen years, volunteering for local associations such as the Rotary Club. The mustachioed assemblyman was a member of the Amateur Comedy Club in New York City, an amateur theater group, and also worked at the Pratt Institute in Brooklyn for two years as a product design teacher.[5]

Marcella Fugle, a teacher from Hamburg, New York, just south of Buffalo, had met Jerabek in the late 1960s, while she was in Albany lobbying for NYSTA. Ron Tills, an assemblyman from her district, introduced Fugle to the Bay Shore assemblyman. When Fugle told Jerabek that she was a teacher lobbying for educational issues, he responded. If you were a good teacher, he said, you'd be back in the classroom, not here. Then he walked away. Fugle told teachers in her school about the unpleasant exchange; none of them had heard of Jerabek.[6]

But once the anti-teacher bills passed, Jerabek's name became the rallying cry for New York's teachers. They would attack Jerabek, and he fired back. It was a battle that would include secret meetings, secret deals, and secret donations—a battle typical of New York politics, except that for the first time, teachers weren't watching on the sidelines. Instead, they were angry combatants, scraping, fighting, organizing.

Jerabek's bills outraged Costello, but he wasn't surprised by the disregard toward teachers that seemed to characterize them. In many ways, Costello had felt disrespected professionally since he began his career as a social studies teacher in 1964. His starting salary was $6,300, more than upstate teachers earned, but meager compared to salaries of other professionals or skilled laborers. An educator's pay was so low that the man who taught in the classroom next to Costello's that fall, a teacher with a wife and two children, easily qualified for food stamps, a new benefit being offered by the federal government. Banks on Long Island, aware of teachers' paltry salaries, were reluctant to provide them with mortgages.

One day in 1969, Costello was visiting his next-door neighbor, when a college friend of the neighbor stopped by. Costello listened as the two men shared news about some of their college buddies. Hey, what happened to "so-and-so"? asked the guest.

He became a teacher, Costello's neighbor replied.

A teacher? Oh my God, said the visitor. Man, that guy, he did so well in school I thought he'd make something of himself. "That's what I heard over and over again," Costello recalled many years later. "Ask me why I got into the union, that's the reason. I was not going to put up with it. I kept saying to myself: This is either going to get better, or I'm leaving. I'm not going to have these people laugh at me."

On the Tuesday following the state legislature's anti-teacher votes, Long Island teachers came together to consider their response. One of the men present was David Miller, a NYSTA director in central Suffolk County, who said he would push for a strike declaration at NYSTA's board of directors meeting, scheduled for the next night. The Jerabek bills had convinced Miller and other NYSTA leaders on Long Island to join ranks with their usual combatants, the United Teachers of New York (UTNY), the statewide organization of the United Federation of Teachers (UFT), which represented New York City's teachers.

For years, rank-and-file teachers had been griping that their leaders—whether in NYSTA or UTNY—spent too much energy bickering and too little time advancing education and their profession. Fred Lambert, NYSTA's membership promotion director, witnessed the debilitating effect this conflict had on the movement. Shortly after the Jerabek bills passed, Manny Kafka, president of NYSTA, held a press conference on one side of a room in the State Capitol, while Al

Shanker, the New York City teacher leader and UFT president, held one on the other side.

"I was talking to a legislator there," recalled Lambert, "and he said, 'You know why the Jerabek bills went through? Because you guys are on opposite sides [of the room]. And you're going to get more of the same.'"[7] Ken Deedy, then president of the Farmingdale Federation of Teachers, a local within UTNY, described the conflict between UTNY and NYSTA this way: "We both had very effective legislative programs. Our program was to kill their program and their program was to kill ours."[8]

In the May 1971 issue of *New York State Education*, President Kafka responded to disgruntled members who had complained about the association's inability to defend teachers from Jerabek's political assault. In an editorial titled "Sordid Friday," Kafka wrote:

> You have asked, "Where was NYSTA when the four Jerabek bills were being rammed through the Legislature?" NYSTA was right there—lobbying and fighting, and we were the *only* group at the capitol even to attempt to block this surprise move. It may seem to some that NYSTA was not on the job for these bills to pass. Nothing could be further from the truth! . . . Some have asked: "Why hasn't NYSTA shown leadership?" In fact, NYSTA *alone* has shown leadership.

Kafka had initially heeded the call for a statewide strike and had asked teacher leaders to get strike authorization from local NYSTA chapters. Only two locals, however, came back with an authorization. Kafka was also reluctant to hold a symbolic one-day strike because according to the Taylor Law, each teacher would be fined two days' pay for every day he or she struck. Kafka had another idea, which he suggested in a letter to NYSTA leaders. Instead of throwing away two days' pay on a one-day strike, teachers could donate a day's pay to VOTE (Voice of Teachers for Education), NYSTA's two-year-old political action committee.[9] "With the goal of one day's pay from every teacher in the state," he wrote, "we would raise a campaign fund better than $5 million—easily enough to re-elect friends of education and defeat those who are opposed to good schools."[10]

Kafka's bid for a political war chest was a bold idea, but it seemed doomed for one simple reason: teachers were notoriously cheap. Costello knew this because the year before he had volunteered to serve as the coordinator for the Central Suffolk County VOTE. His job was to solicit donations from local teachers for local and statewide political campaigns.

"This was the worst job in the entire world," Costello said. "Nobody wanted it. Teachers believed they had no connection to politics. As far as they were concerned, if you were nice to the principal and made him happy, that was all you had to do."[11]

In 1970, NYSTA's leaders had suggested that Costello and the other VOTE coordinators ask for a $10 donation from each teacher. Those few teachers who did agree to give would invariably reach into their pockets and hand Costello some spare change. When it came time to report to the next Long Island VOTE meeting, Costello only had $150 to show for his efforts collecting donations from the three hundred teachers in his district. Embarrassed, Costello even considered skipping the meeting. But once he confessed that he had raised a paltry $150, another VOTE coordinator responded, How did you raise so much money? The other VOTE coordinators had collected even less. In 1970, all of New York's teachers gave VOTE just $7,000, seven cents for every teacher who belonged to NYSTA. Cub Scouts, Costello knew, had better luck soliciting.

In the weeks after Sordid Friday, organized teachers faced a critical strategic decision: Who to blame for the quartet of anti-teacher bills? Jerabek's name was on the four laws, but the Republican-dominated legislature had passed them overwhelmingly. NYSTA's leaders, including Kafka and NYSTA's public relations guru Ned Hopkins, knew that to blame the entire Republican Party would put them in opposition to the majority of state legislators as well as to the governor, who had long been sympathetic to education.[12] NYSTA's leaders decided to focus teacher rage on Jerabek. The strategy was kind to Republican legislators, but it gave teachers a poster boy they could use to raise money. The name Charles Jerabek, once unknown, soon became an epithet on the lips of New York's teachers. NYSTA immediately mailed out a special legislative bulletin, titled "Sordid Friday," accusing the Bay Shore assemblyman of harboring "inveterate malevolence" toward teachers. Harry Wilson, president of the Long Island Council of Teachers, part of the American Federation of Teachers, spoke for many when he declared, "Jerabek was a dirty word, and we hated him."[13]

Jerabek was aware of the efficacy of NYSTA's strategy. "They had their goat," the assemblyman, referring to himself, would say many years later, "and they had him by the short hairs."[14] Teacher leaders would pass him in the hallways of the State Capitol and say, "What are you going to do to us today, Mr. Jerabek?" Soon after the four bills were passed in 1971, Jerabek's four-year-old Ford convertible was stolen and torched. The assemblyman could never prove his suspicion, but he believed for the rest of his days that the culprit was none other than an angry teacher.

In early May, just a few weeks after Sordid Friday, another bill was introduced that put teachers on the defensive. The bill, introduced by both Charles Jerabek and Assembly majority leader John Kingston, a Republican from Westbury, would force public employees to negotiate only salaries and work hours. While the bill targeted all public employees, teachers again suspected they were the bill's prime target. It would forbid them from negotiating many issues, including curriculum, maximum class size, school discipline, and educational goals, all of which were on the table under the Taylor Law. Again, legislators tried to rush the bill through their chambers.

This time, though, in their first major collaboration, NYSTA and the UFT pooled their political resources. On May 7, 1971, NYSTA President Kafka and UFT President Al Shanker met in Albany to coordinate their lobbying, forming what they called the Emergency Coalition of Teacher Organizations. That weekend, teachers flooded legislators with fourteen thousand phone calls and telegrams. "The bill ruined the May 8–9 weekend for at least one legislator whose home phone rang incessantly with complaints from angry unionists," according to the June 2 *New York Times*. The bill was "starred" in the assembly—deferred indefinitely—and never arrived on the floor of the legislature for a vote.

"To defeat that ugly move," Kafka would later say of the Kingston-Jerabek bill, "we mounted the greatest campaign in our history."[15]

To create a war chest for political campaigns that were coming in 1972, NYSTA had asked teachers to donate a day's pay—roughly $50—to VOTE. Costello, Walter Dunn, president of the East Islip Teachers Association (EITA), and Ed Lopez, EITA grievance chairman, decided to ask for VOTE contributions at a meeting about Jerabek they would hold at East Islip high school.

Most of the high school teaching staff showed up for the event, a remarkable success in itself. Dunn and Costello spoke, and then

Costello told the crowd they could hand in their pledge cards on their way out—just in case they didn't have money with them, a familiar excuse. To make sure teachers in attendance would hand in their cards, the men put a teacher at each of the exits to collect them. After the meeting, the three men counted the cash, checks, and pledged money, and found they had raised $15,000. They were stunned. On one night, in one school, they had raised more than twice the amount that NYSTA had raised in the entire state the previous year.

"Almost everybody donated a day's pay," Costello said. "Now, in some cases we had to go back to them five or six times to collect, but still. . . ."

The teacher contributions in East Islip turned out to be more the norm than the exception. Something had shifted in the psyche of teachers. Pledge coupons were placed in all of NYSTA's publications. "Talking is Out . . ." said one coupon. "Action is In!!"[16] In the spring, Kafka traveled to a NYSTA local in St. Lawrence, a fairly low-paying region in the upper reaches of the state, and there, too, a phalanx of teachers had pledged a day's pay.[17] The angriest teachers, though, seemed to come from Long Island, Jerabek's home, and they were also the most eager to contribute. In late April 1971, a Long Island newspaper reported that the 425 members of the West Babylon Teachers Association, also in Suffolk County, had collected $21,500 for VOTE, an average of $50.58 a head. Dan Threatt, the president of that association, said that in the previous year all of West Babylon's teachers had donated only $100 to VOTE.[18]

Six weeks after Jerabek's bills were passed, four thousand teachers descended on Hofstra University in Hempstead, Long Island, about twenty-five miles west of Jerabek's home district, for a rally to raise funds. Many attendees had to sit in the aisles. Signs attached to chairs in the front of the room read "Political Action" and "We've Had It!"

"The schools do have friends in Albany," NYSTA President Kafka said to the overflow crowd. "Their number is not encouraging. You see a great part of them on this platform. That is the most illuminating—and pathetic—comment on teachers in politics that I can cite. The whole point of this rally and of our $5 million fund drive is to change that statistic completely."

The keynote speaker that afternoon was U.S. Senator Charles Goodell, who had been defeated in 1970 by Conservative Party candidate James Buckley. "If there's one thing that a politician understands the day after he's elected," Goodell said, "it's the need for money to run his next campaign." He went on to say, to the delight of the crowd: "I can't think of any force that would be more healthy for our country than a lobby of educators with a budget of five million dollars to distribute among the candidates of its choice."[19]

"It is time once and for all," said Dr. Francis J. White, NYSTA's executive secretary, "that whenever a legislator votes against children, schools, teachers and society's future, he has committed a crime that is politically fatal."[20] During the two-hour rally, teachers contributed another $100,000.

In the September 1971 Legislative Bulletin, Kafka wrote that "checks representing a day's pay [are] pouring in from educators all over the state."[21] Twelve thousand teachers had donated money. Ray Skuse, the NYSTA lobbyist, called the fundraising drive "the most phenomenal out-pouring of grassroots political sentiment" he had ever witnessed.[22] By the end of 1971, NYSTA's teachers had sent change and bills and checks totaling a half million dollars, an average of $4.50 per teacher.[23] While the final tally didn't come close to the association's five million dollar goal, it was still dramatically more than teachers had ever given. By the next spring, over twenty thousand NYSTA teachers had contributed—the lion's share from Long Island. The funds were deposited in savings accounts until the 1972 campaign season heated up.[24]

In the meantime, Costello knew exactly what he wanted to do with at least a small chunk of the bounty: spend it on a campaign to defeat Jerabek. "What we had to do," he said, "was to prove that there was some payback."[25] But did teachers have the political clout to make that happen? The statewide chairman of VOTE, Roy MacDougal of Port Jefferson, was doubtful. "I don't think [Jerabek] can be beaten in the general election," MacDougal told a reporter, adding that teachers were not interested in financing a political "exercise in futility." Jerabek concurred. "I am reasonably certain I can overcome it," he said, referring to the teachers' animosity. "If it became a major threat to me, they'd have one hell of a war on their hands."[26]

Costello and his peers knew that Jerabek belonged not to the Republican Party, but to the Conservative Party. That party had gained power in the late 1960s as an alternative to liberal Republicans such as New York Governor Nelson Rockefeller, U.S. Senator Jacob Javits, and New York City Mayor John Lindsay. Conservatives were antitaxes, antigovernment, and solidly antiunion. Their shining star was James Buckley, a New York State Conservative Party politician, who was elected to the United States Senate in 1970. The Conservative Party had succeeded somewhat by striking deals with the Republican Party to cross-endorse candidates. Conservatives would endorse Republicans if Republicans endorsed a few of their candidates. The alliance proved formidable, especially on Long Island. It was such a cross-endorsement that won Jerabek his first assembly victory in 1968 and his reelection in 1970.

Costello believed that the only chance teachers had of unseating Jerabek in predominantly Republican Suffolk County was to knock him off the Republican Party line on the ballot. But how were they going to get the Republican Party to abandon Jerabek?

Costello was hardly an experienced political operative. He was a Democrat in a Republican County and he had never even lobbied for teacher issues in Albany. Still, the political science teacher was savvy enough about the local power structure to know that the Republican Party in Suffolk County was controlled by Tony Pace, the Town Republican Chairman for Islip who talked out of the side of his mouth.

"If Tony Pace decided to do something," said one teacher from the area, "it was done."[27]

Costello wanted something done. So he phoned Pace at his office and left a message. Pace didn't return Costello's first phone call. Or his second. Or his third. Costello didn't take offense. He knew that Pace had little reason to know about him or VOTE, the scrawny new player in Suffolk County politics. Finally, one afternoon after school, Costello got a phone call from the gruff-voiced leader.

I hear you've been trying to get ahold of me, Pace said.

Well, we've been trying, Costello said.

I heard you've raised a lot of money, Pace said.

Well, we've been trying, Costello said again.

Pace invited Costello to his Republican Committee Headquarters in the town of Islip, located in the hamlet of Bay Shore. Pace held court in the biggest office in the building behind a large wooden desk and listened while the East Islip social studies teacher gave his analysis of the Republican-Conservative alliance in Suffolk County.

The tail is wagging the dog here, Costello said. The Conservative Party, which can't win anything on its own, is forcing the Republican Party to give up jobs that they shouldn't have to give up. If you got teachers on your side, you can win here without the Conservative line. Then Costello moved on to the reason for his visit: Jerabek. You've got so many good people who could hold this job, he said, and you've got this guy who is alienating us for no reason. I don't know if we ever did anything to him. He's just killing us, and it's not just here. He's killing us all over the state. If the Republican Party dropped Jerabek, said Costello, teachers would be happy to help out with any other candidate the party put forward in the district.

Pace revealed little. He didn't agree to dump Jerabek, but Costello left feeling that the county leader was open to the idea. The men would meet again.[28]

Not long after, Tony Prudenti, another important figure in Suffolk County's Republican Party, invited Costello and other teacher leaders to Republican County Headquarters, located on bay-front property just two blocks from Costello's home in Blue Point. Prudenti seated Costello and a few other teachers who came to the meeting in a former banquet hall in what had once been a seaside hotel. Costello was surprised to find that Prudenti had invited about a dozen other Republican players from the county to the meeting.

All the men sat in a circle. Costello knew that money and power were connected, but he was still new to the etiquette of how such political tender was exchanged. The East Islip teacher made the first move, handing out a one-page list of the NYSTA locals from all over Long Island. Next to each local was printed a dollar amount of how much teachers had contributed to VOTE. The Republican leaders, who had been talking among themselves, suddenly went silent when they got the sheets. The only sound in the room was the rustling of the mimeographed fundraising lists that showed that VOTE had raised tens of thousands of dollars on Long Island in just a few months.

Some of the Republican operatives began shaking their heads, as if the figures both impressed and mystified them. Finally, the Republican town chairman from Babylon asked: How did you raise all of this money without a dinner?

Costello would remember the question for the rest of his days. These political veterans hadn't asked him about what issues teachers cared about or even how he and the other teachers felt about particular candidates. What they wanted to know was: How had teachers convinced their constituency to cough up money without the quid pro quo of steak and entertainment? The inseparability of money and politics—what the social studies teacher studied in the classroom—had never been so apparent to Costello. He answered the question: You've got a guy in your party who has alienated thousands of our people and made them angry enough that they're giving a day's pay. Another Republican operative in the room asked, What are you going to do with all the money? We're looking to be reasonable, replied Costello, and we don't want to pick a fight with anybody. But we have to get rid of Charlie Jerabek.[29]

After that meeting, Costello convened with the statewide VOTE committee to decide how they would spend the roughly half a million dollars they had raised for the 1972 election. VOTE gave many campaigns $5,000, $10,000, or $15,000, but the committee was willing to contribute significantly more to defeat Jerabek.[30] Costello and fellow activist Nick Maletta arranged another meeting with Tony Pace in the late spring of 1972. We want to do what's helpful, Costello told Pace, and we want this guy out. Then Costello, again naïve to the art of political etiquette, made a blunt offer: We'll contribute $25,000 to your party.[31]

Pace's eyes went wide. As Costello figured it, this contribution amounted to about four times what was needed to run an Assembly campaign. Again, Pace made no promise that he would knock Jerabek off the Republican line, but he did suggest the men meet again.

Before they left, Tony Pace asked about Maletta's family. When Maletta mentioned his daughter, a senior in high school at the time, Pace asked, Does she need a summer job?

Sure, that would be nice, Maletta replied.

On your way out, Pace suggested, stop by my patronage man.[32]

At their next meeting, Pace told Costello that $25,000 was too big a contribution. He suggested $20,000 instead. And how did Costello want to make the donation? Costello was confused. He assumed he'd just write a check. Pace wanted something more discreet for the donation, which was legal, but might appear somewhat unseemly.

Pace made a suggestion: Why not buy some fundraising tickets to our annual dinner?

Whatever you want to do, Costello replied.

Costello did the math. Each ticket to the local Republican fundraiser cost $100—a hefty sum in those days. A donation of $20,000 would buy two hundred seats. Still, Pace had made no definite commitment to pull the Republican endorsement from Jerabek. Perry B. Duryea Jr., the Republican Speaker of the Assembly, had put a lot of pressure on Pace to keep Jerabek, a political ally of Duryea's. The Speaker was from Montauk Point, which was also in Suffolk County, and he wanted the cross-endorsements of Conservatives and Republicans preserved. It still was unclear whether Pace would find somebody else for the Republican line come the spring primary or buckle under political pressure and again give the line to Jerabek.

On the morning of March 20, 1972, Costello, with his East Islip colleagues Walter Dunn and Ed Lopez, went to Albany to lobby for teachers' issues. They joined hundreds of teachers who gathered at Albany's Hyatt House Motel. It was the first time ordinary teachers had congregated to lobby legislators.[33] They gathered in a banquet room and were given a packet of information that included NYSTA's legislative program, a report card that rated legislators on education issues, and a map of the mazelike state capitol. Tom Hobart Jr., who had recently been elected president of NYSTA, spoke at the morning briefing session. He wore a turtleneck, sideburns, and striped pants. "Teachers are constantly barraged with demands for accountability," Hobart said. "Today, demands for accountability will rest squarely on the shoulders of the legislators."[34]

After the morning session, school buses transported the teachers to the capitol building, where they cornered legislators from their home districts. Costello and other teacher lobbyists were not surprised to find many legislators were absent for the day, "too busy" to meet. While waiting for an elevator, though, he, Dunn, and Lopez found themselves standing next to the one legislator they hadn't planned on visiting. It was Charles Jerabek.

Good morning, Mr. Jerabek, Dunn said. We're three of your constituents. My name is Walter Dunn and this is Lynn Costello and this is Ed Lopez. The men shook hands and then they all stepped into the elevator. A long moment passed before Costello's name registered. Which one of you guys is Costello? the assemblyman growled. Dunn pointed to Costello.[35] Jerabek glared at him, obviously agitated. You have some gall, he shouted. Who do you think you are, intimidating town and county leaders? Apparently Jerabek had found out that Costello was trying to convince Republican leaders not to endorse the assemblyman. As the tirade continued, Costello kept wondering: When the hell is the elevator going to stop? It finally did, and Jerabek, putting his foot in the door to keep it open, yelled, your plan is not going to work. You think you had trouble with me before? Wait until I'm reelected! You'll be sorry you ever did this to me, Jerabek shouted as he released the door.[36]

Dunn, a good friend of Costello's, couldn't stop laughing. Lopez, ignorant of his friend's machinations with Islip's Republican Party, was flabbergasted. He didn't consider the small-framed social studies teacher with a cackle for a laugh a hardball political operator. God made you to look like a Boy Scout, Costello's wife, Sharon, once told him, which disguises what you are really like. The Boy Scout had evolved into a crafty grassroots activist.

"It became a personal thing," Costello said. "He scared the crap out of me. I didn't know what he could do." One of the ways that Costello motivated teachers to contribute was to play them the message that Jerabek had used on his office phone, in which he talked with pride about his anti-teacher bills. At a Suffolk County event in the fall of 1972, at which UFT President Al Shanker spoke, Costello played the tape from Jerabek's answering machine. He also recounted the elevator story. If Jerabek wins, he told the teachers, I'll be on a slow boat to Australia. Unbeknownst to Costello, a reporter from *Newsday*, who was there to listen to Shanker's speech, had stuck around and taken notes on Costello's presentation. The next day, teachers in his school teased Costello about taking a "slow boat to Australia"—his words had been printed in *Newsday*. "That was one more incentive to work," Costello said.[37]

At the end of March 1972, the same week as NYSTA's first lobbying effort, Costello came home from school, opened his copy of *Newsday*, and jumped from his chair. "Islip GOP Rejects Jerabek Bid," read the headline. The GOP executive committee for Islip had unanimously refused to give Jerabek its endorsement. Pace, who often shied away from the press, made an exception after this decision, telling reporters that Jerabek was "a political fluke" who "would seek the endorsement of any political party as long as it would perpetuate him in office."[38]

"Jerabek has a lot of people mad at him, especially teachers," Pace said. "But anyway, he's not up to our high standards." Costello was jubilant. Not only had teachers denied Jerabek the endorsement he needed to win; they had also demonstrated something Costello wanted to prove since he had learned that Jerabek sponsored the anti-teacher bills: Mess with teachers, and there was payback.

The Islip Town Republican Committee held its "Annual Dinner Ball" on Tuesday evening, June 6, 1972, at Colonie Hill, a country club in Hauppauge, part of Islip. The guest of honor was Anthony Pace. Costello and his crew decided that to send two hundred teachers with the tickets bought with their $20,000 donation would have been a little too ostentatious. Teachers, as well as Pace, wanted to keep a low profile about their new alliance. So about fifteen teachers attended, enough to fill one of the 166 tables in the ballroom that night. As soon as he was seated, Costello noticed that the men sitting at other tables, most of them local businessmen, would occasionally turn their heads to glance at the strange faces at table 62. Costello ignored them as the Tony Forlano Orchestra played the National Anthem, the Reverend Donald McPhail made an invocation, and then the meal was served.

The businessmen, politicians, and teachers sliced into their roast prime ribs and forked their potatoes browned in fat. As he ate, Costello, the teacher from the working-class background in central New York, thought he could have bought a similar meal in one of Islip's restaurants for $6 or $7—on the rare occasions he would have sprung for dinner out. He could have spent even less on the more typical teacher's meal, a hamburger rather than prime ribs, French fries rather than rissole potatoes, and the string beans not followed with the adjective "amandine." This night out, hardly Broadway and a meal, had cost teachers $20,000, about as much as it cost to pay two Long Island teachers to work for a year. All along, Costello knew what the well-heeled representatives of Islip Town gazing at his table were thinking: Who were these newcomers? Costello thought: We are teachers. And now we're sitting in the center of the room, cutting our prime ribs and spooning out our Ice Cream Bombe Fantasy with the Big Boys. And the thought made him cackle.[39]

As the November election approached, teachers volunteered to work the phones for the new Republican candidate, John Cochrane. Christine Brennan, a nurse in the East Islip high school, organized the effort. She and a handful of other teachers from her school had attended the Hofstra rally to raise funds the previous year. Afterward, over a few beers, she and some of her teacher friends from the high school vowed to volunteer to defeat Charles Jerabek. Here was their opportunity. Each Monday through Thursday night for a few weeks that fall, they had twenty to twenty-five volunteers phone the few thousand teachers who worked in their district.

Finally, election day arrived. As expected, President Richard Nixon trounced George McGovern nationwide, winning every state but Massachusetts. In Suffolk County, Nixon took 316,000 votes to McGovern's 131,000. The Assembly election in the sixth district was also a landslide. Cochrane received 14,220 votes, easily defeating Robert Morrison, the Democrat, who received 9,161 votes. Finishing a distant third, with 7,651 votes, was Jerabek. His vote count was only one-third of what he had received in the previous election.

In time, the four Jerabek bills were overturned. The five-year probationary period was turned back to three years in 1974, before any teachers were affected by it, and the other three laws—eliminating sabbaticals, gutting minimum salaries for teachers, and requiring professors to spend a minimum number of hours in the classroom—were also overturned. After the election, Jerabek got a job in state government. He never again ran for statewide office. The only time he turned up again in the newspapers was as an amateur actor.

"He convinced a lot of people that it was a good thing to pay attention to who was elected," Costello observed many years later. "Before him there was no connection. He put government right in their face." Jerabek also was the last New York politician who tried to win a local seat by pillorying teachers. "They may have disagreed with us on some things, may have voted against some things," Costello said of state politicians who have followed Jerabek, "but we've never had a public attack on teachers again."

Years later, an assemblyman from Glen Cove told Costello about a conversation he had had with Jerabek after his anti-teacher bills had become law. Charlie, the assemblyman had said to Jerabek, you're stupid. All you can do is lose by doing this. Those people don't ever get involved. All you're going to do is wake them up.[40]

PART II

Growing Up: The Merger

CHAPTER 4

Planting the Seeds of Unity

Although teachers had turned back the attacks of Long Island Assemblyman Charles Jerabek in 1972, his middle-of-the-night legislative assault against their profession had made it plainly clear that teachers in New York State were politically feeble. In New York City, the United Federation of Teachers (UFT), that city's teacher union, had clout when it came to the decisions made about New York City's schools. But Al Shanker, the UFT's president, had found time and again that the union's muscle dissipated in the halls of the state capitol building in Albany, and he and his allies could rarely muster a majority of legislators to pass any legislation. Shanker and other teacher leaders in the state hadn't even known about Jerabek's anti-teacher bills before they were passed—evidence of the disregard shown teachers.

The cause of teachers' political impotence, Shanker believed, was the division of New York State's teachers into two antagonistic groups. In New York City and in a few pockets in Westchester County and Long Island, teachers belonged to unions affiliated with the American Federation of Teachers (AFT). Upstate teachers, though, belonged to the New York State Teachers Association (NYSTA), part of the National Education Association (NEA). And like teacher leaders in the AFT and the NEA, those in New York's two groups distrusted and often disliked each other. But Shanker imagined a remedy. To make it happen, he knew he'd have to convince upstate teachers to reimagine who they were, but before he did that, he'd have to ask unionized teachers closer to home to do the same.

One of the key leaders he had to persuade was Walter Tice, president of the Yonkers Federation of Teachers (YFT), the largest group of unionized New York teachers outside of New York City. The two men met when Shanker helped the YFT become the collective bargaining agent that represented Yonkers teachers in the mid-1960s. Over the years, the respect between the men, both voracious readers who shared an interest in philosophy, had only grown.

Still, Tice was surprised to be invited to Shanker's Putnam Valley home, an hour north of New York City. The Shankers had moved there because conflicts over community schools in 1968 had made life in the city more difficult for the family. They also believed the town was a good place to raise their children—the Appalachian Trail, which Shanker had walked as a boy, wound through it. Tice, though, like many of Shanker's union colleagues, had never socialized with the man at his residence. Why was he being invited now?[1]

After dinner, Shanker took Tice aside and gave the Yonkers leader a lesson in politics that he would never forget. Right now, Shanker began, the politicians play us one against the other. That wasn't news to Tice, who had lobbied state legislators on education issues. He had learned firsthand that politicians often put off both the UFT and NYSTA, saying they couldn't pass one bill because the other group had a different bill pending.

Next, Shanker proposed that the UFT, and all unionized teachers in the state, should merge with NYSTA. The idea startled Tice, as it would have almost any teacher in New York State at the time. Tice, like other unionized teachers, viewed NYSTA as the enemy. He had battled against a NYSTA local in Yonkers to win the right to represent teachers in negotiations, and he was aware that his battle was but one in the ongoing AFT-NEA organizational wars across the country. Teachers made up the UFT; administrators still dominated NYSTA. The UFT's teachers struck to win what they wanted; NYSTA was still wary of strikes. Elected leaders ran the UFT; staff ran NYSTA.

These differences were exaggerated because the two groups demonized each other. To Tice, the institutional warfare was akin to the Cold War. From his perspective, teacher unionists represented the Free World; NYSTA and the NEA were not unlike Soviet bureaucrats. To NYSTA's members, of course, the stereotype was reversed: NYSTA represented the Free World and union members were the equivalent of Soviet apparatchiks. Shanker was proposing far more than détente; he was suggesting that the two groups merge into a united political juggernaut.

A merger, Shanker maintained, would do more than combine the two group's existing membership. It would also entice the one hundred thousand or so teacher "fence sitters" in New York, who were not members of either group, to join the movement as well, expanding the organized teacher rolls to three hundred thousand. Such a group would be more powerful than any union in the state, and perhaps even more powerful than the corporate lobbyists who held sway in Albany.

It was a grand scheme, but Tice was wary. Wouldn't NYSTA, with its larger membership, dominate the unionists in a merger? We have better ideas, was Shanker's reply, and our better ideas will predominate no matter how large the pond.[2]

The vision that Shanker offered was grounded in his experience helping shepherd dozens of New York City's teacher organizations into the UFT. In 1962, teacher salaries in New York City started at $4,800; in 1973, twenty thousand teachers would make better than $20,000 annually—a tripling of their income in real dollars. Teacher pensions improved, and the teachers' welfare fund provided benefits once unimaginable for teachers, including dental coverage. "You can tell New York City teachers by their good teeth," Shanker once bragged.[3]

Unity was the foundation of teacher power in the city; Shanker believed that unity could produce the same result statewide. Moreover, as Shanker explained to Tice, a merger in New York State would be like the first domino that fell for a national teachers' merger that would eventually produce a political giant consisting of three million educated, persuasive people who resided in virtually every election district in the country. Such a group could set the national agenda for education. It could change the ebb and flow of all national politics.

As Tice drove home that evening, he felt that he had experienced the vision of a man as intelligent as any he would ever meet. Like most labor leaders, Tice was usually preoccupied with pressing local issues—union elections or individual grievances or the next teachers' contract. Shanker, like a chess master, had imagined the future. He also had the persuasive power to convince others of his vision—and Tice was convinced. In one evening, the Yonkers leader became a convert to the cause of teacher unity in the state and across the country.[4]

In short time, Shanker was able to convince almost all the other downstate unionists that a statewide merger would be in their best interest. The question became whether Shanker could persuade his enemies—many of NYSTA's leaders and members—of the same.

In March, an enterprising reporter for *Inside Education*, the monthly magazine put out by the state's Education Department, asked two men, leaders of New York State's two rival teacher groups, for an interview. They were Shanker and Emanuel Kafka, president of NYSTA and a former social studies teacher from Long Island. The journalist no doubt hoped to provoke a stimulating debate, and queried the men about a laundry list of educational issues. Should public vouchers be granted to parents to help pay for private schools? No, both men agreed: vouchers would further divide the haves from the have-nots, making the public schools "a dumping ground" for the poor, Kafka said. Would more paraprofessionals, such as teacher aides, be a boon to teachers in public schools? Both agreed again: Teachers could use such help in the classroom. What about replacing certified teachers with noncertified ones, a suggestion that had been made by legislators to save money in the schools? Again, both men agreed. The legislators had it backward: Certified teachers should be hired to replace noncer-tified ones, not the other way around. The reporter finally put down his prepared questions, looked at the two men, and asked the question that was hard to ignore: So what is the real difference between your two organizations?

Once again, the men agreed: Except for the internal structure of their respective organizations, the groups had similar philosophies and followed agendas that were mirror images of each other. Shanker then turned to Kafka.

When are we going to sit down together and talk merger?

Anytime, Kafka said.

I think we should do it soon, Shanker said.[5]

Years later, Kafka would say that simple exchange had "planted the idea of merger in my mind."[6] What was unclear, though, was whether that idea would grow or wither.

By June 1971, Kafka had met with Shanker and had publicly sup-ported a merger in New York State—a position no NYSTA president had taken previously, and one for which he was "crucified by the board." NYSTA board members grilled Kafka: How dare he publicly endorse a merger with the New York City unionists without getting the board's prior approval? "If I had to come back and get an okay first, you're not going to get anywhere," Kafka told them. He couldn't con-vince NYSTA's board to endorse a merger, but he did persuade them to begin merger talks.[7]

But both sides undercut discussions almost as soon as they began. In October, NYSTA leaders pursued another political alliance to gain more clout, and formed what they called the Public Employees Legislative Alliance, or PELA. The group included the American Federation of

State, County, and Municipal Employees (AFSCME, AFL-CIO), the independent Civil Service Employees Association (CSEA), and units of the Fire Fighters Association, the Policemen's Benevolent Association, and several smaller unions. Despite a much-ballyhooed kick-off, NYSTA was never able to convince the other groups to combine their legislative agendas. CSEA president Ted Wenzle and the executive director of AFSCME in New York City, Victor Gotbaum, both admitted later that they decided to join the alliance to discourage NYSTA's merger with the New York City teacher unionists. They feared the merger would make teachers powerful enough to siphon off a disproportionate amount of money toward education, hurting their own unions.[8] Though PELA didn't take off, it did stall the merger talks for the teachers' groups. The discussions lost further momentum because Kafka was a lame duck; a new NYSTA president would be elected in November.

What threatened to kill the talks altogether—and what also propelled them forward—was Shanker's move to rejuvenate the largely impotent statewide offshoot of the UFT, the Empire State Federation of Teachers (NYSFT). The organization's structure had led to political infighting and its feeble dues structure had left it with little money with which to organize and lobby. The New York City labor leader wanted to reinvigorate the group so it could compete with NYSTA in numerous jurisdictional battles to represent teachers in school districts across the state. The name of the statewide group was changed to the United Teachers of New York, or UTNY, which held its inaugural convention on October 22, 1971, at the Concord Hotel, a resort in Kiamesha Lake that was a ninety-minute drive northwest from New York City. Since the 1950s, the resort had become a favorite vacation destination for first- and second-generation New York City Jewish immigrants as well as visiting celebrities. In the 1950s, Buster Crabbe, the Olympic swimming champion who played Tarzan in the movies, was hired as the resort's swimming pro. In the 1960s and 1970s, New York baseball stars, such as Yankees player Joe DiMaggio and Mets pitcher Tom Seaver came to smile and sign autographs.

This weekend, Shanker was the resort's celebrity. He was idolized by teachers who buttonholed him in the hotel's hallways, wanting to know: Are you really Al Shanker? Some shook his hand and wished him well; some asked for his autograph.[9] The delegates unanimously elected him UTNY's president. He ran unopposed.

"Ten years ago," the New York City leader told the 450 cheering teacher troops, "no one would believe that this could come to pass."

Shanker predicted that day that UTNY, with its 72,000 members, would merge with the 105,000 members of NYSTA within two years, because there "no longer are ideological differences, only historic hostility" separating the two camps. The NEA-associated NYSTA no longer preferred "professional negotiations" to "collective bargaining." They had learned to strike, just like unions. Shanker explained that UTNY's immediate objective was to win members from the rival association to "tip the numerical balance" of the two groups and hence enhance the chances of merger.[10]

"We had a new image and new stationery," said Ken Deedy, the Farmingdale teacher leader who was elected one of UTNY's vice presidents. "There was a sense of a new birth. We thought that we were right and that we'd prevail."[11]

Two weeks after Shanker launched the retooled statewide teachers' union, NYSTA delegates gathered for its convention in Syracuse at the Onondaga County War Memorial Building. It was clear from the opening address made by Frank White, NYSTA's executive secretary, that NYSTA's leaders were watching UTNY in their rearview mirror. "New York City's new statewide union is no paper tiger," White said. "It is a very real threat to the existence of many of your locals, and to the existence of this state association. . . . Organizationally, if jurisdictional warfare does not end—for one reason or another—we are about to enter a fight for our very lives."[12]

Emanuel Kafka, NYSTA's outgoing president, reassured the 1,200 delegates that the association had already begun to prepare for the UTNY invasion. In the previous year, NYSTA had won four of five local elections against the unionists to represent teachers in negotiations. He described how NYSTA, "which only a few years ago seemed outmoded, archaic, out of touch with the needs of its members, has in a short span of time become 'where the action is,' the firing line, the front line of defense for every teacher in the state." In 1971, NYSTA had doubled the number of field reps from eighteen to thirty-four, expanded its PR office from one to five, and expanded its lobbying office from one employee to four. In September 1971, two months before NYSTA's convention, NYSTA had also launched a newspaper called the *Challenger* "that goes out to every single member in the state," Kafka stated.

Kafka ended his speech by expressing his hope that the competition between New York's teacher groups could still be transformed into a momentum toward an alliance. "In the late spring, I met personally with Al Shanker for preliminary exploratory talks on merger," he said. "Both of us clearly saw the need and we discussed the difficulties. Shanker had discovered that, based in the city alone, he could not put enough pressure on the state legislature. I was aware at that time of plans of a state federation which came into being only last month. . . . Their rush to build a state organization so late in the game, and to raid our locals, seems to indicate that they would like to talk merger from greater strength. . . . I hope you will direct whoever is President and the Board of Directors to continue to work toward this goal."[13]

UTNY's leaders heard these speeches while standing in the back of the auditorium. They had crashed the convention and NYSTA's leaders had provided them with no seats on the convention floor. But they did not come to watch; they came as missionaries eager to win over NYSTA's delegates to the union philosophy.

On the evening of November 7, 1971, after NYSTA's first business session ended, a group of UTNY leaders organized a cocktail party in Hospitality Suite 738 at the Hotel Syracuse, where most of the delegates were staying. Dan Sanders, Shanker's old friend from Astoria Junior High School in Queens, told the press that as many as 250 NYSTA delegates, about one in five of those attending the convention, had stopped by the party.

"Some probably came out of curiosity," wrote a reporter from the *Evening Press* in Binghamton, in the next day's newspaper. "More were undoubtedly lured by the generous bar of top-quality potables the UTNY people had set up." The use of alcohol as a recruitment tool was a throwback to the whiskey sour cocktail parties that Shanker held in his Queens apartment to cajole teacher colleagues at Astoria Junior High to join the Teachers Guild. The party had switched locations, but the goal was the same—to bring in recruits.

At the party, a rumor circulated the Shanker was "waiting in the hotel for the right moment to march into the nearby auditorium and propose a merger."[14] Deedy remembers that many NYSTA teachers came to the party to meet or just catch a glimpse of the teacher star— but he wasn't there. The rumor that Shanker was present persisted on the convention floor as well. One delegate rose to a mike and insisted that Shanker was at the hotel; another pushed to have Shanker speak during the convention. "I repeat I have no request from Mr. Shanker or any of his representatives, that he is here or that he would like to address this group," Kafka replied.[15]

While Shanker wasn't there, his followers distributed a seven-page letter he had written. In it, he wrote about the attack against teachers by Jerabek and the other conservative legislators in April of 1971.

"The tide having turned against us, we can easily see the possibility that all we have won can be taken away. The sense of dignity, which came from our participation in the decision-making process, has been replaced by a growing sense of weakness. . . . At a time when not only our recently won gains but the very future of our profession is at stake, *teachers need unity.*" Shanker suggested that New York teachers merge before the 1971–1972 school year ended, just seven months later.[16]

Sanders told the *Evening Press* reporter that many of the NYSTA delegates who came to UTNY's party also wanted a merger. "I'm not claiming they represent a majority viewpoint," Sanders told the reporter. "But there is a feeling there."[17] One local association president at the party asked for two hundred copies of Shanker's letter to distribute to the members of his teacher local.[18] Lee Willette, secretary of UTNY, bragged to one reporter that "militant" NYSTA delegates would introduce a motion to instruct NYSTA officials to meet again with Shanker. Indeed, on the last day of the convention, upstate delegates introduced Resolution C. 63, which read: "Resolved, that the New York State Teachers Association continue and expand discussions leading to a possible merger of all teachers in the state into a single organization and that the Board of Directors report to the next House of Delegates the results of those discussions."

Delegates might have been influenced by their downstate colleagues. Or they might have been just as frustrated as Shanker was by the lack of influence teachers had in the face of an anti-teacher state legislature. Either way, they passed the measure overwhelmingly.

Which NYSTA leaders would emerge to pursue the negotiations the teachers so clearly wanted? Kafka was stepping down as president, bowing to the unwritten tradition within NYSTA and the NEA that a president serves only two one-year terms. In 1971, three men were running for NYSTA's top elected position, all of whom publicly supported merger negotiations: Carl E. Hedstrom, NYSTA's second vice president; Paul Cole, a social studies teacher from Lewiston who had run Catharine Barrett's NEA presidential campaign in July 1971; and Thomas Y. Hobart Jr., president of the Buffalo Teachers Federation, who had served two terms on NYSTA's board.

Hobart had begun teaching industrial arts and social studies in Buffalo, but he went on to become a guidance counselor, a position he held at South Park High School in Buffalo at the time of the 1971 NYSTA election. He had a lot going against him in his first bid for president. In an organization full of gray-haired leaders, he was thirty-four years old, and his skinny build and his schoolboy face made him look even younger. He also had a weak power base. By the 1970s, NYSTA was largely run by suburban teachers from upstate or Long Island; Hobart was from Buffalo.[19] Still, he received more votes on the first ballot than Cole and Hedstrom, but fell 30 votes short of the majority he needed to win. Hedstrom backed Hobart in a run-off against Cole, and Hobart won by a margin of 540 to 444, hardly a landslide.

The elections for the two vice president positions were just as close. Antonia Cortese, who had led a successful strike by Rome teachers in September, ran for second vice president as a "spokesperson for teacher militancy," said Jimmy Wood, one of her Rome supporters. Cortese won a plurality on the first ballot, receiving more votes than William Cea of Rockland and Edwin Robisch of Wappingers Falls. But like Hobart, she also failed to win a majority, falling 57 votes short on the first ballot, and won in a run-off. Ed Rodgers, the candidate for first vice president from North Babylon on Long Island, was the only NYSTA officer who won his office on the first ballot, though he did so by just 3 votes.[20]

The three new officers made for an odd leadership team. Just as teachers were supplanting administrators in their organization, a guidance counselor, a social worker, and a truant officer were elected to its leadership. These were school employees that many classroom teachers referred to as "Coffee Cup Teachers," because they could walk down the hallway holding a cup of coffee rather than an armful of books. Hobart was the youngest president in NYSTA's 126-year history. Cortese was twenty-seven. If pictures of Hobart or Cortese had turned up in a college yearbook, no one would have blinked. Rodgers, square-jawed and always friendly, was, at forty years old, the trio's elder statesman.

A photograph taken after the convention, printed in the *Challenger*, showed the three new officers standing arm-in-arm after the convention, looking almost triumphant. Later, though, when asked how the three leaders had emerged from the 1971 Syracuse convention, Hobart admitted they hardly had a mandate. "We limped out," he said.[21]

CHAPTER 5

Merger Negotiations Begin

On Friday, April 14, 1972, as twilight descended upon Albany, the three elected leaders of the New York State Teachers Association (NYSTA)—President Tom Hobart Jr., First Vice President Ed Rodgers, and Second Vice President Antonia Cortese—converged on the Hyatt Hotel to strategize for that evening's NYSTA board of directors meeting. All three officers knew that it would be the most important board meeting since they had been elected five long months ago—and perhaps the most important of their tenures. That night, the three would try to convince NYSTA's board that a merger they had brokered between NYSTA and United Teachers of New York (UTNY), the state teachers' union that included the United Federation of Teachers (UFT) in New York City, was sound. It would be a tough sell. They were asking that the board members expand their affiliation beyond the National Education Association (NEA)—although many of the board members, well into their fifties, had always identified with that group. They were also proposing that the board members join a New York City union—although many on the board distrusted both unions and New Yorkers. Furthermore, they wanted NYSTA to join forces with the American Federation of Teachers (AFT)—although many board members considered that group the enemy.

For advice on how to approach their board, the officers had invited Clyde Cook, NYSTA's treasurer and a veteran of the organization. Hobart thought Cook, a speechwriter, might be able to draft a presentation that was both persuasive and politically savvy. Hobart also assumed that Cook was one of a few members on the thirty-four-member NYSTA board who supported a statewide merger. A wordsmith, an ally, and a voice of experience: these were the things the three new officers needed for the 9 p.m. board meeting.

After Hobart and the other officers had congregated at the hotel, Hobart called Cook's room to see if the treasurer had arrived. The phone rang, unanswered. As the three officers discussed their presentation, Hobart, distracted, repeatedly reached for the phone to call

Cook's room. Each time he called he got the same response: a persistent ringing. Seven o'clock came and went. Where the hell was Cook? At eight o'clock, their advisor still absent, the president tried the front desk: Was there a message from Clyde Cook for Tom Hobart? No, he was told. No message.

Hobart eventually surmised what had happened: Cook, bowing to the board's near-unanimous opposition to the proposed teachers' merger, had stood them up. Experience would not come to their aid. They were on their own.

Before he walked into the board meeting, Hobart made one final preparation: to the lapel of his jacket he pinned a yellow smiley-face button, that symbol of friendliness that had just come into fashion. To Hobart, though, the pin was not a gesture of goodwill. It was the defiant act of a rebel about to go toe-to-toe with the powers-that-be. When Hobart walked into the NYSTA conference room with Cortese and Rodgers, he spotted Cook leaning back in a chair.

Cook wasn't wearing a smile on his lapel. As Hobart could see, it was on his face.[1]

Hobart, Cortese, and Rodgers were facing the board that April day because five months earlier, in November 1971, NYSTA's delegates, at their annual convention, had directed their leaders to pursue a teachers' merger. The three new leaders were well aware that the alternative to a merger was organizational warfare. In October 1971, just before the annual convention at which they were elected, NYSTA's staff took a hard look at the expected UTNY-AFT jurisdictional challenges around the state. An internal document titled "Proposal for Joint NEA-NYSTA Projects" revealed just how vulnerable the association's leaders felt.

"The American Federation of Teachers (AFT) plans a major offensive in New York State," the analysis began. "Its goal is to become the dominant teacher organization. . . . The AFT in New York is stronger than its record indicates—stronger even than the AFT itself may realize." The report noted that the New York City AFT affiliate, the UFT, was not merely the largest teacher local in the nation; it was the largest union local under the entire AFL-CIO umbrella. Its power was magnified because the union was based in the media capital of the country and had a charismatic leader in Shanker.

UTNY planned to raid higher education facilities where NYSTA represented teachers, such as the City University of New York

(CUNY). Many of the challenges were expected to come from western Long Island and Westchester County, areas close to UTNY's New York City power base, where NYSTA was least established. "From this base," the NYSTA report warned, "UTNY would try to expand throughout the State."[2]

Through the 1960s, New York's unionized teachers had restricted jurisdictional challenges to about six school districts each year, only a fraction of the over seven hundred NYSTA locals. NYSTA figured that UTNY would make from fifty to one hundred challenges in its first year and "will have the money and staff to carry through." Even if NYSTA dedicated a million dollars to fighting off such raids, they still could lose thirty to sixty fights.[3]

In a telegram Hobart sent Shanker immediately after the NYSTA convention he wrote, "NYSTA sets no preconditions for these [merger] talks and is prepared to consider every alternative." But Hobart revealed his real intention—and that of much of NYSTA's leadership—in a memorandum he gave to NYSTA's board of directors on his first day in office. In it, he stated that Shanker's pleas for merger during the Syracuse convention had won the New York City leader "great publicity" and that UTNY had "emerged as the leading advocate of teacher-unity."

"His initiative—if not countered by NYSTA—will damage us in representational contests (and membership recruitment) everywhere, and is a particular threat in the coming CUNY election," wrote Hobart, referring to a challenge that UTNY was expected to make for the allegiance of the eight thousand faculty at CUNY, a NYSTA affiliate at the time. He knew that advocating a merger, even without the intention of agreeing to one, was a good way to win teacher recruits from the enemy.

"Several of us in NYSTA knew that you couldn't be opposed to everybody being together," Hobart said many years later. "But at first none of us were too enamored with the prospect of merger. In the NYSTA campaign of 1971, all of the candidates were in favor of teacher unity, but not giving up the fine tradition of our organization."[4]

In the *Challenger*, NYSTA's newspaper, Hobart accused UTNY leaders of doing exactly what he was doing—negotiating in bad faith. "So far we are disappointed that Mr. Shanker appears to be using the theme of 'teacher-unity' not to bring about unity, but as a campaign issue in representational elections. He appears less sincere about merger than about *calling for unity* in order *to foment division*—by raiding

NYSTA locals that are doing a fine job of representing their members' interests."[5] Hobart might as well have hurled such aspersions at himself.

In his first press release, President Hobart offered to begin negotiations with Shanker "on any ship, in any sea." Shanker responded that he would be in Africa representing the AFL-CIO on the date that Hobart offered. Doesn't Mr. Shanker know that there are blacks *in America* who need to have strong unions to represent them? Hobart replied.[6] Shanker didn't take the bait, replying that he'd gladly come to Albany to begin negotiations on November 30. Judging from the rhetoric, though, a teacher merger in New York State was about as close as peace in Vietnam.

Frank White, NYSTA's executive secretary, wanted to impress UTNY's leaders, so he scheduled the first negotiating session at the Fort Orange Club, an elite men's club in downtown Albany. But when President Hobart found out about the choice, he was furious. The club didn't admit women, which meant that Antonia Cortese, NYSTA's second vice president, would be prevented from attending. Hobart believed White had picked the Fort Orange Club as a way of excluding one of the association's key officers—making sure that he, and not the elected leaders, ran the show.

The friction between the two men, which would bubble up often over the next four months, was more than personal. It was institutional, part of the struggle that surfaced in the late 1960s over who would run NYSTA: the elected officers—led by the president—or the executive secretary, who was a staff member appointed by the board. From 1892 to 1972, NYSTA had had just six executive secretaries, and they were the ones who ran the organization.[7] NYSTA presidents were largely figureheads. That was largely because they served one-year terms, becoming lame ducks as soon as they were elected, as a "president-elect" was voted in simultaneously to replace them. Despite these obstacles, Catharine Barrett, Kafka's predecessor, had been NYSTA's first strong president, becoming the first who worked full-time at the job and who acted more like an administrator than a figurehead. Hobart wanted elected officers to wield even more power. Hobart asked for his own secretary; White explained that *he* was the president's secretary. Hobart thought that White might come to his office at times to discuss business; White insisted that all their business happen in his.[8]

The president also insisted that the first negotiating session be moved so that all of NYSTA's elected leaders, including Cortese, could sit at the negotiating table. White moved the meeting to The University Club, a second home to many politicians located just up the street from the New York State Education building, where New York's educational bureaucrats, many of them former school administrators, decided policy for teachers and schools.

The teacher negotiators who met at that first negotiating session were strangers to each other. The UTNY team included Al Shanker, Dan Sanders, Walter Tice, Abel Blattman, and Ken Deedy (Sandra Feldman would join the group later). By comparison, the NYSTA team was woefully inexperienced. The three officers had been elected less than a month before. White and membership promotion director Fred Lambert, also party to the negotiations, had worked at NYSTA for just over a year, as had Ned Hopkins, who would join the negotiations later.[9] Cortese, the Rome strike leader, was perhaps the greenest of all. When she drove to Albany to attend her first NYSTA board meeting, she got lost downtown and had to call the association's office for directions.

Before negotiations began, Cortese was nervous, but she was eager to meet Shanker, whom she had only read about in newspapers. "There wasn't anybody I had ever met," Cortese said later, "who wielded the kind of power he did." At the first meeting, Cortese felt like a country bumpkin compared to the more sophisticated looking and sounding UTNY team. Cortese was also struck by Shanker's intellect. He was not only well read; his mind was nimble. He never drew a line in the sand over some negotiating issue; he always had a pocketful of compromises that he would suggest to avoid a deadlock. Cortese also was impressed by what a great teacher he was; he explained his points simply and logically.[10]

Hobart, too, was watching Shanker, who sat across from him at the table. NYSTA's president had heard that the New York City leader ran the UFT as a labor boss who permitted little dissent. But at the meeting, the Buffalo leader noticed that the other UTNY negotiators spoke their minds without fear. Shanker made no demands; he didn't bluster. Hobart came away thinking Shanker was personable rather than tyrannical.

And yet, the meeting was cut off after three hours by what the *Challenger* would refer to as "an unfortunate scheduling conflict." Shanker had to catch a plane to Niagara Falls to urge teachers there to vote for the UTNY-backed teachers' union rather than the NYSTA affiliate in the upcoming representational election. There, Shanker skewered the notion that teachers would want to be the kind of professional defined by the NEA or NYSTA. "A professional, as defined by boards of education, is someone who doesn't rock the boat, someone who doesn't criticize," he told Niagara Falls teachers. "A professional is the closest thing there is to a dead person."[11] To further convince the two hundred teachers who attended the gathering, UTNY treated them all to a hearty steak dinner—and free cocktails.

"Shanker's early departure from a unity meeting to attend a warfare meeting," the *Challenger* observed, "struck the NYSTA unity team as an intense paradox."[12]

To Shanker, the juxtaposition was not paradoxical, but a carefully planned political strategy. A vote for the UTNY local, he told Niagara Falls teachers, would "bring pressure on NYSTA to merge." Shanker had warned that, if necessary, he would speak to every NYSTA local in the state to pressure the association's leaders to put a merger to a member vote.

Just two weeks later, Shanker traveled to East Islip High School to speak to three hundred teachers, including Walter Dunn and Lynn Costello, veterans of the battle against Assemblyman Charles Jerabek, the sponsor of antiteacher legislation early in 1971. It was his first direct appeal to Long Island teachers—four thousand of whom belonged to UTNY and eighteen thousand to NYSTA—to support a statewide teachers' merger. "While our unions spend millions fighting each other, they're killing us in Albany and Washington," he said to applause. "It's about time this foolishness stopped. . . . The sentiment seems to me very strong here for a merger. It's stronger on Long Island and Westchester than anywhere else in the state."[13]

Shanker also condemned NYSTA's seven-point merger plan, which suggested that the two rivals ally themselves to create a joint educational lobby. "They're looking for an affair rather than a marriage," Shanker quipped. By this time, the two groups had conducted two negotiating sessions, and Shanker said that the talks were going "very poorly." All that NYSTA's officials would agree to, he said, was that "they accept the merger in principle." He said he still believed that a merger was possible in 1972, "but only if you let them know you want it."[14]

Increasingly, NYSTA's rank-and-file teachers made it known that they were bothered by the costs of organizational warfare. In January 1972 in Levittown on Long Island, teachers voted for the third time since the passage of the Taylor Law in 1967 to decide which group would represent them. Two years earlier, the Levittown Federation of Teachers (LFT), part of UTNY, lost the election by eight votes. This time, it won by one vote.[15] Afterward, LFT president Martin Collinan sent a telegram to Shanker stating that what the evenly split vote by Levittown teachers had revealed was their desire for a merger.[16]

Teachers at Wappingers Falls, just south of Poughkeepsie, had their representational election on January 31, 1972. Martin Maslinoff, president of the Wappingers Falls Central School Faculty Association, said that most teachers there didn't want to choose between the two groups. "In the name of teacher unity, teachers in Wappingers Falls, instead of coming together, are being made to fight each other," Maslinoff said. "This is an election no one really wants and one which should not be taking place."[17] After Maslinoff's local won, he wrote Ralph Capasso, president of the UTNY-affiliated local. "Local rival leaders should, in the best interest of all teachers, sit down and make an attempt to accommodate their differences."[18]

The wastefulness of such jurisdictional battles was wearing on Hobart as well. In the 1969 jurisdictional campaign in Buffalo against a UFT-backed group, two NEA representatives brought Hobart a suitcase that was filled with $50,000 in cash for the jurisdictional battle. Hobart told the men he'd put some guidelines together about how to spend the money and make sure he kept receipts. He was told that no guidelines or receipts were necessary. NYSTA and the NEA, which considered Buffalo a key battleground in the state, hired twenty people and spent $200,000 to help the BTF win the election—which it did by 626 votes. Looking back at the 1969 Buffalo battle, Hobart figured that the victory cost the winners about $300 for every vote that had gone their way, an expenditure that had little to do with improving schools or educating students.

The absurdity of the teacher wars became even more apparent to Hobart after he campaigned in jurisdictional elections that NYSTA eventually lost in Schenectady and Elwood, on Long Island. Teachers told Hobart that they were making their minds up on which teachers group to vote for based not on the politics or educational philosophies of the two groups, but on the personalities of the respective local leaders. We'd vote for you guys, one Elwood teacher told Hobart, but your local representatives are bad leaders and bad teachers.[19]

When Hobart looked into the future, all he saw were more battles in local school districts and at state colleges and universities. He estimated the jurisdictional battle at the State University of New York alone, scheduled for 1973, could cost each side a quarter of a million dollars.[20] In a blunt article published in the *Challenger* on March 3, 1972, Hobart confessed that the teachers' battles were fruitless, destructive, and wasteful.

> Almost everything NYSTA does, almost everything we publish, almost every staff assignment we make, almost every program we adopt or reject, almost every position we take and every statement we make—in fact our whole operation is colored by, "How will this help us against the union?" or "Can we protect ourselves against a union attack by doing so-and-so."
>
> Our public relations staff, for example, spends relatively little time thinking up means and messages of convincing the public to support education. They are too busy evaluating our moves in terms of the union's threat, or looking for ways of taking advantage of the union.
>
> When we send 20 field representatives to Niagara Falls for a month, or 10 field reps to Wappingers Falls, the cost is far greater than it might seem. Instead of helping one group of teachers fight another group, they might be assisting a local to negotiate a better contract for all teachers, or processing a grievance to defend the rights of an individual teacher.
>
> Our newspaper, our research, every NYSTA unit—must keep one eye off the interests of teachers to keep it on the activities of the union. . . . Because UTNY is almost as large as NYSTA, our jurisdictional warfare is the bitterest in the nation and the most costly.
>
> Four years ago, when I came on the Board of Directors, we were still different from the union. But today, only our long-standing rivalry separates us. We, like they, believe in collective bargaining. . . . No different ideology or method separate us from our fellow teachers in the union.
>
> There is no reason we should not get together.
>
> There is every reason we should.

Hobart had changed. He was no longer a NYSTA missionary who paid lip service to teacher unity while battling the infidel teachers of UTNY. In just a few months at the helm of NYSTA, his vision had grown broader. He had converted into another type of missionary: one who believed in beating teacher swords into ploughshares. And he wanted not just peace between New York's two teacher groups. He wanted unity.

From the first negotiating session in November 1971 until mid-January, most of what the two negotiating teams did was exchange merger proposals that largely mirrored their own structures.[21] But toward the end of January and into February, the two groups began making headway. NYSTA's leaders agreed to give up having delegates elect officers by secret ballot, a procedure that the NEA believed protected representatives from retribution by leadership. Instead, NYSTA's leaders would adopt the UTNY model of using public roll-call votes in elections and on other policy matters. "Shouldn't your representative be held accountable on important votes?" Cortese would say many years later. "We believed it made for a more democratic and transparent system."[22]

Most of the time, however, the two sides resorted to creative compromises designed to deflect charges that one group was being taken over by the other. For example, UTNY excluded administrators; NYSTA and the NEA included them. Instead of coming down on one side or the other, the negotiators let each local decide whether to include administrators. Should the new organization elect at-large delegates to represent them, as UTNY did, or should it elect delegates who represented geographic regions, as NYSTA did? The negotiators compromised again: for every two positions that were geographically based, an at-large member would be created. The new organization would have thirty-six board members elected from specific places, with eighteen elected at large.

For their first March negotiating session, Shanker invited the upstate teacher leaders to meet at the Motel-on-the-Mountain, a middle-class vacation spot built on a ridge off of the New York Thruway in Suffern, New York. But the rooms were drafty and cold, not what was wanted from a motel in March, so Shanker suggested they move to the Arden House, a conference center in Harriman owned by Columbia University. The house was a ninety-six-room mansion that was built in 1909 by E. H. Harriman, the railroad tycoon and financier. "It was like being in Citizen Kane's house—and we were all alone," Tice said later. "It was overpowering, but because it was so empty, we were forced together. We had to talk personally."[23]

The negotiators shared an intimate dinner in an upstairs dining room, wood burning in the fireplace, that the Harrimans had used for small informal gatherings. After dinner, the upstaters surprised the UTNY crew by ordering a cake they had asked the Arden House staff to make for the birthday of Dan Sanders, Shanker's longtime friend. As they sang "Happy Birthday," Cortese could see that Sanders was moved.[24]

Afterward, they retired to an informal bar tucked under the stair-case in the building's east wing. The conversation flowed, with Tice, a ninth-grade social studies teacher, describing how much he loved to teach—which he would do until he retired in 1997. The superinten-dent in Yonkers had offered him release from his responsibilities as a teacher so he could attend to his responsibilities as president of the Yonkers teachers' union, but Tice had refused. If I was president of the world I wouldn't leave the classroom, Tice told the upstate leaders. I'm interested in teaching three classes a day no matter what. Tice could see that Hobart and the others were surprised that he was as devoted to teaching as any association "professional."

"We still had this view that they were unionists who would sabo-tage the factory," Hobart explained later. "And the factory in this case was the school."[25]

When Hobart began talking about his admiration for organized labor, it was Tice's turn to be taken aback. He had bought the propa-ganda that all NYSTA members hated unions. Maybe the NYSTA negotiating team didn't see him as a Teamster leader.[26]

Their informal time together at Arden House helped dissolve the prejudices both sides had of each other. After that evening, the two teams no longer approached each other as competitors trying to win concessions. "That night, we became union leaders—all together," Cortese would say later. "It wasn't us versus them any more."[27]

Still, one major issue threatened to kill the merger talks: whether NYSTA leaders, and its members, would ever agree to affiliate with the AFL-CIO. At NYSTA's 1971 convention, outgoing NYSTA President Emanuel Kafka had told delegates that the affiliation with organized labor was the roadblock that stood in the way of a New York State teachers' merger. "Our members, by and large, are not prepared to join the AFL-CIO," Kafka told NYSTA's teachers, "and Shanker is too insecure to leave it."

Two of NYSTA's new leaders were sympathetic to labor unions. Ed Rodgers came from a union family. So did Cortese. Her father was a shop steward for the Mechanics Educational Society of America (MESA) and her uncle was a shop steward for the American Federa-tion of Government Employees. Another uncle of Cortese's had lost his finger in factory machinery, and many men in Rome, her home town, had missing fingers from such accidents. Cortese believed that unions were the best protection against such industrial accidents. And during the September 1971 teachers' strike that Cortese led in Rome, AFL-CIO members volunteered to walk picket lines.

Of the three leaders, Hobart was the most hesitant about joining the AFL-CIO. Through most of the 1960s, the guidance counselor shared the opinion common among New York's suburban and rural teachers that teachers were professionals who were superior to labor unionists. His bias was apparent in an NEA-sponsored flyer that he would distribute in 1967 as president of the Buffalo Teachers Federation during a campaign to defeat the AFT teachers affiliate. The top of the flyer read: "Which organization would you rather belong to and associate with?" One column showed carpenters, butchers, and plumbers; a second column showed doctors, lawyers, engineers, and musicians. Hobart pushed to have the flyer distributed to all one hundred schools in the district. Though the BTF won the election that year, a teacher at the BTF's next delegate assembly stepped up to the mike to condemn the flyer's message.

Who do you think our fathers are? she asked. Doctors and engineers and musicians? You're talking about our fathers, and they are plumbers and carpenters. What work do you think paid for our college educations? Hobart started to defend the flyer, but he was soon silenced by the parade of teachers who stepped up to denounce it.[28]

At about the same time, Hobart received another lesson about teacher unionism from his mother, Anne Malloy. Hobart was working as a guidance counselor in an elementary school in Buffalo for a starting annual salary of $3,500. Like many teachers, he took a second job to support his family, working evenings in the circulation department of the *Buffalo Evening News*, where he made $3,900 a year. Reporters at the *Buffalo Evening News* would often cover stories about the Buffalo Teachers Federation, and headline writers would refer to the BTF as a "union."

The label drove Hobart mad. You can't call us a union, he'd complain. Why don't you just call us the Buffalo Teachers Federation? It didn't fit, they replied. Why don't you call us the BTF then, Hobart countered. Nobody knew what the BTF was, he was told.

After one such demoralizing exchange, Hobart took his complaint to his mother, whom he lived with. We are not a union, he told her. Well, you probably are a union, she replied. No we're not, her son said. We're an *association*. Hobart's mother went looking for artillery and found it in a dictionary. Locating the entry for *labor union*, she triumphantly read her son the definition. "An organization of workers formed for the purpose of advancing its members' interests in respect to wages, benefits, and working conditions." Then she asked: Is that what you do? Hobart had lost the debate; it was the last day he challenged the *Buffalo Evening News* headline writers over the word *union*.[29]

During the merger discussions with UTNY, Hobart had told *Newsday*, the Long Island newspaper, that AFL-CIO affiliation is "no hang-up with me. . . . It is with some people we represent. I don't see it as an insurmountable issue, but it will take a while to sell."[30]

Unbeknownst to him, there was a spy within his ranks who would do the selling for him.

On February 8, 1971, New York City teachers had come up to Albany for a negotiating meeting and stayed at the DeWitt Clinton Hotel, located near the capitol building. That night, Shanker told his negotiating team that NYSTA's opposition to AFL-CIO affiliation— the sticking point in the negotiations—would soon evaporate. An article would appear, he told his friends, in an upcoming issue of NYSTA's newspaper, the *Challenger*, that would be very sympathetic to the AFL-CIO. His team wanted to know: How had he received this inside information? I can't tell you, Shanker said. But that evening, well after midnight, a fire alarm sounded at the hotel. Ken Deedy, an UTNY negotiator, remembers coming down to the hotel's lobby in his pajamas. Standing there with Shanker was one of NYSTA's members Deedy had met during the negotiating meetings. The man looked like a spy; it was a rainy night and he was dressed in a dark hat and a trench coat, both wet, as if he had stepped out of a classic film noir. He was Ned Hopkins, NYSTA's public relations wizard, who was acting as a NYSTA mole, spying for Shanker.[31]

But Hopkins was up to more than spying. On one of the first days of March 1971, after four months of negotiations, NYSTA executive secretary Frank White came marching down to Hobart's office. Have you seen this? White asked, waving the March 3, 1971, issue of the *Challenger*. No I haven't, the president said. White opened the newspaper to its center spread. In capital letters across the top of the page was the headline, "AN INTERVIEW WITH TOM HOBART," summarized as, "Hobart's views on affiliation with the AFL-CIO."

"The AFL-CIO is the strongest lobby in the nation," Hobart was quoted as saying, "just as it is the strongest single lobbying force in New York State." By adding teachers to the AFL-CIO "we can ensure more certainly that the AFL-CIO will continue to fight for more money for education, and greater benefits and rights for teachers." An affiliation with the AFL-CIO might even open the doors of the White House to teachers, according to another quote.

"One of the biggest concessions made by each side in the merger talks was on the issue of affiliation," he was also quoted as saying. "NYSTA agreed that the new state organization should be affiliated with the American Federation of Teachers (AFT), which is itself an AFL-CIO affiliate." But no such concession had been made; the two sides were still trying to figure out how to resolve the issue of labor affiliation. Hobart was stunned. The interview had been completely fabricated. The piece never said who was asking the questions, but Hobart knew immediately who had written both the questions—and the answers.

This again was the work of Hopkins, who was the *Challenger*'s writer, editor, proofreader, and publisher, an intense man with an energy that was apparent in his eyes, made larger by his thick eye-glasses, and a shock of unruly hair that looked electrified as it brushed across his head. No one doubted Hopkins' intelligence—he received his master's from Harvard and had taught in Japan and France—but they did doubt his integrity. Coworkers often referred to him as the Evil Genius. "His typewriter was his machine gun," said Robert Allen, the NYSTA administrator, "but I don't think truth was ever on his plate."[32] In this case, he had fabricated an interview to encourage the merger he strongly believed in.

Did Mr. Hopkins show you this before it was printed? White asked.

Yeah, I saw it, Hobart replied. Years later, Hobart said this lie was based as much on pride as on principle. "I didn't want to admit that I wasn't in control of the newspaper," he said.[33] While he didn't admit it to White, Hobart believed that the article "was devastating to our [negotiating] position."[34] The article had Hobart giving away in public the one major bargaining chip that NYSTA was holding back on in private negotiations.

Privately, Hobart asked Cortese and Rodgers what they thought about the fictitious article and the alleged concession to affiliate with the AFL-CIO. Neither blinked. "That's what we believe anyway," Cortese said, suggesting that the article would be extremely educational to upstate teachers who had strong prejudices against the national labor affiliate. She believed that the challenge was to convince the membership and the board that "they weren't being sold out" or "taken over by this giant called Al Shanker" and the article helped do that.[35] "It was a turning point," Hobart would say of the article many years later. "But I had nothing to do with it."[36]

Following White's office visit, Catharine Barrett, the former NYSTA president who was soon to become the president-elect of the NEA, requested that Hobart and the other NYSTA leaders come down to the NEA's Washington, D.C., office to discuss the *Challenger* article and their apparent decision to affiliate with the AFL-CIO. Hobart flew to Washington, D.C., arriving in the capital on a cold and snowy day. Barrett had a limousine bring them to the NEA office on 16th Street. She had little time for small talk. She tossed the *Challenger* article at Hobart. What is this? she asked. She called on her successor to refute the article as a lie and then fire Hopkins, whom she also suspected had printed the article without Hobart's consent.

Did you know Mr. Hopkins had done this? she asked.

Sure, the Buffalo leader lied. I know everything that goes on in the organization.

We can't believe you knew about this, she persisted. Why would you take these positions about the AFL-CIO if you know the NEA is strongly opposed to AFL-CIO affiliation?

Well, I'm not, the Buffalo teacher responded. With that declaration, Hobart indicated that he'd made a full conversion from teacher professional to teacher unionist. The meeting ended abruptly. Hobart asked whether the driver would bring the NYSTA crew back to the airport. He was informed the limousine was no longer available.[37]

Through the late winter, Deedy noticed that President Hobart was doing more of the talking for his negotiating team and that Secretary White was less of a presence. The Farmingdale leader was witnessing a slow evolution in NYSTA's power structure. White had not only alienated Hobart by wanting sole authority of the organization, he had alienated the board as well, which finally withdrew its support for him. On March 17, the executive secretary announced his resignation. The president had finally deposed the executive secretary. On White's last day, Hobart would proudly make one of the most important announcements in New York teacher history.

On Saturday, April 1, 1972, reporters packed a press conference at the Sheraton in Manhattan to hear Tom Hobart and Al Shanker announce what one journalist would call "one of the great turning points—not just in the history of teacher organizations—but in the history of public education in America."[38] The press conference was held exactly one year after "Sordid Friday"—the day in 1971 on which the four antiteacher bills, pushed by Assemblyman Charles Jerabek, sailed through both chambers of the New York State legislature. AFT President David Selden, Shanker's old friend and mentor, flew from Washington, D.C., to attend, expressing great satisfaction at "the achievement of this historic and important merger" and calling for a national merger between the NEA and the AFT.

Hobart and Shanker, two men who had disparaged each other publicly just five months before, now stood before the press as allies. In a short statement, the two leaders announced that a merger agreement had been signed that would result in "the largest state teachers' organization in the nation."

"We have dissipated hundreds of thousands of dollars contesting each other in representational elections," the statement continued. "That money—and the time and energy that accompanied it—we will now commit to raising the status of the teaching profession and to working for better education for all people of this state. Above all, the merger will permit teachers to speak with one voice in the Legislature; to participate as a united profession in the politics of this State; and to carry our story, and that of public education, to all the people."

The statement implied that the merger was a done deal. An interim coalition would be "operational today," according to the announcement, and "brings the merged organization into existence this summer," although approval was still needed by NYSTA and UTNY members.[39]

But the deal wasn't done. The most important and perhaps most difficult hurdle still stood before them: a meeting of NYSTA's board of directors, who would render their verdict on the merger agreement. Many board members learned about the merger signing from the press, and many fumed when they received the news. How could Hobart announce an agreement without first running the proposal by them? The president was supposed to serve at their behest; they were not a rubber stamp for his decisions.

The board meeting where directors could raise these questions was set for April 14, 1972. On April 10, 1972, Hobart picked up his home-town newspaper, the *Buffalo Courier Express*. It carried an attack on the proposed merger by Tom Pisa, a board member, who vowed to "fight Tom Hobart and his proposal right down the line." It looked like the backlash against the merger agreement would come from Hobart's hometown, where Pisa had replaced Hobart as president of the BTF, NYSTA's largest local, comprised of 3,700 members.

Pisa's objections revealed that the old prejudices that had divided upstate and downstate teachers remained. He charged that the proposed governance structure would give New York City teachers the upper hand and allow their union to control upstate members. The agreement was "a gift to UTNY at the expense of the rest of the state," Pisa said, disparaging UTNY as "just a paper organization in the AFL-CIO."

Pisa attacked the legitimacy of the agreement, charging that Hobart, Cortese, and Rodgers had overstepped their authority. He believed that delegates had authorized their officers to pursue a merger—not to sign one on their own. Pisa also said that the leaders of several of NYSTA's largest locals, after hearing about the proposed merger, had threatened to pull out of the state association. When the agreement came up for review before the board the next weekend, it would come under heavy attack, he predicted, and NYSTA's House of Delegates, which would have final authority, would never ratify it.

That's how Tom Hobart came to be facing a tough NYSTA board meeting with a smiley-face button. On the evening of Friday, April 14, thirty-three board members, all but one, were present at the meeting, which was held in NYSTA's new offices on Albany's Wolf Road. At 9:10 p.m., Hobart called the meeting to order. A few dozen people crowded the conference table, which was covered with scattered agendas and copies of the proposed merger, and more people sat behind them in chairs pressed against the walls.

Hobart sat at the table's head, flanked by Cortese and Rodgers. The president began the meeting by calling attention to the tape recorder in the room that would, for the first time ever, record the proceedings, a requirement of a new law that required nonprofits to keep verbatim copies of board proceedings.[40] The board immediately moved Item 5 on the docket, "Discussion and Action concerning the Unity Agreement," to the top of agenda.

Hobart, like a boxer who slips off his robe prior to a match, pulled off his suit jacket and began his presentation. He didn't have a prepared script—that was what Cook, NYSTA's treasurer, was supposed to help him with, but he'd never shown up at the hotel before the meeting. So Hobart began by reviewing the chronology of the negotiations, repeating the direction that NYSTA's leaders had received from NYSTA's members at the 1971 House of Delegates to "continue and expand discussions leading to a possible merger of all teachers in the state into a single organization." Again and again he circled around the same message: This is a good deal. He also announced that the executive board of UTNY had met and approved the merger agreement. More than once, Chuck Raccuia, of the Cloverbank School in the town of Hamburg, admonished board members who pecked at Hobart's presentation with pointed questions and criticisms. Let him talk, said Raccuia, we'll have our turn.

Rodgers and Cortese then summarized the main points of the agreement. The new group was democratic and teacher controlled, they explained, and it safeguarded against domination by any individual or local. The ultimate say over any important decision was given to the entire membership.

When they finished, board members representing almost every educational district of the state went on the offensive. Ciro Matarazzo, from Carle Place High School on Long Island, complained, as Pisa had, that the negotiators had overstepped their authority. Margaret A. Simmons, from the Shenendehowa school district, said that the board wanted secret ballots and was strongly opposed to roll call votes at delegate assemblies, as was proposed. Seymour R. Horowitz, from the St. Marks Avenue School in Bellmore, on Long Island's south shore, protested that the agreement gave too much power to the position of president in the new organization. Robert B. Cherrington, from Brockport High School, a town just south of Lake Ontario, grumbled about the "raving speed" of the negotiations.

Many members are not even aware that merger talks are going on, he griped.

Why do we have to do the whole thing by June? asked Raccuia.

The anti-education forces are gaining, Hobart replied. There's no time for delay.[41]

Gary Duesberg, from the Beekmantown Central School in Plattsburgh, a town at the far northern reaches of the state, wondered out loud if the merger was an attempt by Shanker to gain resources and funds to help him wage a New York City strike. Constance T. Densmore, from Madison High School in Rochester, asked Hobart whether the rumors were true that the ballots for the merger had already been distributed to NYSTA's membership.

"No ballots are out," Hobart stated.

After twelve board members had attacked the merger, Dave Whitelaw, from Williamsville Senior High School, a Buffalo suburb, and one of the few proponents of merger on the board, complained that the board's discussion was "too emotional" and said the fear of New York City and Al Shanker was overblown. "In my area," Whitelaw said, "people are demanding a merger. People want us to put it together. They're not worried about all the little details."

Matarazzo responded that the delegates from his district didn't consider their objections "little details." Marguerite S. Belden, from Dunkirk High School, which was just south of Buffalo on Lake Erie, believed that only 10 percent of the members in her educational district would approve the merger agreement.

Doug Matousek, of North Syracuse, then made an emotional plea to support the merger, complaining that they, the upstaters, had been the divisive ones—and provincial in their concerns. "We must realize we're all in the same boat, and the boat is sinking," Matousek said.

Then the assault began again. As Cortese listened, she marveled that Hobart answered each question, refuted each challenge, and doggedly defended the agreement, something that she doubted she would have done if the onslaught had been directed at her. The meeting broke just before 2 a.m.

At 9:25 the next morning, Hobart again called the board meeting to order. This time, the heat was on Shanker, whom Hobart had invited to speak. Board members peppered the New York City leader with questions.

Board member: "Can the merger document be reopened?"

Shanker: "If it was, there would probably be no chance that it would change."

Board member: "What happens if we don't merge? Are we at war?"

Shanker: "If you see a chance to take a piece of our turf, you will. We'll do the same."

Paul Fuller, from Harrison High School in Westchester County, called upon a wedding analogy to express his feelings. "I feel we're being pushed down the aisle," he said.[42]

That Saturday afternoon, the board crafted a recommendation to deliver to NYSTA's House of Delegates. They asked that the delegates endorse just "the concept of merger" and receive the merger agreement "with reservations." The board also voted to have themselves, not the elected officers, "establish procedures and conduct a referendum of any proposed Constitution/Bylaws" and "to call a special House of Delegates for the purpose of acting on the proposed Constitution/Bylaws." The board, believing their elected leaders had botched the negotiations, wanted the reins of power returned.

The meeting might have been adjourned before dinner Saturday if not for one more motion that Simmons, of Shenendehowa, made that was unlike any the board had ever passed. She proposed that the board forbid all of NYSTA's elected officers from making any public statements on the merger to the news media before the next board meeting. Although the motion was never passed, this so-called gag order would come up again during the merger debate.

Simmons then asked NYSTA's public relations staff to prepare a press release concerning the board's recommendations. "I want to know exactly what will be published," she said, and asked that it be submitted to the board that evening for review. It was well into Saturday evening when the press release returned, and the board changed just a few words: The title, "NYSTA Board Votes to Endorse Merger," became "NYSTA Board Votes on Merger."

The last issue was whether Shanker would be invited to speak at the House of Delegates meeting. Virginia S. Greer, of the Baldwin Public Schools, made a motion that UTNY's president be allowed to speak only if the House of Delegates decided to invite him. Hobart replied that under NYSTA's constitution, only he, as NYSTA's president, had the power to decide whom to invite to the House. Shanker, he said, would be granted his turn at the podium. Some of Hobart's allies on the board insisted that he also make a presentation; the board voted the motion down.

NYSTA's board finally adjourned at 1 a.m. Saturday night.[43] Despite the constant hostility and the refusal of the board to endorse the merger plan, Hobart left the room feeling relieved, if not quite victorious. The board hadn't endorsed the agreement, but neither had they overtly damned it. They knew the delegates had asked NYSTA's officers to pursue a merger, and they didn't want to appear like obstructionists. Instead of condemning the merger agreement, the board figured they could strike a fatal blow to it at the House of Delegates. Hobart also welcomed putting off the battle, believing rank-and-file teachers would be more sympathetic to a merger than the older NYSTA members who dominated the board.

But Cortese left the room that night feeling tired, depressed, and hopeless. *It's over,* she thought. *The merger is dead. When this comes up for a vote at the NYSTA convention this coming spring, we're going to lose, lose, lose.*

CHAPTER 6

The Concord Convention:
From Two Enemies, One Union

On Friday afternoon, April 21, 1972, teachers from all over the state began to arrive at the Concord Hotel in Kiamesha Lake in the Catskill Mountains for the annual convention of the New York State Teachers Association (NYSTA). It would be the most important teachers' meeting since 1845, when 185 educators had come together in Syracuse to create the state association and declare that "the best interests of every community are founded upon sound and thorough elementary education, and that without unity of feeling and concert of action on the part of teachers, this can rarely, if ever, be attained." NYSTA became the first permanent state teachers' association in the country, and New York teachers were leaders in the national effort to found the National Teachers Association in 1857, which later became the National Education Association (NEA). NYSTA became known as one of the NEA's most progressive chapters, and played a central role in the fight for teacher pensions, tenure, professional standards, as well as the establishment of a free public education system.

Now the organization was at a crossroads, and at this brief convention its members would have to answer a fundamental question. Did their interests lie in remaining independent from unionized teachers—most of whom taught in New York City—who were represented by the rival teachers' group, the American Federation of Teachers (AFT)? Or should they merge with their New York City brethren, gaining power, but giving up an identity that was a century old?

To decide, teachers arrived from places such as Rome and Naples, Troy and Ithaca, Chautauqua and Chittenango, Amityville and Pleasantville, even Sweet Home and Eden. Before the weekend was over, the delegates would hear rousing speeches, witness public betrayals, and watch political drama of the kind rarely witnessed at educational meetings. One delegate, Doug Matousek, a teacher from North Syracuse and a NYSTA board member, was shocked to realize after the convention ended that he had been so absorbed by the unfolding events that he had not left the hotel once, although it was spring in the Catskills.[1]

Promotions staff from the Concord had appeared before NYSTA's board more than once in the late 1960s to convince the group to hold its state convention there. But marketing the Concord to upstate educators, who included few Jewish teachers, was a hard sell. Inevitably, remembers Tom Hobart, a board member at that time, someone on NYSTA's board would interrupt the presentation with a variation of the same question.

Can I have eggs and bacon for breakfast as well as cream in my coffee?

The question, of course, was rhetorical. The questioner undoubtedly knew that the Concord observed kosher dietary laws that forbade the eating of meat and dairy at the same meal. Despite nondairy creams and imitation bacon, the NYSTA board, more rural and Christian than urban and Jewish, as were their New York City colleagues, repeatedly secured other sites. But finally, in 1972, in part because the Concord was one of the few places outside of New York City that was large enough to accommodate NYSTA's growing membership, board members selected it for their April 1972 convention.[2]

On the morning of Saturday, April 22, NYSTA's teachers gathered for business in the Imperial Room—where performers such as Woody Allen, Perry Como, Jack Benny, and Sammy Davis Jr. had performed during the 1960s. Shortly past 9 a.m., Tom Hobart, the former Buffalo guidance counselor who had served as NYSTA's president for only five months, stood at the podium. Although he usually wore turtlenecks or polyester leisure suits, this morning he wore a suit and a tie, aware that many delegates seated in the room were evaluating not only the wisdom of a merger, but also whether Hobart, who had pushed so hard for it, was a leader they should trust. This was his first major meeting as NYSTA's president, and most of the people in the crowd had worked in schools longer than he had, but the thirty-four-year-old felt no jitters. Of all those gathered, in fact, Hobart might have been the most confident that NYSTA would vote for a statewide teacher merger.

"When I was young," Hobart recalled later. "I never thought I'd lose a vote."[3] Based on the hostility NYSTA's board had shown toward the merger agreement the previous weekend, others were not so optimistic. "All my buddies on the board were against [the merger],"

Matousek said. "I didn't expect it would pass."[4] Antonia Cortese, NYSTA's second vice president, was also convinced that her dreams of a merger would probably "go nowhere."[5]

Hobart began the proceedings by introducing NYSTA officers and board members, seated in the audience. He also mentioned Catharine Barrett, the former NYSTA president and now the NEA's president-elect, who had worked hard to derail the merger over the previous five months and who was expected to make a stand against it later in the day.

The delegates unanimously passed a motion to move the merger discussion to the front of the docket. Hobart then quickly summed up the recent history of the merger talks. "Last November in Syracuse," he began, "this House of Delegates adopted resolution C. 63. The resolution said, and I quote in full: 'RESOLVED, that the New York State Teachers Association continue and expand discussions leading to a possible merger of all teachers in the state into a single organization and that the Board of Directors report to the next House of Delegates the results of those discussions.'" He reminded the delegates that Emanuel Kafka, the NYSTA's former president, had begun merger talks almost ten months earlier. He read the recommendation made by NYSTA's board of directors the previous weekend to endorse "the concept of a merger," but that also damned it with the caveat that the merger agreement of March 30, 1972, be "received with reservations." The board, in its recommendation, also stated that the "board of directors"—not the president or the House of Delegates—"establish procedures and conduct a referendum" and generally control how the merger would proceed. In his speech, the Buffalo leader didn't reveal what he suspected: that the board wanted control over the merger process so they could kill it.[6]

Many of the board members undoubtedly winced when Hobart added that "last weekend your board voted to invite Mr. Shanker to present his views on merger to this meeting." Hobart, not the board, had insisted on inviting the most famous teacher in America to make a pitch for a teacher merger. Then the president relinquished the podium to Second Vice President Antonia Cortese, who introduced Shanker. Many delegates respected the New York City leader, but regarded him with suspicion, fearing his power and disapproving of the strong-arm union tactics he had used so effectively in New York City. Cortese had no such ambivalence. "If a man's actions are the measure of his philosophy and commitment," began Cortese, "there can be no denying that Mr. Albert Shanker is both a teacher advocate and a teacher leader." She mentioned that he had abandoned his PhD in philosophy to become a math teacher at two junior high schools in New York City. She neither side-stepped nor soft-pedaled his militant past, mentioning his leadership of the 1967 UFT strike, which earned him a fifteen-day jail term, and the controversial 1968 strike that followed. Finally, she called him up on stage as "one of the outstanding teacher leaders of our nation, Albert Shanker."

According to one reporter at the assembly, the delegates gave Shanker "a cordial reception." He was used to speaking to largely sympathetic teachers, but he had a different challenge this day. Too much rabble-rousing might feed the "angry militant" stereotype upstate teachers had of him and New York City teachers. That would lose votes for the merger. Yet too milquetoast a speech would win few converts. Shanker came to the podium and he grabbed the sides of the lectern. At 6'3", he had to lean over to speak into the mike. "Mr. Chairman, officers, members of the house," he began, "I want to express my appreciation for this opportunity, although I have two separate speeches here because I'm still not sure if I was invited to a wedding or the first part of a know-your-enemy program."

He did not have two prepared scripts—or even one. Instead, he used notes he had scribbled on the back of an envelope.[7] As was his habit, he started his speech without much emotion, rocking slowly back and forth. He began with a history of the teachers' rights movement.

> For years we did not enjoy the rights of collective bargaining or negotiations. We didn't have written agreements. We did not have very effective grievance procedures. The Forties and Fifties were a very bad time in terms of economic gain. Then, in the 1960s, things changed. All of us became more militant. And we saw year after year our negotiating committees coming back from the bargaining tables with better salaries, better working conditions, things that improved our own life as teachers, and many which have improved conditions for children and for the school system. And so, there was a great feeling of optimism in that decade. . . . And then the last few years came and reversed that feeling of optimism and of hope.[8]

Then he tried to allay fears that the merger was a New York City takeover. "What we have tried to do is preserve what is good in both organizations," he said of the two negotiating teams. "Merger agreements, like collective bargaining contracts, are compromises. Whenever I have returned from the negotiating table to a membership meeting of our organization, I have always, at the very beginning, informed my members that I could have written a much better contract myself. The trouble is that there were other people at the table and they didn't permit me to write it myself."[9]

Then he described the troubles that could befall teachers if they made a poor decision, a technique he often used in his speeches. Shanker reminded his listeners that in 1971 and 1972 legislators had tried to water down teacher pensions, allow uncertified teachers to take their place, and limit contract negotiations to just salaries. Legislators had also tried to eliminate sabbaticals and undermine tenure and institute a voucher program that could undermine the entire institution of public education. As Shanker gathered steam, his swaying picked up speed and his voice began to convey his passion for a merger. Now he was speaking in a mesmerizing rhythm that some described as almost chantlike.

> We stand at a crossroad. One way, one road is a road to disaster. It's a road of continued conflict. It's a road of you trying to take a little piece of our territory and we trying to take a little piece of yours while the world falls in around us. It is a world of insanity in which our historic fears and rivalries prevail over the realities of the situation that surrounds us.
>
> We're not just facing a struggle. We're all used to that. We're not just facing an uphill battle. We're used to that. We are literally at the point where it is not an exaggeration to say that five or six or seven years from now there may not be very much left of public education in this state or in this country. There may not be a school system. And there may not be public education. And it is in that context that your leadership and ours came together. Not out of the history of cooperation, which has not been there. Not out of love or affection, which has also not been there. But out of plain, common, brutal necessity. And self-interest. The interests of teachers and of children and of public education. Because if we continue during this time to fight each other, there will be nothing to fight over within a very short period of time.[10]

He pushed the delegates not to delay a vote by quibbling over details, for if negotiations were prolonged "three months or five months or one year or five years," he said, "we will come back with essentially and substantially what you have now."

Then, shifting gears, Shanker emphasized the success that was within reach. "One, or two or three years from now teachers in Michigan and in

Massachusetts and in California and Ohio and in Pennsylvania and in Illinois should look to New York and they should say, 'There's Tom Hobart and there's Al Shanker and there are the union people and there are the association people and neither side has destroyed the other. Neither side has dominated. They're living well and they're doing well for their members and their school system. And if they can do it in New York, we can do it throughout the United States of America and build the most powerful force of good schools that has ever existed within this country.' That's the issue."

Shanker's voice now rose above the gathering applause: "Vote your fears and schools will go down while we're busy fighting each other. Vote your hopes and your dreams, and there's nothing we cannot accomplish together."

At that moment, you might have thought that the teachers were cheering for Frank Sinatra or one of the other entertainers who usually stood on the stage in the Imperial Room late on a Saturday evening. Instead, these upstate educators were applauding a teacher who was a labor unionist, an unapologetic New Yorker, and a militant. While he had not used the word *union* once in his speech, he had clearly invited NYSTA teachers to join one. Riding on a wave of emotion, many of the pro-merger teachers might have thought that Shanker's half-hour speech had just won the battle for the merger. But the battle had yet to begin.

Soon after, Paul Cole, a social studies teacher from Lewiston, walked to a mike located in the back of the room. To many who opposed the merger, Cole was the man, a tall, mustachioed former college quarterback, who would lead the counterattack. He was one of the best-known delegates at the convention, and the quintessential NEA soldier. The social studies teacher had been chairman of NYSTA's Council of Classroom Teachers, a national group inside the NEA that had worked to shift power from school administrators to teachers. With Ned Hopkins, who was in charge of NYSTA's public relations, Cole managed Catharine Barrett's successful campaign for presidency of the NEA in July 1971, just eight months prior. Everyone knew Barrett, the former NYSTA president, was opposed to the merger. Cole was her friend.

The merger opponents also expected Cole would lead the charge to avenge his loss to Hobart in the election for president in November 1971. Many in the anti-merger crowd had buttonholed Cole before the convention and urged him to lead the rally to defeat the merger, promising in return to support him for president in the next election. By Saturday morning, Cole had made up his mind what he would do. But he told no one, not even his wife, Lynne, about his plans. Hobart saw his former opponent and recognized him to speak.

As Cole began, one thousand delegates turned their heads to the back of the room.

"Resolved," Cole read from a prepared text, "that the House of Delegates of the New York State Teachers Association approve the merger agreement signed by the presidents of the New York State Teachers Association and the United Teachers of New York." Many of the delegates were stunned. Cole then called for a referendum on the merger by all NYSTA members in May, then for a special meeting of the House of Delegates in June to make a final decision. Cole included a defiant gesture to NYSTA's recalcitrant board, which had a week earlier wanted to prohibit Hobart and the other NYSTA officers from campaigning for the merger: "Resolved, that to permit members to fully understand the issues involved, the House of Delegates withdraw from the Board of Directors any authority to restrict the freedom of speech of the president and vice-presidents of the New York State Teachers Association."

Simple logic had led Cole to his surprise position. He had grown up in Lockport, just north of Niagara Falls, a big United Auto Workers town, so he had inherited none of the antiunion prejudices of other upstate teachers. When he had arrived at the convention, he had listened to both sides, talking at length to Dean Streiff, a NYSTA official who was part of the merger negotiating team. A former Colorado teacher who had worked as a national field rep for the NEA, Streiff was low-key and thoughtful, an insider with integrity. Of all the things that Streiff told Cole in their discussions, one point stood out: The proposed structure of the merged teachers' group was not written in stone.

"Now the agreement obviously is not perfect," Cole told the crowd. "Mr. Shanker is not completely happy with it, nor am I perfectly happy with it. And, I would not guess that there is one individual in this house who is completely happy with the agreement. We will and we can work to change any specific aspects of this when we convene, in terms of by-law changes. I think that we have the ability to do that. The important thing is that we have a democratic structure."[11]

Hobart was one of the few people in the room who was not surprised by Cole's stand. Cole had let Hopkins and Streiff know what he was going to do and they, in turn, had told the president. Hobart had been peering out from the podium to find his former rival that morning because he knew that Cole was pro-merger, and he wanted a pro-merger motion on the floor for delegates to debate rather than an anti-merger one.

Cortese, pessimistic about the chances of merger when the convention had begun, saw that the political winds had changed, and were blowing steadily in the direction of a teachers' merger. Shanker's speech had drawn a standing ovation, Cole had switched sides, and Tom Hobart, her new friend, was keeping firm command of the convention. The president had even wisely ignored a persistent heckler in the front row.

But then Cortese felt the political winds in the chamber suddenly shift again. As soon as Cole finished, Herb Carlone, one of NYSTA's board of directors who had serious reservations about the agreement, jumped to a mike directly in front of the podium. "I caution you not to be stampeded by an emotional speech, into an action, that once you take, is done," Carlone warned the delegates. "I would hope that you would vote down . . . the amendment so that another motion could be made, to present to this body, to find out if you believe in your board of directors or not."[12]

Lorraine Bennett, a delegate from the town of Highland, located in the Hudson River Valley south of Kingston, followed with a simple request. "I would like to know . . . the reservations of the board of directors."[13] She was referring to the reservations that the board had attached to the proposed merger the weekend before. Hobart had to think fast.

"I am in an extremely difficult position," he confessed. "I am unable to enumerate a total list [of reservations]. . . . There are board members who might wish to give this. I would be very happy for them to come to the podium and enumerate them."

Cortese sunk in her seat. What a huge tactical mistake, she thought. Tom has given the opposition an open-ended forum to parade their reservations—and has invited them to do so at the podium, no less. She braced herself, knowing that verbal arrows would now come raining down upon the merger agreement she had helped forge.

One board member objected to the provision that allowed delegates to come to meetings with proxy votes for absentee delegates. Another objected to the replacement of secret ballots with public roll calls. Another complained about the "commingling of monies" with

UTNY "when we don't know what funds they have." Hobart, seeing the lines of board members around the room and perhaps having second thoughts about the forces he had unleashed, ruled to limit each board member to three-minute statements rather than the usual five-minute ones. Immediately, a delegate objected to the time limit. Another board member complained that a thorough "legal analysis of the ramifications of the merger" should be done before a vote. Another opposed the creation of a special assistant to the president, believing it was a political patronage post.

As one after another of the board members spoke, Cortese's mood shifted. Hobart's decision to let board members speak without constraint, she concluded, had not been folly. It had been a stroke of political genius, intended or not. Far from turning the delegates away from the merger, the board members' statements were convincing them that the board's objections were largely trivial. Many arrows were launched, but most were flimsy and fell short.

At the lunch break that Saturday, the delegates settled down to one of the bountiful kosher meals for which the Concord was famous. For Paul Cole, it should have been a celebratory meal; he would later call the speech he gave that morning "the most important thing I've ever done" as a unionist. But he did not spot any people—Hobart, Cortese, Streiff, Hopkins, or even some old friends from the Lewiston-Porter Education Association—who might have given him a slap on the back. Instead, he spotted the woman who might have been more bothered by the stand he had made for merger than any other delegate: NEA President-Elect Catharine Barrett. After he sat down with his old friend, the two were joined by Tom Pisa, who had succeeded Hobart as president of the Buffalo local, and who was also strongly opposed the merger. Looking back on that lunch years later, Cole didn't remember what food he ate or the details of the conversation. He remembered only that the lunch was long. Very, very long.[14]

The anti-merger delegates felt their hope now lay with Barrett, the president-elect of the 1.1-million-member NEA, the umbrella group for NYSTA. She was the one person who had the clout to torpedo the merger. At the NEA convention in Detroit in July, three hundred New York delegates, "resembling a tightly disciplined battalion of marines," according to the *Challenger*, had rallied to make the Syracuse teacher the first New York president of the NEA since 1924. The same article referred to Barrett as "Catharine the Great," and her full name—

Catharine O'Connell Barrett—did sound like royalty.[15] At the end of 1971, Representative James M. Hanley, a Democrat from New York, praised her in the Congressional Record as "one of the most remarkable women it has ever been my pleasure to know. . . . Winning has been a way of life with Catharine Barrett. She has taken her winning ways to the places where they count—City Hall, the State Legislature, and the Congress."[16]

Her powers were especially apparent on a podium; she was an articulate debater with a booming voice. Delegate Doug Matousek went so far as to call her "the female Al Shanker."[17] And like the NEA leadership she represented, she was dead-set against a merger.

But where was she? She had arrived for lunch, but as the afternoon session began at 2:30, she was still not in the Imperial Room. A short while into the afternoon session, Donald Peterson, a delegate from Burnt Hills, a northern suburb of Albany, asked whether Barrett was at the convention. Delegates on the floor shouted that Barrett was indeed there. "Since we have had some very valuable input from Mr. Shanker and hopefully some very valuable input from your position," Peterson continued, referring to Hobart, "would it also be valuable input to hear from Catharine Barrett, representing NEA?"[18] The request, disguised as a question, elicited applause.

"It appears to be the consensus of the body and I would concur," Hobart said. "We will try to find Mrs. Barrett and invite her to give her input."

The promise of a Barrett appearance emboldened the opposition. One delegate moved to substitute Paul Cole's resolution for merger with the four-point recommendation that the board voted for at their last meeting, but it was defeated. Others demanded that two-thirds of the membership, rather than just half, be required to pass the merger.

Meanwhile, Hobart sent aides up to Barrett's room to fetch her, and while no one answered her door, they were convinced she was inside. She was, along with Dan McKillip, a NYSTA staffer who opposed the merger, and a few others. They told Barrett that the only way a merger could be prevented was if she gave a strong anti-merger speech. When McKillip left the room he was convinced she would publicly condemn the merger.[19]

On the floor of the convention, Hobart said it was time for a vote. Now Ciro Matarazzo, from Carle Place High School on Long Island, stepped to a mike. "Mr. Chairman," he said. "I don't mean to delay the house. But I would think that it's just a simple matter. Does the house *want* to hear Catharine speak first, or does the house *not* want to hear Catharine speak first?"

A voice vote on whether to wait was too close to call. Hobart called for a standing vote, asking all the delegates who favored taking a vote on the merger without hearing from Barrett to stand up. As heads were being counted, Catharine O'Connell Barrett strode into the Imperial Room, her head held high. Barrett's long and luxurious gray hair was swirled up in a large bun on top of her head. She wore horn-rimmed glasses and a heavy herringbone tweed dress with a pelerine shawl that she draped over both her arms, a corsage on her lapel. She resembled a formidable and elegant schoolmarm marching into her classroom.

The standing delegates who wanted to move a vote for the merger without hearing from Barrett felt like schoolchildren caught in a prank. So they tried to make amends by applauding. Barrett's supporters also rose to their feet. The delegates offered their second standing ovation of the day. Catharine the Great had finally arrived.

"Would the house please come to order," Hobart said, banging his gavel. Then he stepped aside.

"Mr. President, officers, and staff of this great state association, and members of this historic house of delegates," she said, "I am indeed happy to be here."

"For those of you who do not know me, I'm Catharine Barrett. I'm an elementary teacher on leave of absence from the school system of Syracuse, New York. Some of you may not know that I am past president of the New York State Teachers Association. . . . NYSTA was turned around for those two years and became a very active association."[20]

Barrett went on to note that NEA officials had met twice with the NYSTA officers and staff about the statewide teachers' merger. "This was the involvement of the NEA. Now you have a very great decision to make here today. It is a historic decision."

Yes, yes, yes, Cortese thought. And now the attack.

Barrett suggested that all members should have "the financial assets and liabilities of both associations. And delegates should have a statement of the total membership of each group, who the staff are, and guarantees that the governing structure be democratic. And do these proposed constitution and bylaws protect the individual member? Does the proposed agreement guarantee the autonomy of the local associations?" Moans and groans, audible to the podium, began to percolate in the crowd as the NEA president began casting her doubts.

But her complaints stopped soon after they began. "Now I would urge you to make a decision that is based on fact. . . . I would urge you that the decisions made here today be based solely upon what is best for the teacher profession across this country. Which, in turn, will determine the fate of the youth of our country. Thank you very much."[21]

It was over; the speech lasted about five minutes. Everyone in the room stood up and cheered New York State's first lady of education. For some, including Cortese and Hobart, the cheers came from relief that Barrett, the most dangerous opponent to merger, had not assaulted it. Barrett had feinted at the merger, but never even tried to deliver a knockout hook. After she spoke, many in the audience were unsure whether Barrett was for or against the merger. Anti-merger members, including McKillip, were deeply disappointed.

Then the man in the front row who had been heckling Hobart mercilessly during the day's proceedings raised his voice again. "Hey, Tom," he yelled up to Hobart, misinterpreting Barrett's position. "If Catharine's for it, then so am I."[22]

Many who were in the Imperial Room that day would long wonder why Barrett didn't use her bully pulpit to kill the merger. Cole suspected that Barrett, as politically savvy as she was, might simply have been avoiding a battle she knew she would lose. Ken Deedy, one of the UTNY negotiators who was in the room watching, thought that Barrett might have backed away from her assault when her criticisms from the pulpit elicited groans from delegates. Hobart believed that the standing ovation with which the delegates greeted Barrett's arrival gave her the impression that they were similarly opposed to the merger.

"The only thing I've ever been able to figure," Hobart recalled later, "is that when she saw everybody applauding she thought, 'My job is done. All I have to do is appear.'"[23] After Barrett spoke, Hobart called for a vote. It was just past four in the afternoon. "The only comment that I would make is that the delegates have a free and unemotional choice on the issue before us," he said. Hobart asked those who supported the Cole Resolution for merger to stand. Even Hobart, the optimist, was shocked by what he saw. Teacher after teacher stood up. No roll call was necessary. The *New York Times* put the majority at about three to one; the magazine *The Saturday Review* pegged it at almost four to one.[24]

The delegates began applauding again, this time for themselves, a group who had decided that the enemy until then, unionized teachers from New York City, were not the enemy at all, but allies worth joining. That day, they voted for peace and unity rather than continued organizational warfare, and the Concord had proved true to its name, which meant "an agreement, a contract, a covenant." It had taken the teachers just six hours to make their historic decision.[25] Afterward, the Brooklyn teacher, Jeanette DiLorenzo, remembers sitting in the lunchroom of her school, Junior High School 142, and saying to her fellow teachers, We are on the eve of one of the most important things that has ever happened to teachers. We from New York City and the teachers of upstate New York—we're going to get together. The NEA and the AFT are getting together in New York State.[26]

Before the convention ended on Sunday, April 23, 1972, the delegate Edward Zwick made one final resolution to "express appreciation and gratitude" to a man whose efforts "did more in one year to give birth to a truly united teaching profession in New York State than did the efforts of any single person," and whose "wisdom brought widely varying interests . . . into one narrowly focused target for genuine teacher unity. His sense of timing and the magnitude of his actions was only exceeded by the relative speed with which we as teachers have reacted to his accomplishments and taken significant action as a result."

The recipient, recognized for his "singular, monumental, indirect contribution to public education in New York State" was not Tom Hobart or Al Shanker. It was Charles M. Jerabek. The attacks by the Republican assemblyman from Long Island had led New York State teachers to call a truce and then merge their two rival groups. The joining had created the largest single state organization of public employees in the United States and the only example until then of a statewide merger between an NEA and an AFT affiliate.

The resolution to honor Jerabek drew wild applause from the remaining delegates. Delegate Emil Schweissing then asked the last question of the convention. "I would like to inquire of the Chair if the appropriate resolution will be sent to Jerabek's office and possibly to the papers?"

"Yes it will," responded Hobart. Then he adjourned the convention.

In May 1972, more than 67,000 teachers, an impressive two-thirds of NYSTA's membership, mailed back their secret ballots on the question of merger to the American Arbitration Association (AAA). On Monday, June 5, 1972, staff at the AAA, on West 51st Street in Manhattan, counted votes. Cortese felt a sense of euphoria as the yes votes rose in stacks on the tables. When the counting was finished, 46,106 had voted for merger; 19,510 had voted against it. The UTNY referendum, conducted by the Honest Ballot Association, was even more lopsided: 34,171 cast yeas and only 1,706 cast nays. All that was left were formalities. A special NYSTA House of Delegates met in Syracuse on June 17, 1972, to pass the merger. UTNY delegates did the same at the AFT convention in St. Paul, Minnesota, on August 22, 1972.[28] The New York Congress of Teachers, soon to become New York State United Teachers, was born.

After the merger was approved, Sylvia Matousek, a teacher in the North Syracuse Education Association, never again used the word *association*. "The first time I used the words 'teachers union' together in the same sentence, it was harsh to even my ears," she said. "But I persevered."

In the summer of 1972, the union's leaders still worried that prejudices of both upstate and New York City teachers would undermine the fragile unity. Hobart waited impatiently each day in his Albany office, fearful that teachers would abandon the ship they had launched. He knew that upstaters had a deep suspicion of New Yorkers, and he feared that this antipathy would trump teachers' common interests. He also worried that upstate teachers would abandon the new group because it had aligned itself with organized labor by joining the AFT and the AFL-CIO. Some also suggested that New Yorkers, feeling their militancy had been diluted by their alliance to the more conventional upstate teachers, might also wander from the fold.

"We held our breath," remembered Hobart, "because we didn't know if any dues would come in."[29] Shanker, though, was confident. He knew that it was continuous bickering between the UFT and NYSTA that had convinced many teachers to shun both groups. During the campaign for the merger, Shanker found a mathematical equation to express his conviction that unity would attract the teachers who had long avoided joining any teachers' group. "One plus one," claimed the former math teacher, referring to the two groups, "equals three, not two."

In September, when teachers returned to school, the dues and membership forms began to appear at NYSUT's offices. Shanker had been right: not only did the former members of both groups stay with NYSUT, but teachers who had avoided joining now enrolled. Membership soared from approximately 167,000 in September 1972, the first month of combined operations, to an estimated 207,000 at the time of NYSUT's first Representative Assembly in Montreal in early 1973. Shanker had guessed that total teacher membership would rise by 33 percent, a prediction that proved only slightly excessive; in just eighteen months the membership roster increased 25 percent.[30] New York's teachers had not only joined together; for the first time, many of them had simply joined.

At the 1973 spring convention in Montreal, at NYSUT's first, members would select just one president to succeed Hobart and Shanker, copresidents during the previous year. Shanker's friends in New York City, as well as many rank-and-file teachers there, thought their local hero and America's best known teacher should be the state union's first president. But Shanker, who understood the fragility of the new marriage, had other plans. During the merger negotiations, before any agreement had been signed, Shanker asked Walter Tice, the Yonkers unionist, a telling question: What would you think if we made Tom Hobart president? Tice looked at Shanker as if he had lost all reason. In Tice's mind, Hobart was still the leader of the enemy camp, and he was afraid that if Hobart assumed the presidency, the upstate teachers, with their larger membership, would dominate the downstate UTNY teachers. Oh my God, Tice said, They'll swallow us.

No they won't, Shanker replied, reminding Tice what he had told him when he first presented the idea to the Yonkers leader. Our ideas are better. We can't lose. We have to reassure them. They're more frightened of us than we have a right to be of them.

Shanker was right: in many ways, upstaters had more to fear from the new teachers' union than did New York City teachers. While on paper, the merger resembled a marriage between equals, it had been an ideological coup d'etat by the New York City teachers. The new merged teachers' union had wrested control from staff, abolishing the association's most powerful staff position, the executive secretary. After the merger, the most powerful positions in NYSUT were the president and the other elected officials, whose terms were extended from one year to two. These elected officials now could run for three terms (the election limit was later eliminated), giving them time to learn the job and to grow in stature. An organization once controlled by bureaucrats had become an openly political one controlled by elected officials.

If democracy was one cornerstone of the new teachers' political house, another was solidarity with organized labor. Shanker had succeeded in convincing upstate teachers to join the AFL-CIO, the extended family of American labor unions. The affiliation with labor was a rebuttal to the idea that teachers were professionals who were better than working-class Americans, an idea that had been fiercely defended by the NEA and many NYSTA teachers.

At the Montreal convention in April 1973 NYSUT's delegates elected leaders from both upstate and downstate. From NYSTA, Hobart was elected the first president of the new statewide union; Cortese was elected second vice president; and Rodgers was elected secretary-treasurer. Two UFT members were elected as well: Dan Sanders, Shanker's old friend, was elected as NYSUT's first vice president. Shanker chose the most influential post short of president: executive vice president. The new group had fifty-four members on its board of directors. The leadership of the two groups, like the membership, had become one.

At their first convention, New York State Governor Malcolm Wilson displayed a deference to New York's teachers that was new among the state's powerful politicians. "Had you been meeting in Saskatchewan," he said, "I would have traveled to Saskatchewan."

A small item in the June 16, 1972, issue of the *Challenger* showed just how far New York's teachers had come. "Thomas Hobart, and his wife, Dottie, were guests of Governor Rockefeller . . . at a dinner party for labor leaders at the Governor's Pocantico Hills estate in Tarrytown," the article stated. "The dinner guests also included UTNY President Albert Shanker and his wife, and some 20 other AFL-CIO labor leaders and wives from New York State. Hobart described the dinner as 'very relaxing and pleasant' with no business discussed, but with 'rapport established' for future talks with the governor."

Teachers had suddenly become inside players in New York politics—a position almost unimaginable even a year earlier. They were no longer city or suburban teachers; unionists or professionals; Republicans or Democrats; college professors or elementary school teachers; upstate ladies in tennis shoes or Jewish militants who had never left the island of Manhattan. Now they were all just teachers who had joined together into the largest local in the AFL-CIO and the largest single state organization of public employees in the United States. But in the minds of these unionists, this wasn't the end. It was just the beginning.

Merger Chronology

- 1970: UFT President Al Shanker puts out feelers about a statewide teachers' merger to NYSTA leaders and is rebuffed
- March 1971: UFT President Al Shanker suggests to NYSTA President Emanuel Kafka that they begin discussions about a statewide teachers' merger; Kafka agrees
- April 1971: The New York State legislature passes four anti-teacher bills, sponsored by Assemblyman Charles Jerabek, that shock the state's teachers
- June 1971: Preliminary merger talks between UFT President Al Shanker and NYSTA President Emanuel Kafka begin
- October 22–24, 1971: UFT President Al Shanker launches the United Teachers of New York (UTNY), a statewide teachers' union, to challenge NYSTA statewide
- November 7–9, 1971: NYSTA delegates narrowly elect three officers at their annual House of Delegates convention who will lead NYSTA's merger discussions: Tom Hobart Jr. (president), Ed Rodgers (first vice president), Antonia Cortese (second vice president),
- November 30, 1971: Official negotiations between NYSTA and UTNY begin
- April 1, 1972: UTNY President Al Shanker and NYSTA President Tom Hobart announce they have reached a merger agreement
- April 14–16, 1972: NYSTA's Board of Directors votes for the "principle of merger," but endorses the actual merger agreement "with reservations"
- April 22, 1972: NYSTA's House of Delegates meets and overwhelmingly approves the merger agreement
- May 15–19, 1972: Shanker and Hobart barnstorm through the state to campaign for the statewide teachers' merger
- May 31, 1972: UTNY membership officially approves the statewide merger by a vote of 34,171 to 1,706
- June 5, 1972: NYSTA membership officially approves the merger by a vote of 46,106 to 19,510
- June 24, 1972: NYSTA Special House of Delegates convenes to support merger

- November 1972: John Cochrane, a candidate supported by teachers, trounces Charles Jerabek in the election for the Assembly seat in the sixth district on Long Island
- April 1973: NYSUT holds its first Representative Assembly in Montreal and elects its first leaders: Tom Hobart, president; Al Shanker, executive vice president; Dan Sanders, first vice president; Antonia Cortese, second vice president; and Ed Rodgers, secretary-treasurer

Members of the two negotiating teams who created NYSUT. Seated from left, are: Sandra Feldman, UTNY vice president; Ed Rodgers, NYSTA first vice president; Al Shanker, UTNY and UFT president; Tom Hobart, NYSTA president; David Selden, AFT president. Standing, from left, are: Emanuel Kafka, NYSTA past president; Ken Deedy, UTNY vice president; Dan Sanders, UTNY executive director; Abel Blattman, UTNY vice president; Antonia Cortese, NYSTA second vice president; Walter Tice, UTNY vice president.

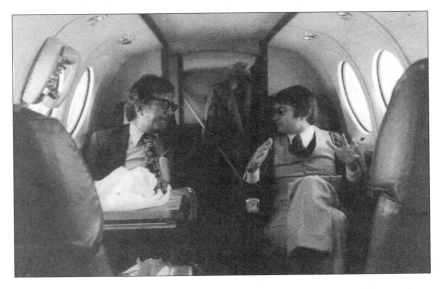

Al Shanker, then UTNY and UFT president, and Tom Hobart, NYSTA president, criss-cross New York State by plane in 1972 in an effort to promote a merger of their rival unions.

Shown here is NYSUT's first slate of officers, elected in 1973. From left, are: Ed Rodgers, of North Babylon, secretary-treasurer; Tom Hobart, president; Dan Sanders of New York City and Antonia Cortese of Rome, vice presidents; and Al Shanker of New York City, executive vice president.

Bob Allen (on right), the Rome teacher who took part in the increasing militancy of upstate teachers during the 1960s, is pictured here with Manny Kafka, former NYSTA president (center), and John DeGregorio, the regional staff director for Suffolk County (left).

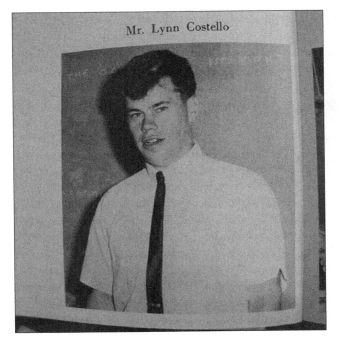

Lynn Costello, a social studies teacher shown in this photo from the 1967 yearbook at East Islip High School, helped defend teachers from the attacks of New York State Assemblyman Charles Jerabek.

Oneonta teachers, shown here picketing in 1975, were one of many NYSUT locals who went out on strike in NYSUT's early years to earn respect and better working conditions.

NYSUT members cast over 100,000 ballots in a 1976 poll on NEA affiliation. Observing the vote were, left to right, Paul Cole, a NYSUT director, NYSUT officers Antonia Cortese and Tom Hobart, and Dean Streiff, assistant to the president.

At the 1976 NYSUT convention, Al Shanker galvanized NYSUT members by comparing the young union to an intricate clock that could be crushed by NEA's attacks. "Keep the Clock," printed on buttons, became the members' rallying cry.

Al Shanker, the long-time UFT and AFT president, is shown here at the 1976 NYSUT Representative Assembly, where he rallied members to defend their 4-year old union with one of his most memorable speeches.

Roughly 12,000 members of NYSUT, which is affiliated with the AFL-CIO, attended the first Solidarity Day in Washington, D.C. in 1981. Wearing the tie is Dan Sanders, the long-time NYSUT officer, and sporting the beard to his right is Emanuel Kafka, the NYSTA president who began merger negotiations with Al Shanker in the early 1970s.

In 1990, members of the Federation of Nurses and Health Professionals, one of the groups of non-teachers who have joined NYSUT, lobby at the Legislative Office Building in Albany.

Bill Clinton meets with NYSUT officers after his 1992 election as U.S. President. From left, are: Secretary-Treasurer Fred Nauman, Second Vice President Walter Dunn, Executive Vice President Herb Magidson, U.S. President Bill Clinton, NYSUT President Tom Hobart and First Vice President Antonia Cortese.

NYSUT retirees—one of the fastest growing groups in the union—go to Washington, D.C. in 1999 to communicate their views on pending health care legislation.

In 2002, Tom Hobart celebrates the first recipients of the Not for Ourselves Alone Outstanding Leadership Awards, AFT's Sandra Feldman and NYSUT's Antonia Cortese.

On May 3, 2003, NYSUT led the organizing effort that brought 40,000 people to the Empire State Plaza in Albany—the city's largest rally ever.

Alan Lubin, NYSUT's executive vice president, speaks to the 40,000 people gathered for the May 3, 2003 rally in support of public education and its funding.

Frances L. Brown, the former paraprofessional who became a teacher for 21 years in the South Bronx, and Peggy Atkins, are shown at the 2004 NYSUT convention where they sold pins to raise money for the AFT-Africa AIDS Campaign.

Monserrat Banda Arteaga and five other Mexican teacher unionists from Guanajuato, Mexico, attended the 2005 NYSUT Representative Assembly, where they presented this gift to outgoing NYSUT President Tom Hobart.

NYSUT Officers, 2006

Pictured are the NYSUT's officers as of 2006. From left to right are: Alan B. Lubin, Executive Vice President; Kathleen M. Donahue, Second Vice President; Richard C. Ianuzzi, President; Maria Neira, First Vice President; and Ivan Tiger, Secretary Treasurer.

CHAPTER 7

A National Merger?

In June 1972, just weeks after merging into one union, New York's teachers invaded Atlantic City, where the National Education Association (NEA) was about to begin its 110th annual convention. The New Yorkers came to the resort city eager to preach the gospel of national teacher unity inside the mammoth organization that all the New Yorkers now belonged to. Like rebels high on their local success, they wanted to export the revolution, and they believed that history was on their side. The NEA and AFT affiliates in Flint, Michigan, had merged in 1969. In Los Angeles in 1970, the Association of Classroom Teachers (ACTLA) and AFT Local 1021 merged to form the United Teachers of Los Angeles, a group that had more than fourteen thousand members. In March 1972, teachers from AFT and NEA affiliates in Gibraltar, Michigan, a medium-sized suburb, announced they had merged. There was talk that teachers in cities such as Detroit and Baltimore would follow, as would teachers in states such as Rhode Island and Illinois. Then in June 1972, New Orleans teachers merged.[1]

But the merger that inspired New York teachers most was their own. David Selden, the New York City organizer who had become president of the AFT in 1968, had been trying to broker a national teacher merger for years. But by the spring of 1972, Selden admitted to a *New York Times* reporter that he had "finally despaired" over a national merger, largely because NEA staff were reluctant to engage in discussions.[2] But his despair lifted after the New York merger, which granted the New York City champions of teacher unity access to NEA conventions, with possible election to its board and executive committee and even to its top offices. It was as if the revolutionaries had gained access into the court and castle of the enemy. For Selden, it was an almost unimaginable breakthrough. The army of unionized teachers in New York, he believed, would destroy the more genteel NEA "like a bowling ball in a room full of teacups."[3]

The upstate New Yorkers had been to NEA conventions before, but New York's newest delegates, the unionists from New York City,

115

immediately sensed they had entered foreign territory. The NEA conventions were nothing like the more sober ones held by the United Federation of Teachers (UFT) or the American Federation of Teachers (AFT). One New York City teacher described the convention as a gigantic Girl Scout meeting; another, more generous, said it had the festive feel of a political party's national convention. Floating everywhere were brightly colored balloons advertising the names of candidates for NEA's top offices. NEA delegates—seven thousand of them—sat clustered in state delegations in the massive hall, many dressed in colorful costumes to distinguish their state's delegations. The Texas women wore cowboy hats and boots, and fringed skirts and matching vests. Walter Tice, the Yonkers leader, said the event felt like "cartoon land."[4]

At a midnight merger forum, Shanker and Hobart spoke of the advantages of teacher unity to roughly a thousand NEA delegates. However, NYSUT's leaders didn't come to preach; they came to organize. They strategized with NEA delegates about how to bring about a national merger between the AFT and the NEA. Joining in the discussion were Marge Beach, the president of the NEA's National Coalition of Urban Education Associations; Roberta Hickman of Illinois and George (Jerry) Gumeson of California, both members of the NEA's executive committee; and Thelma Davis of Georgia, a longtime NEA leader who had lost to Catharine Barrett in the campaign for NEA president the previous year.[5]

Despite finding allies, the New Yorkers were greeted coolly at the convention, especially by the NEA's staff. On the third day of the convention, Sam Lambert, who held the NEA's highest position, executive secretary, for five years, used his annual report to disparage the merger forged in New York just weeks earlier. "This may be the last report I'll ever make to an NEA Representative Assembly," an angry Lambert began on June 27, 1972. "After I say what I *must* say, I may be unemployed. But come what may, the things I am going to say here today are going to be the real gut feelings of Sam Lambert, and I don't really care what the personal consequences are. In this final week of June 1972, we face the most important turning point in NEA history. This time we have to be right because the very life of this great organization is at stake."

He belittled the very idea of unions. "The mentality of the old days of the family store, when a father automatically turned over the business to a son, lives on in the unions. Friends and relatives are rewarded with jobs." He wondered aloud what would happen in New York State after the teachers' merger. "Who will speak for teachers of New York next year in the national arena? Catharine Barrett, Dave Selden, Al Shanker, or George Meany, or will it be some type of mixed quartet?" Applause rose from the delegates. "My guess is that all will speak, and I suspect there will be a few discordant notes in this unfinished symphony. Can you imagine George Meany consulting Catharine Barrett? It is a well-known fact that George Meany has little interest in public employees, including teachers. . . . Very soon the teachers of New York will see how democracy really works in a big union."

Lambert glared down at Shanker, who was seated in the front row. "One-man control of the teachers of New York is inevitable," Lambert said, "and the president of the AFT in New York City, I predict, will be the man in not less than two years. I don't want [the NEA] to become nothing more than another labor union under the complete domination of any one man."

Lambert attacked the decision of the New Yorkers to affiliate with organized labor. "The hottest issue is not the merger per se but AFL-CIO affiliation which goes contrary to our belief in a completely independent teaching profession," he stated. "Our leaders have stated firm positions on independence and autonomy over many, many years." The executive secretary then cited the results of a recent poll of NEA members asking if they would stay in the NEA if it merged with the AFT and the AFL-CIO. "Of our members responding, 61 percent said No. Of state presidents, 79 percent."[6] Applause again filled the hall.

Lambert went on to urge the delegates to pass New Business Item 20, which had been approved by the NEA's Board of Directors just before the convention. The item forbade the NEA or any of its city or state associations to enter into any more mergers with AFT affiliates that required joining the AFL-CIO. The NEA's leaders grandfathered in all previous and pending mergers, such as Los Angeles, New Orleans, and the New York State merger, which would soon deliver over $3 million of additional dues to the NEA. Despite these exceptions, NEA leadership had made their wishes clear: they had no interest in stepping into the House of Labor.[7]

The NEA's leaders had other organizational quarrels with the New York teachers' union. The NEA required its local leaders to have minority representation; NYSUT did not. The NEA required all officials to be elected with secret ballots, but NYSUT preferred open ballots. The

NEA also had term limits for its officers, but NYSUT would soon eliminate theirs. During the convention, Cortese and other delegates speculated in private about other sources of the unfriendliness inside the NEA. Was it the knee-jerk prejudice that so many Americans felt against New Yorkers? Was it the prejudice of middle-class teachers who looked down on labor unionists, even those who were teachers? Cortese even suspected some measure of old-fashioned anti-Semitism directed against the largely Jewish teacher workforce that dominated New York City's schools.[8]

Much of the hostility was directed at Shanker, the only nationally known figure at the convention. During one meeting about a potential national teachers' merger, Lauri Wynn of Milwaukee, chair of the association's black caucus, asked Shanker to explain what she called his "racial activities and lack of public relations among New York city's blacks and Puerto Ricans." She was referring to his battles with the leaders of black-operated schools in the Ocean Hill–Brownsville district in Brooklyn in 1968. Shanker said that "no one should be judged on what the newspapers say," and then argued his record on race relations, but his reply apparently won over few of the black NEA teachers and administrators in the room. They walked out en masse.[9]

One morning during the convention, Cortese watched proudly as Shanker, a hero of hers, walked into the convention hall. As the teacher leader made his way down the long, sloping aisle to take his seat with the New York delegation, Cortese heard a few conventioneers begin to boo and hiss. As they did, more delegates turned their heads to see what the commotion was and when they spotted Shanker, hundreds of others joined in the hostile cheer. By the time Shanker reached his seat the hisses and boos were tumbling through the hall like a cold, noisy wind.[10]

After Lambert's address, the anti-merger Business Item 20, which forbade mergers that required AFL-CIO affiliation, dominated the convention. The debate was heated. On the last day of the convention, just before the vote was taken on the item, Shanker made his plea to the NEA delegates.

> Mr. Chairman, I believe that the major issue before each of the teacher conventions this summer is the question of whether or not we can turn to the interests of the teachers of this country in spite of the fears and the historic rivalries, in spite of the political problems, the staff suspicions, and so forth.

If we can in each of our conventions do something to bring all of us closer together in a single united organization that will be able effectively to deal, as we are not now able effectively to deal, with the dangers of vouchers, of performance contracting, of deteriorating standards, of massive unemployment, of an attack on tenure and on pension systems, and of massive fines and the jailing of teachers—these are the issues.

Now, the unfortunate thing is that we are devoting tens of thousands, hundreds of thousands, yes, millions of dollars not fighting conservative school boards and legislators, the enemies of education, but fighting each other and viewing each other as an enemy. And I am here to say that I am not your enemy and you are not mine.[11]

Then NEA President Don Morrison told Shanker his time was up. Three years later, Shanker, looking back at what had transpired at the Atlantic City NEA convention, said to a crowd of NYSUT leaders, "All we asked was one thing . . . Give us a chance as a minority, as a small minority, to come here and argue with you and convince you so that those few other people in other cities and states who agree with us can go the same road that we decided to go [and merge]. Don't make it an act of treason if others do what we did. Don't say you will chop their heads off. Don't say you will expel them. Allow this to be decided democratically by people's wishes. That's all we asked. . . . We said: Don't adopt a rule where you will throw people out if they disagree with you. That's exactly what was done, though."[12]

New Business Item 20, the measure forbidding local and state mergers with AFL-CIO affiliation, passed 3,723 to 2,051. Then Catharine Barrett, who had vehemently opposed the New York teachers' merger, assumed the presidency of the NEA.

As the convention came to a close, the New Yorkers made an exuberantly defiant gesture. It came in the morning, when the convention organist would strike up patriotic songs to rouse the spirits of the conventioneers. That morning, the organist played the "Battle Hymn of the Republic," and the NEA conventioneers sang along. But the New York contingent broke into an alternative set of lyrics, written in 1915, which replaced the religious imagery of the original with the labor anthem, "Solidarity Forever." Walter Tice, the Yonkers leader, remembers the singing as the highlight of the convention. The New Yorkers may have been battered by their first national encounter with the NEA and its leaders, but their spirit was still strong because they knew they had placed the issue of a national merger at the center of the NEA table. The last stanza of the labor hymn expressed the New Yorkers' commitment to their cause:

In our hands is placed a power greater than their hoarded gold,
Greater than the might of armies, magnified a thousand-fold.
We can bring to birth a new world from the ashes of the old
For the union makes us strong.

Solidarity Forever
Solidarity Forever
Solidarity Forever
For the union makes us strong.

Singing "Solidarity Forever" at an NEA convention in 1972 was a bit like quoting Karl Marx at a Republican Party convention. Some NEA delegates were aghast; some laughed good-naturedly.[13] The New Yorkers didn't care, though. They had come on a mission, and their sense of unity had only been strengthened by the attacks against Shanker and their union. The antiunion NEA would soon be reduced to ashes, they believed, and the new world would be theirs.

After the 1972 NEA convention, the New Yorkers campaigned for national unity, hoping to build momentum for a teachers' merger as the 1973 NEA convention approached. "[What teachers] have done in the state in the past few months is one of the most exciting events in American education," Shanker told teachers at the Polish Hall in Riverhead, Long Island, in September. "With your help, it's going to work, be great and be a national model. I think we are part of something that will build an organization of three million teachers across the country."[14]

David Selden, the general behind the movement for a national teachers' merger, had a plan based on the strategy he had used to unite the dozens of teachers' groups in New York City in the late 1950s. Selden and the other young leaders of the Teachers Guild had sought out a subset of high school teachers from a rival group who believed in merging with the guild, creating a core constituency for unity who eventually became the UFT.

"I was convinced that what had worked in the city would work nationally," Selden wrote in his memoir, The Teacher Rebellion. "I thought that once the unity goal had been set before them, the nation's teachers would demand that the two organizations work out an amalgamation. Then, if the Association's controlling cadre of state executive secretaries, administrators and national officials did not respond to teacher demand, militant individuals and whole associations would break away. . . . I call the strategy 'merge or split.'"[15]

Selden found the "militant individuals" in the NEA who wanted to press for merger within the National Council of Urban Education Associations (NCUEA), a sub-governance group within the NEA that represented about four hundred thousand teachers who worked in cities. Through the 1960s, this progressive group clamored for the NEA to support collective bargaining and had led the drive to reverse NEA's antistrike policies. Early in 1972, NCUEA adopted a resolution that called upon the NEA and AFT leaders to explore the possibilities of a national merger, but NEA leadership largely ignored the measure.[16]

In December 1972, Selden and Marge Beach of Oakland, California, the NCUEA president, established the National Coalition of Teacher Unity (NCTU). The group consisted of both AFT and NEA members who claimed to represent seven hundred thousand teachers nationwide. Beach, one of the chairs of the NCTU, said that the group had formed to create "a groundswell for merger" and stated its intention to get a million teachers to sign a petition calling upon the AFT and the NEA to start negotiations. The goal was to bring about an NEA-AFT merger "within the next two to three years."[17]

"We find it astonishing and almost incomprehensible," Beach stated, "that the last three presidents of the NEA have found it both possible and desirable to visit the Soviet Union—and at least to meet with the president of the Russian Teachers Association—but they find it impossible and undesirable to sit down and talk with the president of the AFT." Beach argued that the NEA's position against AFL-CIO affiliation was just a smokescreen to hide the real fears of the NEA, which Beach described as "fear by professional staff members that they will lose their control of the organization since the merged group will be firmly in the hands of the elected—rather than the appointed—leaders."[18]

NEA leaders dismissed the group and President Barrett contended that if the AFT were "truly interested in unity, it would join with the NEA and other public employee organizations through the Coalition of American Public Employees [CAPE]," a loose alliance formed in March 1972 that included the American Federation of Federal, State,

Municipal and County Employees (AFSCME). She charged that the AFT had simply created a "rump group within NEA to intervene in our policy decisions." That was just what Selden had planned.

By the summer of 1973, NCTU had solicited three hundred thousand teachers to sign the petition calling for national teacher negotiations, giving some measure of hope to New Yorkers going into the NEA convention in Portland that summer.[19] Switching fewer than a one thousand votes among NEA delegates—what would have been necessary to overturn the anti-merger Business Item 20 in 1972—seemed possible. It seemed even more attainable given that the membership of the New York delegation had expanded with the addition of seventy thousand New York City teachers. The recent membership drive to have local and state members join the NEA—a project called "unification"—also added tens of thousands of new members to the New York union. This expansion translated into 950 New York delegates at the NEA convention rather than 250, and 11 members on the NEA board rather than 2, which both gave the New Yorkers greater political weight in the association. With the hope of swaying the NEA, the New York union also decided to run two of their officers for two NEA posts. Antonia Cortese would run for vice president/president-elect of the NEA—the association's highest elected office—and Walter Tice, the Yonkers leader, would run for the NEA's ten-member Executive Committee. The masthead for their stationary showed Cortese and Tice, fashionably suited and striding right toward the reader. "No gimmicks," their masthead read. "Just answers for the real issues and an effective NEA." Her campaign, Cortese said, "will be based on leading all teachers into a single professional organization, unencumbered by duplication or rivalry."[20]

"If our election bid fails this year," Tice said, "we expect to run again next year, and the year after that—and so long as it may be necessary to get these issues before the NEA convention, and to get a real debate on them."[21]

Despite these hopes, New Yorkers who traveled to the Portland NEA convention again received a cold welcome. Robert Paliwodzinski, a NYSUT staffer, noticed that many of the delegates from other states were seated in mezzanines and balconies high above the New Yorkers seated on the ground floor. Often, when a New Yorker stood to address the delegates with comments or a speech, boos and hisses would come cascading from above. Paliwodzinski said it was as if the other delegates were watching the New Yorkers and waiting for them to speak, "ready to take shots at you."[22]

Tice found that many NEA delegates expected he "wouldn't be able to speak coherently." The reason? He belonged to a union, something many of the delegates believed made the New Yorkers "diabolical, even evil." Tice tried to disarm his opponents and critics with humor, beginning his presentations to state caucuses by turning his back to the audience.

Look, he'd say, no tail. Then he'd turn around and point to the top of his head.

Look, he'd add, no horns.

A few chortles would rise from the crowd, although some of the long faces just grew longer with the joke. After his presentations, Tice always took questions from the delegates. One of the Mississippi teachers made a comment that Tice had heard many times. We're *professionals*, the teacher said, implying that he and the other members of NYSUT were not.

What's your maximum class size? Tice asked, and received the answer he expected: there was no stipulated limit to the size of any class within Mississippi. Well, it's thirty in our high schools and twenty-eight in Kindergarten and first grade, Tice said. It says so here. At that point he lifted up his Yonkers contract and waved it.

What do you professional teachers get paid? he asked next. The answer from the Mississippians, as from teachers in other states, was a variation of the same: they were paid a pittance. Tice would always volunteer his salary, which was invariably higher than the nonunionized teachers earned elsewhere. Now, Tice would conclude, who has more professional conditions?[22]

Tice might have won the debates with NEA members, but he didn't win many converts to the merger cause. He wasn't even able to get on the ballot; the NEA rule-keepers deemed Tice ineligible to run for the executive committee because he hadn't belonged to the NEA for five years. Cortese finished a distant third in a race with three candidates for vice president/president-elect. An attempt to get the NEA delegates to drop the prohibition against NEA teachers from affiliating with the AFL-CIO failed by a vote of 4,912 to 2,905, an even greater margin than the previous year.[24]

Despite these defeats on the convention floor, Selden had a breakthrough right before the 1973 convention. Until then, the overtures he'd made to the NEA's leaders to begin merger talks had yielded nothing; two weeks before the NEA convention, he thought "the situation could hardly have looked bleaker."[25] Then, Selden got a call from Don Morrison, the former president of the NEA who had spoken in defense of the New York teachers on the floor of the 1972 NEA convention. He and Selden had met while working together in Educators for McGovern-Shriver, a teacher group that backed the 1972 Democratic presidential ticket. Morrison told Selden that the NEA was holding its last executive committee meeting before the convention and that he wanted to introduce a motion that the NEA open merger negotiations with the AFT.

Morrison asked Selden about the obstacle of AFL-CIO affiliation. Selden proposed a compromise: What if each NEA local was given the option of paying dues to the AFL-CIO?[26] And what if NEA members could join the AFL-CIO on a trial basis and could revisit the decision a few years down the road? By Selden's account, the proposed solutions were enough to convince Morrison and the NEA's board of directors to recommend to the NEA's delegates that they vote to begin merger negotiations. It was the breakthrough Selden had dreamed of.[27]

The delegates voted to direct their leaders to pursue a merger, but did so with three clear preconditions. "We prefer not to characterize them as 'preconditions,'" said Barrett, "but rather as reflections of what the NEA stands for and simply is not prepared to relinquish as the price of 'teacher unity.'" They required that any merged teacher organization guarantee minority representation in "all aspects of its governance and operation," what NEA leaders considered affirmative action, and what NYSUT leaders considered a quota system. They also didn't want any new organization to be affiliated with the AFL-CIO. The third provision was that all officers and governance changes be voted in secret ballots, to eliminate pressure to vote according to the leadership's desire, which was often the case in open ballots.[28] "People knew that once you're elected president in a union, you're there for life," explained Ken Melley, an NEA official. "Few challenges are made to union leaders in part because you have to vote in an open ballot where the union's officials can watch you vote against them. That was an offensive prospect to many 'small d' democrats in the NEA."[29]

In response to what he called "this warm, friendly statement," Shanker expressed an eagerness to begin negotiations. Reporters asked him about the NEA's three "reflections." He told them that in the successful New York negotiations a year and a half before, both sides had started with a long list of demands, which they debated and resolved. The implication was that the AFT and NEA negotiators could do the same. "Continued warfare between the two groups would be the height of insanity," Shanker said.[30]

In his "State of the Union" address to the AFT on August 20, 1973, Selden said that the upcoming merger talks with the NEA were the "most significant event" in the AFT's fifty-seven-year history. "We have faced crisis before," he told the two thousand teacher delegates, seven hundred of them from the merged AFT/NEA New York State local, "but none where the stakes were so high and the possible gains for teachers so near and so great."[31]

But as Selden expressed his hope for a merger, he was tumbling from power. He and Shanker, once best friends, had become estranged. Teacher unionism had brought them together through the 1950s and early 1960s; they had commuted together to the UFT offices for years and spent countless hours visiting at each other's homes.[32]

But when both stepped into the limelight—Shanker at the UFT and Selden at the AFT—their different worldviews became more apparent. Shanker described himself as a "practical political man who deals with the possible."[33] Selden was a Left-leaning idealist who pushed for what should be done as much as for what could be done. Again and again, their different worldviews drove them apart. In the Ocean Hill–Brownsville affair in 1968, Shanker risked his reputation—and even his life—defending the rights of teachers who had been fired by African American school administrators. Selden, based in Washington, D.C., was sympathetic to the African American educators who wanted community control over their schools.

The two also differed on national issues. In the 1972 presidential campaign, Shanker did not want teachers to endorse the long shot Democratic nominee, George McGovern, but Selden embraced the candidate. Selden opposed the Vietnam War, arguing that "the war issue was dividing the liberal movement at a time when unity was essential."[34] Shanker was a Cold War liberal and a fierce defender of the war—a position he shared with George Meany, the anti-Communist AFL-CIO president.

In early 1973, the AFT's executive board, seeing Shanker as the rising star of teacher unionism, nominated him, the executive vice president of the AFT, for the next opening on the powerful AFL-CIO Executive Council. Selden took the decision as the slight that it was:

Union presidents, not vice presidents, were nominated for the council. A week after the 1973 NEA convention ended, Shanker confirmed a report in the *New York Times* that he would run for president of the AFT in August 1974, retaining his presidency of the UFT and the vice presidency of NYSUT. "I believe that the likelihood of AFT-NEA merger will be greatly strengthened if the AFT president is someone who has firsthand, recent experience negotiating a union-association merger," Shanker said. "As an officer of the United Teachers and the UFT—which are the largest state and local unions in both the AFT and the NEA—I think I have a perspective and an experience that are uniquely suited to bringing about merger on the national level."[35] George Altomare, the UFT's vice president for high schools, was a friend to both men. "It was like a train wreck," said Altomare. "You could see the two of them coming down the tracks long before they collided."[36]

Despite Shanker's public enthusiasm for a national teachers' merger, Selden believed he and Shanker had even parted ways on that fundamental issue. Selden said he tried to strategize with Shanker before the 1973 NEA convention about how to push the NEA into a merger, but found his former protégé uninterested. The UFT president's lackluster response made Selden wonder whether Shanker had lost his desire for a merger after the rough treatment he had received at the NEA conventions in 1972 and again in 1973.[37] After the NEA delegates voted at the 1973 convention to open merger talks, Selden talked, half-jokingly, about "unity before Christmas." At the AFT convention at the end of August, though, Shanker sounded far less optimistic. Expected talks between the two groups represented "a shot" at merger, he said, but "less than a 50-50 shot." He questioned whether the union and the association would be united in even five to ten years.[38]

Before the first NEA-AFT negotiating session scheduled for October 1973 Selden went to the AFT Executive Committee to discuss negotiation strategies. He was surprised to find the committee, like Shanker, uninterested. For so long, he thought that the NEA staff leadership was the obstacle to merger; now he was beginning to believe that the AFT hierarchy was also an obstacle. "The AFT," Selden said in his memoir, "was proving a reluctant suitor."[39]

The substance of the NEA's proposal offered at that first negotiating session was a repeat of the proposal approved by delegates at their

1973 convention: they wanted no AFL-CIO affiliation; quotas for minority representation; and secret roll call votes. The AFT negotiators caucused for an hour to discuss the offer. Selden lobbied for a counterproposal, but the AFT negotiators, scornful of the offer, couldn't agree on one. A dismayed Selden was forced to send word that the AFT would respond in writing. Negotiations for a merger were proving more difficult than he had ever imagined.

A week following the first negotiating session, the AFL-CIO held its annual convention in Miami and Shanker was named to its executive council. The labor unionist and civil rights leader, A. Philip Randolph, eighty-six years old and a vice president himself, nominated his friend for the post, making Shanker the first educator ever named as a vice president to the AFL-CIO. He had overseen a huge expansion in the number of unionized American teachers, which had lept from 71,000 in 1962 to nearly 400,000 in 1973. Over 100,000 members joined after New York State teachers merged in 1972.

At the same convention, a petition was circulated among AFT vice presidents to support Shanker for AFT president at the 1974 convention, almost a year away. In his memoir, Selden described the event as "a crushing blow." Few in the AFT had much faith left in Selden, who had also developed a drinking problem. Although he was being cast from power, he clung to the dream of creating one powerful teachers' group. At the AFT convention, the union's negotiating committee met again to discuss the NEA proposal, and Selden offered compromises on how to finesse the AFL-CIO affiliation. Shanker objected, saying, "Why give it away?" The AFT's negotiating committee offered no compromises to the NEA. In name, Selden was leading the negotiating team, but no one was following. The NEA received the AFT's weak counterproposal only a few days before the October 30 negotiating session. At that session, Selden found the NEA team lacked enthusiasm. Nobody was moving on anything; Selden was beginning to fear nobody would.

In early December 1973, Shanker sent Selden a telegram telling him that a special meeting of the AFT's executive council, the AFT's board, was scheduled for early December 1973, its purpose unspecified. Selden found out that Shanker planned to accuse him of betraying the negotiations by publicly proposing only a limited affiliation with the AFL-CIO—a capitulation that the negotiating committee had specifically rejected. For that, Shanker was going to ask for

Selden's resignation. Selden would describe what transpired in the meeting, held on December 7, as a "Pearl Harbor Day sneak attack on me."[40] The executive committee, a subgroup of the council, did ask for Selden's resignation, and gave the once-esteemed labor leader half an hour to make up his mind. Selden said he'd need at least a week. The session had been private, but the deliberations became public. The battle between the two former friends was national news. Selden didn't attend the next negotiating session with the NEA, held on December 13, declaring himself "voluntarily absent." Shanker now served as the AFT leader in the negotiations.

On December 19, Selden held a news conference saying he would not resign as AFT's president and stated that the "real source of the present conflict is Al Shanker's thirst for power." Shanker accused Selden of making public statements that would prevent merger and had weakened the AFT's commitment to the AFL-CIO, what Selden called "trumped up charges."[41]

On January 18, 1974, the AFT's executive council released a statement that it "rejects President Selden's proposal that merger be based on a trial affiliation with the AFL-CIO. The concept of trial affiliation suggests a lack of commitment to affiliation with organized labor and creates a misconception that affiliation is of a temporary nature and should be taken lightly. . . . We are committed to the view that affiliation with labor is on a permanent basis, not a temporary one, and is essential." The statement was a clear rebuke of Selden, and an indication that with Shanker in charge, there was no more flexibility in the merger talks on AFL-CIO affiliation.

Despite Selden's hobbled political position, he was able to convince the AFT's executive council to offer one final compromise: to allow any NEA member who was not affiliated with the AFL-CIO to refuse to pay dues to that organization. Selden offered this long-withheld compromise at the February 27, 1974, meeting; NEA negotiators turned it down. The AFT negotiators suggested that a mediator be brought in. The NEA refused. Shanker summed up the negotiating session this way: "Within a single hour, the NEA rejected the AFL-CIO compromise, refused to make a counterproposal, refused a mediator, indicated complete disinterest in the AFT's other compromises, announced it was breaking off the talks, and walked out."[42] It appeared that the NEA group had come to the meeting planning to end the negotiations. The negotiations were suddenly over.

The media had long assumed that a national teachers merger was probable, even inevitable. "The media overlooked the simplest reality of all," Shanker wrote in a column after the collapse of negotiations. "The fact that a given course of action is intelligent and reasonable does not make it inevitable."[43] Hobart called the NEA's break-off of merger talks "totally irresponsible, mindless, and unconscionable."[44] In an open letter to NEA leaders, he argued that the NEA ended the talks because it feared democracy.

> For merger inevitably would mean greater democracy within the organization—both because it would be subject to federal labor law and because the merged organization would necessarily be a compromise between NEA's staff-dominated structure and the AFT's elected leader-controlled structure. And since the elected leadership would have greater authority, the organization itself would be more accountable and responsive to the will of the membership. It is this which the NEA staff opposes.[45]

"The talks have ended," NEA President Helen Wise stated in her February 28 press release, "because the AFT has no flexibility on the issues of AFL-CIO affiliation, minority guarantees and the secret ballot." The major reason for failure, it appeared, was the one that had nearly sabotaged the merger discussions within New York State: teacher affiliation with organized labor. "NEA wants unity," Wise stated. "AFT wants AFL-CIO membership. The two are not compatible. . . . Since the majority of American teachers do not wish to be in organizations affiliated with the AFL-CIO, no teacher unity could be achieved under AFT conditions." Wise added that the talks "have been severely hampered by the inability of the AFT leadership to solve their internal problems privately" and by the way that Shanker and Selden were "flailing away at each other."[46]

The NEA's fear that Shanker and New York State would take over a merged organization also contributed to the merger failure. Shanker once said, "The 1972 merger here in New York . . . created large blocs in both national organizations in favor of a merger. Someone once said that when something happens in New York, it's like having an elephant in your living room. You can't quite say you don't notice it. After all, there are more teachers in New York City alone than in the 11 smallest states in the nation combined."[47] Shanker was proud to be riding the elephant; the NEA leaders were afraid that the elephant would crush them.

Selden admitted in his memoir that his dream of a teacher merger had been somewhat misguided. In the late 1950s and early 1960s, the ire of New York City teachers had coalesced against a "single, clearly visible target," the New York City Board of Education. Nationally, the enemy was far more nebulous, and it was unclear that a national merger would bring teachers the concrete gains that merger had brought in New York City or New York State.

The biggest obstacle to merger might have been the disparity in size between the NEA and the AFT. In New York State, the two rivals that had merged had been of roughly equal size. Nationally, the NEA dwarfed the AFT. Why should the NEA, with well over one million members, merge with the AFT, with less than half a million, and risk being subsumed by them? Selden and the others were never able to present a convincing answer.

In ending the talks, Wise said she did not intend to offend labor. "In rejecting affiliation, the NEA is not rejecting the AFL-CIO among those [organizations] with whom we could have a cordial and beneficial relationship. . . . The NEA can help the AFL-CIO, and they can help us."[48] Shanker responded like an insulted suitor. "If the NEA is to develop the 'cordial and beneficial relationship' it is going to have to go further than a press release. Its actions, if not its words, continue to display contempt for labor. Though two years ago the NEA removed Communist Party membership as a reason for expulsion, NEA leaders are now preparing to expel the NEA affiliate in Miami (Dade County) Florida, for affiliating with the AFL-CIO. That is hardly illustrative of a 'cordial relationship.'"

Shanker was referring to developments in Florida, which New Yorkers hoped would become the next state ally in the national merger movement. Their hopes gained fuel when Dade County teachers, Florida's largest teachers local, voted by a 10 to 1 margin to merge with AFT teachers in the county to form the United Teachers of Dade in December 1973.[49] More than that, the Dade teachers had affiliated with the AFL-CIO, defying the 1972 NEA ban.

"By making clear that we want the AFL-CIO strength that we get by being members of the AFT," stated Pat Tornillo, a longtime NEA leader who was the executive secretary of the Dade County Teachers Association, "we hope to give a significant push to national teacher-unity by proving to the NEA, as Dade County teachers have done here, that teachers want a national merger."[50]

This interest in merger was also strong among the leadership in the NEA-affiliated Florida Education Association (FEA). They invited NYSUT staff to Florida early in 1974 to educate FEA leaders how to bargain collectively, a right that was expected to be granted to teachers by the Florida legislature. Vito DeLeonardis, NYSUT's executive director, brought about ten NYSUT field representatives to Florida for the training, and he hoped the delegation would show Florida's merger advocates that they had natural allies in New York and the AFT. Robert Paliwodzinski, a NYSUT staffer who was sent to Florida, said the New York delegation went over like "a pork chop in a synagogue" with the NEA's national leaders.[51]

On March 17, 1974, the New Yorkers got the breakthrough they had been waiting for: the FEA's board of directors approved a merger with the Florida American Federation of Teachers, Florida's AFT union, which would take effect in September if approved by the FEA's membership. The Florida teachers tried to finesse the NEA ban against AFL-CIO affiliation by allowing each local to decide whether they wanted to affiliate or not.

The NEA would have none of it. Immediately following the FEA board vote to merge, the NEA sent down dozens of staffers to Florida to convince teachers and their leaders to reject the merger at its upcoming annual meeting. FEA leadership wrote that "the NEA hierarchy has loosed an enormous propaganda campaign—not merely against our unity plan, but against FEA elected leaders and staff as well."[52] On April 22, just a few days before the FEA's annual convention, the NEA executive committee expelled Dade County teachers. These teachers were told that they were expelled because their merger was "prejudicial to the best interest of the National Education Association" and had violated the prohibition against affiliating with the AFL-CIO.[53] On April 26, the FEA's Representative Assembly, bowing to the NEA's threat that they would disaffiliate the FEA if they merged, narrowly rejected the merger agreement.

Despite the rejection, the NEA kicked out the 53,000-member FEA from the association in September 1974. The NEA created a new affiliate in the state, the Florida Teaching Profession, or FTP, and worked to recruit members away from the FEA. Only months earlier, Florida teachers had come close to creating one united teachers' organization. Now they were Balkanized. About a third joined FEA-United, the merged teachers' group, which dominated the urban areas; and about a third joined the NEA-affiliated FTP, which dominated the rural and suburban areas. Those two groups would pummel each other for nearly thirty years. The remaining third of teachers, thinking better of getting involved in the mess, refused to join either camp.[54]

Floridian teachers, like other NEA affiliates around the country, had been discouraged from merging by New Business Item 20, passed at the 1972 NEA convention and enforced by NEA leaders. "From that point forward," Hobart would write in a column in *New York Teacher*, NYSUT's newspaper, "New York's cause—the cause of teacher unity— was almost a forbidden topic. Anyone who showed the slightest inter- est in merger was either bought off or ostracized by the NEA staff. Anyone who moved toward merger—the Florida Education Associa- tion, for example—was condemned and expelled. . . . People who had had no direct contact with New Yorkers for a full 12 months assailed us more bitterly each summer."[55]

After 1973, the New Yorkers would continue to introduce pro- merger resolutions at NEA conventions to overturn the NEA ban against local AFL-CIO-affiliated mergers. But no roll call vote, as was used in 1972 and 1973, was necessary. A pro-merger resolution would come to the floor, it would be dismissed with an overwhelming voice vote, a gavel was struck, and the conventioneers went on to other less contentious NEA business.[56]

By 1974, the NEA leadership had grown tired of listening to the New Yorkers preach merger. Ken Melley, a high-ranking NEA official keep- ing an eye on New York and the merger movement, told Hobart: This luxury that you have of being a member of the NEA Board of Direc- tors and going out and speaking up for the AFT and a national merger is over. It's *over*.[57] At their May 1974 meeting, the NEA board of direc- tors passed a motion prohibiting any NEA officials or board members from "expounding the philosophies which are in conflict with official NEA policy," and threatened anyone who did with "censure, suspen- sion as a board member, or removal from office." The motion was aimed at preventing the NYSUT officers from advocating teacher mergers, as Hobart had done in Ohio and Hawaii during the winter and spring of 1974.[58]

Hobart protested the prohibition. "New York State is a lighthouse state on teacher unity," Hobart told the NEA's directors, "and it is quite natural that other teacher groups want to hear from the president of this fully united state organization."[59] Manny Kafka, the former

NYSUT president who had started the merger talks with Shanker in New York State, characterized the NEA attempt to muzzle pro-merger forces as "the beginning of a witch-hunt."[60]

The New York merger advocates were no longer on the offensive; they were in retreat. The New Yorkers had hurled a bowling ball into the NEA to destroy it and create one national teachers' union, but the association's leaders had succeeded in slowing down the ball and finally blocking it. What the New Yorkers hadn't expected was that NEA leaders would pick up a bowling ball of their own and hurl it right at the heart of the merger movement: New York State.

CHAPTER 8

Coming Apart

To most of the leaders of the National Education Association (NEA), the 1973 teacher merger in New York State was not an inspiration, but an organizational disaster. From the day it was founded, New York State United Teachers (NYSUT) and its unionist culture irked NEA's leaders like a rotten tooth. The NEA's new constitution, passed in 1972, required its local associations to guarantee minority representation in all its governance bodies, but NYSUT opposed the requirement, dismissing it as a quota system. The NEA required secret ballot elections of officers, but NYSUT chose public votes, a preference typical of unions. The NEA placed term limits on its officers, but NYSUT would refuse them. Most of the NEA's leaders abhorred unions, and now New York's teachers had become one.

NEA leaders saw New York's teacher merger as a takeover of the entire state by the New York City unionists and expected that the NEA would soon lose over one hundred thousand of their New York members to their national nemesis, the American Federation of Teachers (AFT). And they viewed New York's teacher unionists as hostile troops concealed in a Trojan horse who would try to overthrow their organization from within. NEA's disapproval was laced with distrust, even paranoia, stemming from the decades of institutional warfare with the AFT. In their eyes, NYSUT President Tom Hobart had betrayed the NEA by pushing for the teachers' merger, a tack they believed he had taken to further his personal ambitions.[1] All along, they expected that the New Yorkers would soon disaffiliate with the NEA and remain exclusively with the AFT. Instead of waiting for the New Yorkers to begin the divorce proceedings, the NEA's leaders attacked.

In February 1975 Jim Harris, NEA's president, wrote a letter that complained that NYSUT's publications had "consistently portrayed NEA in a negative manner," that Shanker "misrepresents" the NEA in his statements, and that "some NYSUT leaders have worked for AFT against NEA in representation elections."[2] Harris sent the letter to all of NYSUT's members without the approval of NYSUT's leaders—a breach of NEA etiquette. At the NEA's convention in Los Angeles in the summer, rumors circulated that the NEA was going to expel NYSUT from the association.

In the fall of 1975, John Ryor, the new president of the NEA, flew to New York State to show support for Orchard Park teachers, who were in the middle of a long, bitter strike. Ryor flew to Buffalo and on the drive south to the teachers' rally Shanker and Hobart joined him. It was a tense ride. The marriage between the NEA and NYSUT's leaders, rocky to begin with, had grown more and more hostile over the previous year. As they drove, Hobart and Shanker asked Ryor a simple question.

Had the NEA declared war on NYSUT?

Ryor assured them they hadn't. But when Ryor returned for a subsequent meeting in New York City, he and his associates presented a memorandum outlining what they called the "NEA in New York" project, aimed at shining up the NEA image they believed had been sullied by NYSUT's leaders, including those in the room.

The project included an advertising blitz to enhance NEA's image in New York, direct mailings to educate New York teachers about NEA services, and a program to train two hundred activists in the state as political lobbyists. In the first year, Ryor said, the NEA would contribute $200,000 to pay for the program, which would be run out of the NEA's national offices. Hobart, who was at the meeting with Cortese and Dan Sanders, remembers Ryor telling them that NYSUT "would be kept fully informed of the program's progress."[3]

Hobart and the others assumed they were being handed a blueprint of how the NEA planned to destroy the merger. "They were coming at us with both barrels loaded," Hobart said. As they saw it, the "NEA in New York" project was designed to bad-mouth NYSUT using advertising and direct mailings to New York's teachers, thereby winning converts to the NEA and preparing the ground for the establishment of a rival NEA group in the state. The gall of it, thought Hobart, was that Ryor had also asked for a $50,000 NYSUT contribution to the plan.[4]

In a November 12, 1975 letter, Hobart told Ryor that the executive committee of NYSUT had rejected the "NEA in New York" project. "The Project is consistent with NEA actions in Florida just before the Florida Education Association was disaffiliated 14 months ago," Hobart wrote. "Do you think we know nothing of what the NEA did in Florida—establishing just such a network, then creating an 'NEA-

Florida' headquarters, and finally converting that network and head-quarters into a rival organization?

"The NEA plan will fail," continued Hobart. "New York is not Florida. Our members have had three years' experience with unity with labor affiliation. They know that unity works. They have seen NYSUT roll the probationary period [for tenure] back to three years, make pension benefits for upstate teachers permanent, win $500 million in additional state aid the past two years despite the recession and the fiscal crisis, and provide the most extensive and competent field and legal services in the nation." Hobart compared the New York teacher union-ists to the founding fathers, who had also separated from their perceived oppressors.

"In this bicentennial year," Hobart wrote, "that lesson needs no lengthy exposition."[5]

Confronted with this possible rebellion, Ryor asked to speak at the NYSUT Board of Directors meeting in Syracuse, New York, on Friday morning, November 21. Ryor opened the meeting by saying that the NEA wanted New York teachers to remain with the NEA, and that the "heart of the problem" was that the NEA had an "inadequate visibility" among New York teachers. The NEA's president said that when he read NYSUT publications, "I can't help but perceive a deep sense of alienation and disaffection from NEA itself," and that the "NEA in New York" program was intended to correct the NEA's "image problem" in the state. After Ryor finished his brief statement, NYSUT board members spent the next two and a half hours badgering, probing, and attacking him.

Robert Cherrington, a board member from Brockport, asked whether "this NEA program will go into New York State with or without the consent and cooperation of New York State United Teachers?"

"That is true," Ryor responded. "That is necessary."

Paul Cole, the social studies teacher from Lewiston-Porter United Teachers, believed that the NEA would have no choice but to eventually kick out the New Yorkers. "If New York is not in compliance with the section in the NEA Constitution that calls for state elections by secret ballot [and for racial quotas] and we are reviewed and are found not in compliance in September of 1976, then in my judgment the NEA has no alternative other than disaffiliation from New York."

"That is true," Ryor said.

Doris Blank, a NYSUT and NEA board member from Port Chester, asked a question that was on everyone's mind. "Could not this money that you are planning to spend in our state for ostensibly such pure and motherhood-type reasons be the very basis of an attempt to set up that other NEA affiliate in New York State?"

"This is not my intention, Doris," Ryor replied. "I repeat that."[6]

Few in the room believed Ryor. At the end of the question and answer period, Paul Cole introduced a unity resolution that pledged NYSUT to fight "any effort . . . to divide New York's teachers" and that "deplores and condemns any attempt, by any organization or individual, to split NYSUT and weaken the state's teachers." It was fitting that Cole introduce the unity measure; as a delegate at NYSTA's 1971 convention, he had called on the state association to merge with downstate teacher unionists to form NYSUT. The NYSUT board passed the measure overwhelmingly, and the next morning, the board voted to recommend to NYSUT's Representative Assembly that the union remove the requirement in its constitution that it stay affiliated with the NEA. The vote was 52 to 6.[7]

"No one was planning on dropping out of the NEA," Hobart recalled. "We just didn't want to be bullied." Cortese said it was a case of defending the organization that NYSUT's leaders had worked so hard to build over the last four years. "Before you let all the foxes into the henhouse," she said, "you have to protect yourself."[8]

In a December 1975 NEA board meeting, the eleven New York members of the NEA's Board of Directors offered a potential compromise. What if the NEA grandfathered in NYSUT and its constitution, exempting the union from the requirement to follow the NEA policy on racial quotas and secret roll call votes? The NEA board rejected the compromise. The vote, excluding the New Yorkers, was 112 to 1.[9] "There is now no hope of a reconciliation," Hobart wrote in his December 21 column in *New York Teacher*, NYSUT's newspaper. "The teachers of this state will not permit the NEA to ruin what it has taken us 100 years to put together."

In the last months of 1975, *New York Teacher* was full of letters from angry teachers. Joseph Sano, the president of the Guilderland Central Teachers Association, called the "NEA in New York" project a "declaration of war." His mother, Josephine Sano, the president of the Albany Public School Teachers Association, stood up at an Albany-area meeting of NYSUT in December and said, "I'll have you know that the working man built this country. If I am forced to choose between George Meany and John Ryor speaking for me in Washington, I'd take Meany any day."[10] She also wrote a letter to Ryor that was reprinted in *New York Teacher*. "Stop spending our money to cut our throats and yours," she wrote. "New York will not be a second Florida. We will not take it."[11]

But behind the scenes, NYSUT's leaders were nervous. NYSTA, the NEA-affiliate in New York, had brought well over one hundred thousand members into the merged teachers' group in 1973. If the NEA returned to the state, would those members rejoin the association? A Harris poll completed in February 1976 reported that if NYSUT split, 17 percent of the members would go with the NEA affiliate, while another 19 percent were unsure, which meant more than a third of the union—roughly eighty thousand members—weren't committed to sticking with NYSUT. If defections of that size occurred, New York would again become the home of two ineffective teacher organizations engaged in constant battle.[12]

As expected, the NEA moved to establish an NEA affiliate in New York State. One part of the NEA strategy in New York State was to recruit teacher leaders in the hope that rank-and-file teachers would follow.[13] The NEA had won over Pisa, the Buffalo teachers' leader, and a few others, such as Edwin Robisch of Wappingers Falls, but few others. The second strategy was to woo away NYSUT staff, many of whom had previously worked for the New York State Teachers Association (NYSTA) before the merger. The idea was that teachers were more likely to follow a person—especially field staff who helped negotiate contracts and handle grievances—than to follow one teacher bureaucracy or another. This tactic proved more successful. In January 1976, President Hobart noticed three white envelopes on his desk—resignation letters from defecting staff members.[14] And each morning thereafter, Hobart's assistant, Jimmy Wood, would check to see who else had left a resignation letter in the president's office. Hobart told himself that he worked for an organization, not a family, and that "these things happen," but the institutional battle became bitter and personal. At one meeting, a defector told Hobart: We are going to destroy NYSUT—and you. And when you lose your job, we're going to be living in your house.

"That was the atmosphere," Hobart remembers. "They were assuming they'd be able to wreck our organization and supplant it."[15]

Robert Allen, the former Rome, New York, teacher who had risen to the position of assistant director of field services, remembers

NYSUT's staffers "dropping like flies" in the early months of 1976. Employees would seek out Allen and ask him which teachers' organization they should choose. Well, I only know what I'm going to do, Allen, a man of few words, would respond. I think the organization that's here is going to survive. It's institutionalized. It's together. I'm sticking with it.[16]

On January 16, 1976, Dan McKillip, NYSUT's assistant director of field services for four years, left his car keys on Allen's desk, went out to lunch, and never came back. He left, he said, because of "what, in my mind, was a carefully calculated plan on the part of the AFT to take over—lock, stock and barrel—all the teacher organizations in New York State." He believed that NYSUT's officers had sided with the AFT in the national dispute with the NEA and had expected the staff to do the same.[17] Day after day, Allen found car keys on his desk.

On a Wednesday, February 25, 1976, NYSUT's entire Vestal office, about a half-dozen people, who served one hundred school districts in ten southern counties from Binghamton to Elmira, handed in their letters of resignation. Only a secretary was left behind. The Vestal staff said that they were acting on the wishes of teachers in their area who had a deep allegiance to the NEA. Many of the NYSUT staffers had started their careers in NYSTA and felt that they would be more protected from the vagaries of politics if they remained in a staff-dominated organization like the NEA.[18]

"We don't think of ourselves as turncoats," said Ronald Crawford, one of the departing Vestal employees told the *Binghamton Press*. "We've converted, not defected."

NYSUT leaders didn't make that distinction. They were fighting for their professional lives—and for a unified teachers group that they believed best served teachers. The stakes were high—and they fought accordingly. The group of departing Vestal employees intended their resignations to take effect after they had taken accrued vacation time. Their NYSUT superiors had other plans. On the day the Vestal field representatives quit, Crawford was in the Susquehanna Valley arbitrating a NYSUT case. "I came back to the office after five o'clock to drop off some material and pick up some more things I needed, and the lock on my office door had been changed." On that Friday the same field representatives were sent letters on NYSUT stationary saying they were fired, effective immediately, and new staffers were hired to replace them.

Gary Slater, another Vestal field representative who had left NYSUT, was outraged. "This action is inconsistent with why NYSUT exists. If a school board had done to teachers what they did to us, the wrath of God would be down on it."[19]

Allen said NYSUT's leaders were "wandering around and wondering how many shoes were going to drop."[20] Frank Squillace, the NYSUT staff director in Syracuse, started calling Allen every day to make sure *he* hadn't left. Allen started traveling around the state to talk to NYSUT's members, especially ones where field representatives had left, to urge patience. Don't get swept up in this, he told teachers. You're still getting services. Hell isn't going to freeze over tomorrow.[21]

Robert Paliwodzinski, who managed the Rochester office for NYSUT, decided to leave NYSUT for the nascent NEA group. Two days later he got a call from Ken Melley, the NEA point person in charge of establishing a new presence in New York. Melley asked him whether other Rochester employees were going to leave with him. I don't know, Paliwodzinski told him. I haven't talked to them. Talk to them, he was told.[22]

Paliwodzinski invited the staff over to his home, and by the end of the meeting, the entire Rochester staff decided to leave, believing the future of education in New York State and in the country lay with the NEA.[23] Antonia Cortese, the second vice president of NYSUT, remembers the phone call she received about the Rochester office defection while in a meeting with Shanker, Hobart, First Vice President Dan Sanders, and Secretary-Treasurer Ed Rodgers. She was told the entire Rochester office was gone except for the secretary, who walked in one morning and found the desks bare and the chairs empty. Palidwodzinski and the others had set up a shadow office for the NEA right down the street from the office they abandoned.

When she relayed the news to Shanker, Cortese remembers watching the blood drain from his face—a response she had never seen from him before. To Cortese, the flurry of defections felt like an ocean wave that was retreating into the sea, taking the very ground she was standing on. Oh my god, she thought, we're losing the whole organization.[24]

At the end of January, the NEA opened an office across the street from NYSUT's Albany office and staffed it with four employees. The NEA's New York campaign was originally budgeted for $200,000, but in February, NEA staff said that even more had been committed. NYSUT publications that same month suggested it was a half-million-dollar campaign; Hobart claimed the NEA was spending a million.[25]

During these first months of 1976, debates between the NEA and NYSUT representatives sprung up all over the state. The NEA sent in President Ryor and Lauri Wynn, a Wisconsin leader and the chair of the NEA's black caucus. Paul Cole, Shanker, Hobart, and Cortese defended NYSUT and the AFT. Cortese learned once that a few NYSUT local leaders sympathetic to the NEA had invited Ryor to give his perspective on the conflict at a teachers' meeting in a Buffalo suburb. Cortese showed up, carried a chair from the audience up to the stage, and placed it next to Ryor as he spoke. Then she started responding to his comments.

One of the local leaders interrupted and told the Rome leader that they had invited *Ryor* to address the teachers, not *her*. People in the audience began shouting, Let her speak, let her speak, and the organizers backed down. Cortese had turned the address into another debate.[26] "The stakes were high," Cortese remembers. "We weren't going to have the NEA running around telling things that weren't the truth."[27]

By the time NYSUT held its 1976 convention in March, the NEA had hired away 35 of NYSUT's 306 staff members and opened sixteen offices across the state. The biggest question at the convention was whether to take the NEA affiliation requirement out of NYSUT's constitution. The NYSUT leaders were confident that such a resolution would pass, but they wanted an overwhelming mandate, believing that would help keep teachers from defecting. During the debate, several delegates rose to urge delay or a reconsideration of the affiliation vote, arguing that teacher unity was too important a goal to sacrifice without attempting a compromise.

Others, though, warned that putting off the decision would only hurt NYSUT, and their arguments were not always civil. "We all sat back and we said in 1939, 'Oh, Hitler is a reasonable man, all he wants is a little bit of this territory.' And we agreed [that] all he wanted was peace. The NEA only wants peace—a piece of New York City, a piece of Rochester, and a piece of Buffalo," said delegate Donald LaBombard from Carle Place, Long Island. "It is like the situation where I find that I have walked right into the middle of someone making love to my wife. Should I hand him his pants or his teeth? I think we should hand the NEA its teeth."[28]

The 3,400-member Buffalo Teachers Federation had voted overwhelmingly during the convention to disaffiliate from NYSUT and join a statewide NEA group if NYSUT delegates voted to cut its constitutional tie with the NEA. Thomas Pisa, the Buffalo leader who was aligned with the NEA, told the gathered delegates that "NYSUT has already lost some of its teeth," referring to the staff that had defected to the new NEA group. "[NYSUT] has been strong for three and a half years. . . . It has been strong for one reason: It has not had to fight another organization. Once it has to fight, monies have to be reallocated, staff has to be reallocated, we have to begin to develop strategies and lies about each other. We have to begin to compete. . . . That is what is going to happen if you continue with this madness. Speaking for the Buffalo Teachers Federation, Tom Hobart's home local, it's been nice being with you, we'll miss you, but if you go ahead with this, 'Good-bye.'"[29]

From 5:15 to 6:15 p.m. on the evening of Friday, March 5, 1976, locals voted and brought their results back in envelopes to be tallied in the convention's main hall. On Saturday morning, Jeanette DiLorenzo, a longtime UFT activist, read the results: 157,400 voted for removing the NEA affiliation requirement from NYSUT's constitution and 37,729 voted against. Over 80 percent of the New York delegates had voted to eliminate the affiliation requirement with the NEA. While NYSUT never officially disaffiliated from the NEA, and the NEA never officially kicked NYSUT out of its association, the two groups had separated. Immediately after the results were announced, Annette Bonder stood at a mike for a chance to speak.

"It is with great pride that I report to this assembly that ED [Educational District] 17 voted unanimously for the disaffiliation resolution. We believe, as did our forefathers, that if we don't hang together, we will surely hang separately."[30]

Shortly after the vote, a few hundred delegates who were NEA sympathizers left the hall. They reconvened at the Sheraton Hotel, where they officially established a new NEA group in New York, which they called the New York Educators Association (NYEA). The defectors included delegates from Syracuse and Buffalo, as well as those from suburbs such as Greece and East Ramapo, and rural areas such as Wayne and De Ruyter. The NEA gave them a multi-million dollar budget with which to wage an organizational war.

The group elected Edwin Robisch of Wappingers Falls and Thomas Pisa of Buffalo to be the group's copresidents. In the packed room that day, Pisa told the teachers who had left NYSUT that "from the moment of the announcement of disaffiliation, a new organization has existed."

Also in the room was the NEA's national president, John Ryor. "Many of you in this room have been predicting this to me and to others for more than three years now," Ryor told the crowd. "Al Shanker has seen fit to destroy the unity enjoyed by New York teachers." He added that "you are here to lay claim to the support and assistance of the 1.7 million American teachers united in the largest and strongest professional association in the world." He said that the NEA had "been in this state supporting New York teachers for more than 100 years and we are going to stay in New York. . . . It is time New York had an organization that devoted its time and money to working inside the state . . . not sending its leaders and propaganda around the nation."[31]

Paliwodzinski believed that NYEA would be able to win away nearly all the state's rural locals and maybe two-thirds of the suburban ones.[32] Pisa also believed that most of New York's teachers would fall away from NYSUT and join NYEA.[33] Daniel C. McKillip, who had left his post as NYSUT's assistant director of field services in January, had hopes that the organization could gain a toehold, and that "if we were lucky," it could become "a viable organization that could be competitive."[34] A headline from the *New York Post*, printed on the first day of the convention, expressed the worst fears of NYSUT's delegates: "Teacher Merger: The End."[35]

The one speech the delegates at the convention would almost universally recall was made by Al Shanker the day after the historic vote. He spoke in front of a wall emblazoned with the words "Standing Together." As usual, he started with doom and gloom, reminding New York's teachers of the dire economic and political straits they and their state were in. If New York City went into bankruptcy, which was possible, and huge cuts were made in the state's education budget, class sizes would go "all the way up, and by all the way up I mean thirty-seven, forty-seven, fifty and fifty-seven and sixty—I don't mean up to thirty. I am talking about classes that are huge." New York teachers also "had no choice" that year but to engage in "the largest number of strikes in the history of this state" against "a massive campaign" on the part of school boards "to take things away that were there long before we had collective bargaining contracts and negotiations."

Then Shanker turned his attention to the enemy, the NEA. He called the NYSUT staff who had defected the NEA's "mercenary army," and he compared them to scabs. "Anyone who walks that street is playing exactly the same role as a teacher after a strike vote who walks through a picket line," Shanker said. "It is a destructive role because the NEA cannot build a united organization in the state. They cannot do it. They can destroy, they can weaken, they can take away this group and that group, they can go to Albany and say, 'Now there are two teacher groups, so don't pass what that other group wants. . . .' They have no chance of having even a majority organization in this state. The only thing that they can do is . . . hurt the majority."

Shanker's spoke for almost an hour. What delegates would recall in later years, though, were just the last few minutes of his speech. It was then that the tough-talking leader began to recount the dark fairy tale "The Most Unbelievable Thing," written by Hans Christian Andersen. Cortese remembers that Shanker slowed down his cadence for effect as he told the story.

> There was a kingdom and in the kingdom there was a king and he had a princess, and he was interested in the progress of the arts. And at a certain point he announced that he would give the princess in marriage to the man who would accomplish the most unbelievable thing. . . . There were many marvelous things, but towering high above them was a truly wonderful mechanism showing the calendar back and forth into the past and into the future, showing the time, and intellectual and spiritual figures of history throughout mankind were sculptured around the clock. And whenever the clock struck, these figures exercised most graceful movements.
>
> And everybody, the people and the judges, said that yes, to accomplish a thing like that was most unbelievable, and the princess looked at the clock and looked at the handsome man, and she liked them both very much.
>
> The judges were just about to pronounce their formal judgment when a new competitor appeared, a lowbrow fellow. He, too, carried something in his hand but it was not a work of art, it was a sledge-hammer. He walked up to the clock and he swung out and with three blows he smashed up the clock, and everybody said, why to smash up such a clock, this was surely the most unbelievable thing.
>
> And that was how the judges had to judge.

"Our organization is a wonderful work of art," Shanker concluded. "If destroyed, it will never be put together again. To each of us goes the responsibility of seeing that it is the clock that survives—and not the sledgehammer!"[36]

The two thousand delegates tossed the convention brochures, flyers, and folders off their laps and stood up, clapping, whistling, and shouting. The standing ovation they offered to their leader lasted five minutes—the longest standing ovation ever given to a speaker at a NYSUT convention. Those who were sitting at the officers' table at the front of the room saw delegates in the crowd weeping at Shanker's call for teacher solidarity.[37] Hobart, knowing a showstopper when he heard one, adjourned for lunch.

As delegates ate, Arthur Cardinali, the president of the Baldwin Faculty Association, drew a picture of a "NYSUT" clock and an "NEA" sledgehammer coming at it. The impromptu button was immediately mimeographed and cut into paper buttons that hundreds of delegates proudly pinned to their shirts in the afternoon. "Keep the clock!" became the rallying cry of the New York teacher unionists. "Keep the clock!"[38]

Terry Herndon, the NEA's executive director, reported to the NEA convention held in Miami Beach in July 1976 "that the New York Educators Association, a faithful and dedicated NEA affiliate, is definitely up in place to stay."[39] When the 152 delegates from New York State—all from the breakaway NYEA—marched single file into the air-conditioned NEA convention, delegates stood and cheered. Often during the convention, the national delegates congratulated the New Yorkers who had severed all ties with the AFT and organized labor.

Since March, these NYEA teachers had worked to win away teachers from NYSUT. The new group claimed that 103 of the 767 local teachers' unions in New York had sided with them, bringing 18,200 teachers into the NYEA. The NEA had given $1.6 million to the new group to aid them in their battles, and $1.3 million more was reportedly promised for the 1976–1977 school year. The NYEA concentrated most of its recruitment efforts upstate, but rumors floated at the 1976 convention that it would try to set up an NYEA chapter in NYSUT's stronghold and Shanker's hometown, New York City. Ned Hopkins, the NYSUT public relations director who was attending the NEA convention as an observer, found the rumors amusing.

"Let them try to get something going in New York City," Hopkins told a reporter. "We'd like to see them try."[40]

The NEA leadership and the NYEA staff set a membership target of fifty thousand by June 1977. NYEA staff focused their efforts on Long Island, Syracuse, and Rochester, as well as in the New York City suburbs of Westchester, Rockland, and Orange Counties.[41] "We almost took for granted that Rochester and Syracuse would stick with the NEA," McKillip said. But the effort was distracted in the fall of 1977, when NYEA's largest local in Buffalo staged a debilitating thirteen-day strike that claimed the attention and resources of NYEA staff. The Taylor Law applied to the new organization as well as to NYSUT, and Pisa, Buffalo's teacher leader, spent thirty days in the Erie County Correctional Facility.

By June 1977, the NYEA had won few other school districts in the state. One of the mistakes the NEA made, believed McKillip, was running the campaign from outside New York. "It didn't look good at all," he said, and it led the NEA to make political blunders that cost the NYEA Rochester and Syracuse.[42] "The belief that NYEA would enroll 50,000 members by the end of its first year was unrealistic," an internal analysis of the NYEA would later state, "and the consequences of that belief were unfortunate. NYEA's failure to attain the impossible produced an unjustified sense of futility and led to widespread demoralization."[43] In March 1977, the NYEA lost challenges in Horseheads and Corning, and in May they lost in Mount Vernon. By the end of the 1976–1977 school year, NYEA still had far fewer than 25,000 members, most of them concentrated in school districts on the southwest of the state.

Still, NYSUT lost thousands of teachers to the NYEA as well as over eight thousand UFT teachers who were laid off after the 1975 fiscal crisis in New York City. Both events reduced dues coming in to the union. In May 1977, the union had to cut back spending and was forced to sell its airplane, a Beechcraft King Air, used to ferry officers around the state. It streamlined its newspaper and laid off sixteen employees, and in the fall of 1977 they had to borrow money for payroll.[44] Despite its financial troubles, NYSUT was, by its spring 1977 convention, largely free from the threat posed by the NYEA. Official T-shirts for the convention read "Winning Together," and the slogan was accurate.

"Just over one year ago," Hobart told the conventioneers in Niagara Falls, "while NYSUT was still a dues-paying affiliate, the NEA raided our staff and began creating its little puppet, the New York

Educators Association, the Pinocchio of teachers organizations. You remember Pinocchio, how every time he told a lie, his nose got bigger and bigger. Well, if NEA's puppet suffered the same problem as Gepetto's did, NYEA would have this tiny little body with a nose a thousand stories high.

"Here are just a few of the NEA-NYEA's bigger nose builders. Eleven months ago, they said they would have fifty thousand members by December of 1976. In October, the claim was down to 30,000. Six weeks ago, NEA's top man said NYEA had 25,000 members. Over four weeks ago an NYEA publication said it already had 22,000 members. On March first, at an open meeting in West Genessee, an NYEA field representative admitted, 'We have actually got between 12,000 and 13,000 members.'"[45]

The NYEA was no longer feared; it could now be dismissed with humor.

NYEA made its last stand in the fall of 1978 when it challenged NYSUT for control over the United University Professionals (UUP), the NYSUT-affiliated union that represented sixteen thousand staff members at state university schools. Nationally, the NEA and the AFT were warring over who would represent professors and staff in higher education, and both sides considered the SUNY battle an important one. Shanker considered the campaign important enough not only to campaign at SUNY campuses, but even to write some of NYSUT's campaign literature.[46]

After a three-week voting period in December 1978, the ballots were counted at seventeen tables by the staff of the Public Employment Relations Board at a tense three-hour session at the Student Activities Center at the SUNY Albany campus. Both sides were uncertain about the outcome; many of the members of the UUP were new and their loyalties hadn't solidified.

The day before, the participants in the election had challenged 310 ballots and they were put aside in case they were needed to decide the winner. They weren't needed. The tally was 6,067 votes for NYSUT and 4,092 for the NEA challengers.

That was the end of the NEA challenge in New York. The NEA leadership in Washington accepted that NYEA was going to remain a 25,000-member organization. The NYEA staff was cut from 120 to 60. Paliwodzinski, who had left NYSUT to join the NYEA over two years before, called this period "the most difficult time in my life." As NYEA's director of field services, he now had to lay off many of the NYSUT staff members he had recruited to join the NYEA effort. Some of the staff found jobs with NEA affiliates in other states; some didn't. Each year until Paliwodzinski left in 1984, NYEA's budget was squeezed tighter as funds from the national office dried up.[47] Among the reasons for their failure, NYEA leaders cited NYSUT's "excellent service program"; Al Shanker's "aura of power"; and the fact that NYEA was established four years after NYSUT had formed.[48]

Hobart, Cortese, and the other NYSUT leaders saw the victory not as NYEA's failure, but as NYSUT's success. After the merger, NYSUT had delivered more money and better services to New York's teachers and become a major player in state politics. Teachers didn't want to go back to having two impotent teachers' groups engaged in continuous fights. Cortese believed there was another reason that NYSUT held its members. "I think we appealed to people's hopes," she said, "rather than their fears."[49]

But while the threat from the outside had been beaten back, internal divisions surfaced within the union the next few years. Some of NYSUT's leaders, including Shanker's old friend Dan Sanders, believed that NYSUT's leadership could be stronger. One of the complaints was that Ed Rodgers, the union's treasurer, was not competent to handle the union's finances. Sanders, in charge of legislation for the union, also believed that he could manage the union better than Hobart could. In late 1977, he announced he would run for NYSUT president in 1978.

The challenge to Hobart's presidency put Shanker in an awkward position. Sanders was his longtime confidante and neighbor. He might have tried to dissuade Sanders from running, and he probably had the power to kill his candidacy, but he didn't. Shanker also knew that a victory by Sanders could destroy NYSUT in a way that the NEA challenge could not. During the merger discussions of the early 1970s, Shanker had to overcome upstaters' suspicions that the statewide teachers' merger was a takeover by Shanker and his New York City union friends. The campaign by Sanders resurrected those fears.

"He was afraid of breaking up the union," Ken Deedy said of Shanker. "Everyone was afraid of breaking up the union."[50] In an attempt to keep both sides in the union no matter what the outcome of the election, Shanker recommended that the loser of the Hobart-Sanders election agree to fill the post of executive vice president. But Hobart would have none of it. Let the chips fall where they may, was Hobart's response.[51] Shanker also suggested that Hobart leave Rodgers off his ticket, but Hobart refused to abandon his friend and merger ally. Shanker then urged Herb Magidson to run for treasurer, and he did, defeating Rodgers.

By the time NYSUT's Delegate Assembly was held in the spring of 1978, Shanker had taken steps to make sure Sanders's candidacy did not tear the union apart. He persuaded teachers in the UFT to abstain from voting in the presidential primary election of the Unity Caucus, NYSUT's dominant political party. That way, whoever was elected as NYSUT's president would be seen as an upstate choice, not a New York City one.

When the announcement came that Hobart had defeated Sanders by a handful of delegate votes in the Unity Caucus primary, Hobart remembers hearing gasps from the floor of the NYSUT convention.[52] Sanders and his allies had expected victory. Teachers had stuck with Hobart rather than risk dividing their union. After Sanders's loss in the caucus, Shanker convinced him to run for executive vice president at the convention, and he did so, and won.

For years, relations between Hobart and Sanders, and their supporters, were strained. Two officers, Cortese and Hobart, were close allies. On the other side were Sanders and Ken Deedy, the vice president from Long Island who had supported Sanders's candidacy. Jimmy Wood, Hobart's assistant, remembers that after meetings of NYSUT's board and its executive committee, the Hobart camp and the Sanders camp would go their separate ways to socialize. At first, Magidson served as a bridge between both camps. The process of healing began after Wood and Dean Streiff, both assistants to Hobart, attended a fundraiser later that same year in Westchester to eliminate Sanders's campaign debt. It was a gesture that Sanders appreciated, and a thaw began in the icy relationship between the two camps. Over the months and years, the distrust faded, as all understood "that the future of the organization was hanging in the balance," said Wood, "and that NYSUT was more important than the personalities."[53]

In three years, the union had withstood three challenges that could have destroyed it. The first was the NEA challenge in New York. The second was a financial crisis, caused by a loss of members to the NEA and exacerbated by teacher lay offs as a result of New York City's fiscal crisis in 1975. The third was the internal power struggle for control of the union. The union survived all three challenges. The NEA in New York never became more than a marginal group, and NYSUT's fiscal problems were solved by steadily expanding membership and the steady fiscal leadership of Magidson and the man he brought in to steady the union's finances, Dan Frasca. Within a year of the election, all of the sixteen NYSUT staff members who had been laid off were offered their jobs back. Within five years, the union could afford to build a new million-dollar headquarters—with cash—and it began expanding its membership services, which would become the envy of many labor unions.[54] The moves were evidence that the union was here to stay, and that teachers wouldn't give up what they had finally earned: power.

Now teachers, politicians, and the public wondered: What would they do with it?

PART III

Maturity

CHAPTER 9

Wielding Political Power

Rachel Moyer, a mother and a special education teacher at the Anna S. Kuhl Elementary School in Port Jervis, New York, had no warning that the evening of December 2, 2000, would descend as the worst night of her life. On this evening, she traveled to the high school in East Stroudsburg, Pennsylvania, with her daughter, Abbie, and her husband, John, to watch their son, Gregory, a fifteen-year-old sophomore at Notre Dame High School, play on the varsity basketball team. Gregory, who stood 6' 3" and weighed 210 pounds, played about ten minutes during the first half. He had only scored a few points and his team was losing, but as he left the court at halftime, he looked up into the stands and made eye contact with his father as if to say: All is okay.

But it wasn't. A few minutes later, one of Gregory's teammates, fear on his face, came running into the stands and said, Hurry up, come with me, it's Greg. The three hurried to the locker room. Rachel expected that her son had somehow hurt himself during the game or in the locker room. When she arrived, however, she found Gregory lying on the floor.

She bent over her son and lifted his head.

Why aren't you breathing, Greg? she asked. What's the matter? Gregory opened his eyes for a moment, gasped, and then fell back, unconscious. The team's athletic trainer conducted CPR for twenty minutes, the time it took for the ambulance to arrive. It took another twenty-five minutes to travel twenty-three miles to Pocono Medical Center in East Stroudsburg. There, a doctor and a team of nurses worked to revive the boy. When they finally stopped, Gregory's father begged the doctor to keep trying. The medical team began again, and then finally gave up. John, the doctor told the boy's father, it's too late.

As Rachel stood over her son's body, Sue Ruehle, a nurse in the emergency room, spoke to her plainly. This should not have happened, the nurse said. There should have been an automatic external defibrillator in Gregory's school. There should be one in *every* school.[1]

It was the first time Rachel had heard the term *automatic external defibrillator*, often called an AED. The device looks a like bulky laptop computer and is similar to the manual defibrillators that actors playing doctors use on television dramas to shock hearts back to life that have stopped beating. Gregory had suffered a sudden cardiac arrest, which kills 350,000 Americans a year, almost 1,000 people every day. The American Heart Association estimates that if AEDs were available in public places, about 50,000 Americans could be saved each year.

Rachel decided that in lieu of flowers, she would ask family and friends to donate money to buy AEDs for area high schools. In the three days before the funeral, people donated about $14,000, which the Moyers used to buy AEDs for the five high schools in Monroe County, Pennsylvania, where Greg's high school was located. The Moyers made the contribution in honor of their son. But Rachel also did it because she was a teacher. "School districts and teachers are not only responsible for the education of the kids," she said, "but also their safety."

Rachel then pushed to bring AEDs to other schools. On April 25, 2001, which would have been Gregory's sixteenth birthday, the Pennsylvania legislature passed a law that funded up to four AEDs in every school district that wanted them. She found, though, that she met resistance as soon as she tried to bring AEDs into New York State schools. In Port Jervis, where she taught, for example, the attorney for the school district told her that they didn't want any AEDs because of possible liability if they were improperly used.

Just imagine the liability if a child dies and I tell them I offered you a free AED, Rachel replied. But her indignation didn't win over the lawyer or the school board.

In February 2002, Rachel learned of another couple, John and Karen Acompora, from Long Island, who had lost their son Louis to sudden cardiac arrest a year earlier when he was hit in the chest with a lacrosse ball in Northport, Long Island. Rachel invited Karen to a fundraiser for Gregory at the Fernwood Resort in the Poconos. Karen was surprised to hear of Rachel's success in Pennsylvania. The Acomporas had gotten a Long Island legislator to introduce a bill nine months earlier mandating defibrillators in school districts with over one thousand students, but the bill had foundered. Before the two couples had mobilized to try to move the stalled legislation, Rachel came across an article that reported that the New York State School Boards Association opposed a law that required schools to buy a defibrillator.

Rachel's heart sank. If school boards were opposed to AEDs, she figured, there was little chance that statewide legislation would be passed. She feared that she would have to fight to bring AEDs into one school district at a time, a strategy she knew would be painfully slow, if it succeeded at all. Then, in February 2002, Rachel remembered Alan Lubin, executive vice president of NYSUT, who directed the legislation and political action network at the union. As a local leader in NYSUT, she had met Lubin in passing a few times, and she hoped he and his contacts might help. What she didn't know was just how well connected he was.[2]

During the 1990s, Lubin had attended two Christmas parties at the White House hosted by the Clintons. At a 2002 fundraising dinner in Manhattan, the union's VP sat next to former President Bill Clinton, and the men talked about Al-Qaida and the South Beach diet. About a year later, after announcing his run for the presidency, John Kerry had called Lubin at home to discuss his positions on education and his political strategy.

"I look back and say, 'Where did I get the right to get these contacts?'" Lubin says. "I'm no genius. I'm just a pudgy guy from Brooklyn. It's because the teachers lend me their power. That's what I say to them all the time. We are as strong as you allow us to be. Their collective power gives me an entrée to a lot of places to promote our issues."[3]

Lubin began as a fourth grade teacher in 1967 at PS 304 in the Bedford-Stuyvesant neighborhood of Brooklyn, one of the most tumultuous times and places in the history of the teachers' movement. "When I first came to work in 1967, I didn't know anything about [Al] Shanker or the United Federation of Teachers, other than I should join. It didn't take long during that first six months that I became familiar with Shanker. We were moving toward the 1968 strike and he started appearing on television a lot and I was extremely impressed with his strength. He would stand up to the superintendent of schools, he would stand up to the mayor, he would go toe-to-toe in media interviews with the governor. He would just consistently stay on target and never lost sight of where we were going."

Lubin became one of the "Class of '68," those teacher recruits who became active in the UFT during the New York City strike that year. When Lubin first started working for the teachers' union, Shanker took him under his wing, sometimes taking him to see Bayard Rustin, the civil rights leader who organized the 1963 March on Washington for civil rights, and A. Philip Randolph, founder of the Brotherhood of Sleeping Car Porters and a mainstay of the civil rights movement. By answering Rachel's phone call, Lubin was acting on one of the first political lessons Shanker had taught him: Listen to teachers. Shortly after Lubin was elected in 1969 as borough rep from Brooklyn, Shanker organized a series of press conferences to try to recover from the public relations debacle of the Ocean Hill–Brownsville conflict. Lubin was asked to bring some bodies to the first event and he gathered two carloads of parents from the Bedford-Stuyvesant neighborhood. Afterward, they all agreed; the event had been a snore. Reporters had floated softball questions at Shanker and his answers had lacked the fire they often contained when he was challenged in public. In the office the next morning, Ann Kessler, another district representative and an old friend of Shanker's, talked Lubin into calling Shanker and relaying the parents' assessment.

He doesn't have to call back, the new district rep sheepishly told Shanker's secretary. I just wanted to let him know that the Bed-Stuy parents weren't very excited about the event and that the real issues weren't hit. Late that afternoon, Shanker phoned. Lubin was nervous: "A lot of people were intimidated by the man."

Shanker wanted to know what exactly the parents said, and Lubin told him. For the next press conference, held the following week, the twenty-six-year-old union rep could only muster one carload of parents. The next morning, Shanker called Lubin and again asked him about the parents' response, which Lubin was sorry to report, was much the same. Shanker thanked him and told him that he and his Brooklyn parents were the only ones who had provided honest feedback. That afternoon, Shanker's secretary called Lubin to tell him that Shanker had cancelled the remaining press conferences.

"It showed me he could listen," Lubin says. "He was bigger than life sometimes and he was powerful, but he was accessible." In all the years Lubin worked with Shanker, the union leader always called him back promptly. It's a responsiveness that Lubin has tried to emulate.

"If you don't hear back from me in two or three days," he tells his constituents, "it means I screwed up."[4]

When Rachel Moyer first called Alan Lubin on that day in February 2002, the NYSUT vice president did what Al Shanker had taught him to do over thirty years earlier: He listened. Rachel explained that she had been told repeatedly that school districts didn't want to pay for defibrillators, and didn't want them in any case because they were worried about liability. She mentioned that the School Boards Association had opposed the defibrillator bill because they didn't want another unfunded imposition on schools. They have defibrillators in prisons, an incredulous Lubin told Rachel, and they're telling you we shouldn't have them in the schools. He also told her that the chances of passing legislation bringing defibrillators into the schools were good. Rachel's sense of hopelessness lifted.

"I knew he was going to help me. It took so much weight off my shoulders. I also knew that he had the support of half-a-million unionists behind him. I felt I could share the responsibility for making New York's schools heart-safe."[5]

NYSUT's membership—the foundation of their power—had grown so large because of another fundamental political lesson that Shanker preached: Expand the membership base. For most of its history, the teachers' movement had a narrow view of who it was. They believed their organizations—whether the American Federation of Teachers (AFT) or the National Education Association (NEA)—should include only skilled education workers, such as teachers, professors, and in the case of the NEA, administrators. It was an organizing model inherited from the American Federation of Labor, the first nationwide federation of unions.

But in the mid- and late-1960s, a new group of employees who had entered the New York City school system challenged how teachers saw their union. At that time, Title I, the federal antipoverty program, injected funds into schools with poor students. Schools used the money to hire teacher assistants—often called *paraprofessionals*—to help teachers in crowded urban classrooms. Most of the people hired were African American and Puerto Rican mothers, few of whom had finished high school. School administrators in New York City took advantage of these nonunionized employees by paying so little that many of them qualified for welfare. In 1969, paraprofessionals, often called *paras*, began to organize and the UFT had to decide whether they would compete with the American Federation of State, County, and Municipal Employees (AFSCME), District 37, to represent them in contract negotiations. Because a large segment of the African American community still resented Shanker from the Ocean Hill–Brownsville conflict, AFSCME thought that it could win a majority vote in a head-to-head election with the UFT.[6]

Also, many New York City teachers did not want paraprofessionals in the union. Some wanted to keep them out because they didn't consider them professionals, and others wanted to exclude this large group of minorities because they had failed to support teachers during the 1968 Ocean Hill–Brownsville teacher strikes. Some even feared that empowering paraprofessionals would create more competition for their jobs.[7]

At a UFT delegate assembly meeting in 1969, Shanker addressed a large minority of teachers who were openly hostile to expanding the UFT's membership. You have to understand, he told the crowd of delegates. I'm not going to be here if I can't be an effective leader. Enlarging our union makes me a more effective leader, and you might want someone else to be your president if you don't want to do this.[8]

Shanker said something else that evening that Lubin would remember. The responsibility of a union, Shanker declared, is to organize the unorganized and to do for others what the union had already done for its own. Organizing paras was neither a selfish act nor an unselfish one; it was both. The union benefited those who joined, and those who joined benefited the union. Shanker argued that adding more members built the union's muscle. By adding the paraprofessionals, the union also broadened its political base, bringing African Americans and Puerto Ricans into a union that was largely white and Jewish.

Offering the privileges of unionism to others in the schools also redefined who could belong to a teachers' union. Instead of just organizing highly skilled workers, the UFT was taking a page out of the organizing book of the Congress of Industrial Organizations (CIO), which had in the 1930s organized unskilled workers in entire industries, such as those in mining or textiles. Shanker was taking the same broad approach to organizing in education.

Shanker's argument prevailed, and UFT teachers invited paras to join their union. In 1969, the paras voted by a narrow margin to have the UFT rather than AFSCME to represent them. When negotiations between paras and the city's board of education stalled, UFT teachers voted to strike. That expression of support moved discussions forward. On August 3, 1970, the paras voted by a margin of 1,461 to 42 to approve their first bargained contract with the Board of Education. The paras' package of wages and benefits increased 140 percent and they received paid vacations, sick leave, as well as health and dental coverage—none of which they had before.[9]

The contract stipulated another benefit that surprised many who had branded New York City teachers and Shanker as racist during the

1968 Ocean Hill–Brownsville controversy. It provided release time with pay—as well as financial aid—for paras who wanted to pursue additional education to become teachers, incentives that are still part of paraprofessional contracts.[10]

One of the women who took advantage of the program was Frances L. Brown, a tall, friendly woman who lived in the South Bronx with her husband, Robert, and her two boys, Chad and Shep. When her boys began at PS 130 in her neighborhood in the early 1980s, she started volunteering in the classroom. "The assistant principal told me there's a new program coming through, and she said 'I think you should get involved, because I think you'd make a very good teacher.'" Brown took a job at the school as a paraprofessional. "The paraprofessional program pulled in men and women from the neighborhood," Brown remembers. "They knew the neighborhood and the children and the parents. The para was like the liaison between the union and the community."

Brown took advantage of the release time and the financial aid provided in the UFT contract to study at City College and Bronx Community College. "Many of us wouldn't have become certified if the union hadn't started the program," she says. During those years, Brown worked in two classrooms with two teachers who mentored her. "When I had to do papers for college, they'd make sure I did them correctly," Brown says. "They taught me everything: roll books, lesson plans, how to work a lesson. These women said to me, 'If you're going to be a teacher, you're going to be a *good* teacher.'" After twelve years as a para, Brown became a full-fledged teacher. She taught for twenty-one more years in the South Bronx.

"I really loved teaching, I loved giving," says Brown, who is now retired. "I used to tell my students, 'When I'm old you're going to be my doctor, you're going to be doing my hair. I'm going to come to you when you have your own business. I'm training you so you can take care of me in my old age.'"[11]

By 1974, practically every teacher's aide had completed at least a high school equivalency exam; over six thousand were enrolled in college. Three hundred had earned teachers' degrees and one hundred had been licensed. "Al Shanker is the man in the United States and the only one I know who has upgraded . . . black and Puerto Rican women through his paraprofessional system," said Bayard Rustin, a good friend of Shanker's. "Many of them are now becoming teachers because he wrote that into his contract."[12]

Paraprofessionals have become a kind of farm team for the teaching profession. Since 1970, more than six thousand paraprofessionals in New York have earned associate's degrees and more than five thousand have gained bachelor's degrees.[13] "If that effort isn't civil rights, what is?" Lubin asks. "Now they are some of our most loyal and fervent trade unionists."

Near the end of his life, Shanker was asked to name his proudest achievements. He mentioned building the UFT, supporting the American labor movement, and fighting for freedom internationally. "But if I had to pick one thing, I'd say it is organizing the classroom paraprofessionals and negotiating for them, not only for better salaries and benefits but for the career ladder that enabled them to become teachers, and to join the struggles of teachers to improve their profession."[14]

Through the 1980s and 1990s, NYSUT steadily expanded its rolls by repeatedly opening the circle of membership to include school-related professionals, such as bus drivers and secretaries, and then professionals, such as doctors, nurses, and psychologists, who often had similar concerns as teachers. Those additions, coupled with the growth of the number of teachers around the state, would more than double the size of the union to over a half million members. "The expansion was part of what Shanker talked about," said Herb Magidson, a NYSUT official for fifteen years. "To the extent you can identify with others and expand the scope of what you're about, the more you can build your political strength."[15]

In a fall 1973 "Where We Stand" column published in the *New York Times*, Shanker looked back on the political achievements that teachers had made not only in New York State, but across the country. He pointed out that in a dozen years, teachers in twenty-seven states had won the right to organize and that 60 percent of teachers in the country had engaged in collective bargaining. Nationwide, teacher salaries had jumped 100 percent. He wrote:

> Prior to the 1960s, teacher organizations rarely participated in partisan politics. They prided themselves on staying out of election campaigns, and actually believed they could keep education and politics separate. Today, teachers are a major political force in several states, and their organizations recognize that every gain and every loss, and every goal and every danger is achieved ultimately—is produced or protected—through the political process. There simply is no separating education and politics. . . .

Teachers, too, realize that they cannot educate children in a sick society. They must work to improve that society—to guarantee that every family has an adequate income, and that every pupil has a home decent enough for him to come to school prepared and able to learn. In short, the problems that teachers face require for their solution, tax reform, aid to education, national health insurance, better housing, full employment and the elimination of poverty and discrimination.[16]

After the New York teachers' merger, Shanker and others relished the challenge of becoming a political player in the statewide arena. "From the first day I met him, Al told me, 'The union has to get involved with politics,'" Lubin remembered. "He said, 'Politics is the key to improving our schools for teachers and students.'" Shanker and the UFT brought strong connections to the Democratic Party into NYSUT; NYSTA, the other party to the merger, brought its connections to the Republican Party, which had long been dominant in many upstate rural and suburban areas. The result was a union that was willing to support Republicans or Democrats—as long as they were friendly to education. One of the first decisions that Dan Sanders made after he became NYSUT's vice president in 1973 was to keep on Ray Skuse, a former Republican Assemblyman, as the union's director of legislation. It was the union's way of sustaining its NYSTA connections to upstate Republicans.

The first sign that the new union had gained political power was how the press reacted to it. Editorial writers and reporters had long advocated better working conditions for teachers—it was a bit like supporting motherhood and apple pie. After NYSUT was formed, though, the press corps turned 180 degrees. The *Albany Times-Union*, expressing the attitude of much of the press, editorialized: "Issue: Is NYSTA to remain an organization of professionalism in a most vital calling, or is it becoming a militant, self-serving labor union?"[17]

Syndicated columnist Victor Riesel joined the *New York Times* and other editorial pages in warning that the 210,000-member NYSUT had become a major political power. "This rolling classroom teachers' power can clobber" its enemies, Reisel wrote, since its "money pool is even more startling than it first appears." He noted that the union's political action fund was likely to exceed $1 million annually; that its defense fund was $3.5 million; and that its annual budget topped $11.5 million. The organization, Riesel warned, "is swiftly turning the teachers into a precinct machine" that would force politicians to become more pro-teacher and pro-education.

Tom Hobart, NYSUT's president, found the column amusing. "What 'startles' Riesel is nothing more than what teachers and their organizations—even the NEA—have long said that we *ought* to be," was Hobart's response. "We want education at the top of the nation's priorities; and what our experience in New York proves is that when teachers stop fighting other teachers, they can do just that. . . . Political power does *not* come out of complaining that you don't have it, but from unity and concentrating our energies on work for teachers and schools," he said. The only thing that teachers had lost by unifying, Shanker liked to say, was pity.

One of the first tests of NYSUT's political power came in the 1974 gubernatorial race. Four years earlier, prior to the teachers' merger in the state, both the UFT and NYSTA remained neutral in the governor's race. In September 1974, though, the merged teachers' union decided to abandon the incumbent Wilson, who had served as lieutenant governor under Republican Governor Nelson Rockefeller. The union wanted to take advantage of the post-Watergate backlash against Republicans and elect a Democratic governor who was more sympathetic to teachers' issues.[18] NYSUT's Board of Directors voted to endorse Hugh Carey, a little known New York City congressman, a risky move that surprised everyone—including Carey. Hobart said the union endorsed the challenger because of his strong voting record for education in Congress, but he also praised the congressman's labor record. NYSUT backing proved crucial in winning Carey the endorsement of the New York State AFL-CIO a few weeks later. That endorsement signaled the end of the long domination of the state's AFL-CIO by the construction unions, which endorsed Wilson, and the ascendance of public employee unions such as NYSUT and Council 37 of AFSCME, which both backed Carey. The day after the AFL-CIO endorsement the *New York Times* showed Shanker escorting Carey into the AFL-CIO session at Kiamesha Lake, just minutes after the labor federation gave Carey its endorsement.[19] Carey defeated Wilson in November. Despite the success, Hobart remembers not all teachers were happy with the union's decision to take sides in contentious political battles.

"Everyone was asking, 'Why are you doing this?'" Hobart remembers. "They said, 'You're supposed to be negotiating contracts.'"[20]

In the 1976 Democratic primary for New York Senator, which had five contenders, NYSUT refused to back the front-runner, Bella

Abzug, because she had opposed the UFT teacher strikes of 1968. Instead, it put its weight behind Daniel P. Moynihan, the former representative to the United Nations, and he squeaked by with a 7,000-vote plurality. Moynihan won the general election as well, defeating the Conservative Party's James Buckley, whom the union considered the most anti-teacher member of the U.S. Senate. That victory was all the sweeter because Buckley had supported teachers' number one enemy in the state legislature, Charles Jerabek, in the early 1970s. NYSUT's winning streak continued into 1978, when NYSUT endorsed Carey again and he won a second term.

Teachers were also getting involved on the national level. In 1976, both the AFT and the NEA endorsed Democratic candidate Jimmy Carter for president—the first time that the two major teacher organizations took a stand in a presidential campaign. In New York and nationally, the era when teachers shunned politics was ending. At the AFT convention in 1976, Walter Mondale, the Democrat's vice presidential candidate and a strong friend to education, called Al Shanker, the AFT president, the "ablest union leader in America today."[21] Four days before he was elected president, Jimmy Carter stopped by New York and met with NYSUT's officers.

Despite doubters, the perception was growing that NYSUT was a political team that could play—and win—at the statewide level. "Ever since the merger, our endorsement has been coveted," Lubin said. Mario Cuomo, Carey's lieutenant governor in 1978, acknowledged NYSUT's power in an entry to his diary, dated March 10, 1982. Cuomo wrote the passage after he had been invited to a meeting with Al Shanker to discuss Cuomo's bid for the Democratic nomination for governor. "Teachers are perhaps the most effective of all the State's unions," Cuomo wrote. "If they go all out, it will mean telephones and vigorous statewide support. It will also mean some money. I would have had them in 1977"—a reference to Cuomo's failed run for mayor in New York City—"if it had not been for a clumsy meeting I had with Shanker. I must see that I don't make the same mistake again."[22] At NYSUT's annual convention that spring, Cuomo earned a standing ovation after he dazzled NYSUT's members with his oratory. Still, NYSUT leaders were inclined to stay neutral in the Democratic primary because New York City Mayor Ed Koch hadn't lost a primary in twenty years and was leading Cuomo by as many as twenty-five percentage points in pre-election polls.

NYSUT's leadership abandoned its neutrality, though, when Koch told NYSUT's board at the New York State AFL-CIO convention that he believed the penalties against teachers in the Taylor Law should be stiffened, not relaxed.[23] Three weeks before the primary, the union endorsed Cuomo, and teachers made tens of thousands of calls for the underdog candidate—"the best phone banks I'd ever seen," Cuomo said. The support helped him squeak out a victory over Koch in the primary in September and then win the general election. Cuomo told New York's teachers: "I never could have won without you."[24]

In 1998, NYSUT's twenty-fifth anniversary year, the union entered another high-profile statewide race. This time they got involved not just because they preferred one candidate over another, but because a U.S. senator decided that the way to get reelected was to attack NYSUT and all teacher unions. Lubin learned that New York Senator Alfonse D'Amato, a New York State Republican senator in his third term, had fired a shot at the teachers' union when a reporter from a local newspaper called him for comment regarding a blistering attack on teachers by D'Amato. "It was the shot across the bow," Lubin said. "We knew it was a declaration of war."[25]

D'Amato repeated his attacks in stops all over the state, including Regents' hearings in Ithaca and Long Island and appearances in Albany and Syracuse. He also launched an ad campaign against teacher unions that ran in September and October 1997, more than a year before the 1998 election. The senator from Long Island apparently felt that he could boost his waning popularity by getting out front on an issue that, according to polls, New Yorkers considered more important than any other: education.

Throughout the fall of 1997, Lubin saw the thirty-second spots on early morning television and heard them on his car radio. "When it comes to education," the voice for the senator's ad said, "Senator D'Amato knows the Liberals are wrong. Our public school system isn't working because Liberals have put union demands ahead of our children. Al D'Amato wants to change that. It's time to expel violent, disruptive juveniles so good kids can learn. It's time for merit pay. That means more for good teachers and getting bad teachers out of the classroom. And finally, it's time we told the teachers' union to put our children first."[26]

The ad campaign marked the first statewide attack against teachers since Assemblyman Charles Jerabek, a Long Islander like D'Amato, had sponsored four anti-teacher bills that became law in April 1971. "He may have awakened a sleeping giant," said John Zogby, the

New Hartford, Connecticut-based pollster, of D'Amato's attack. "In this instance, I thought it was a very risky thing for Al D'Amato to do, especially since Bob Dole failed so miserably in attacking teachers' unions" during the 1996 presidential race.[27]

When Lubin went on the road, angry teachers approached him wanting to know how and when the union would counter the attacks. Society didn't finger police officers for high crime rates, blame doctors for the health care crisis, or blame soldiers when a war wasn't going well, they argued. But D'Amato was blaming teachers and unions for any and all problems in public education. His thirty-second critiques were blind to bad administrators, schools and classes that were too large, the under-funding of urban schools, and even the problems that poverty brought to the classroom. Senator D'Amato was simply teacher bashing.

Lubin knew that a thirty-second TV ad responding to D'Amato would have cost upwards of a million dollars, and wouldn't have educated teachers about the senator, much less mobilized them to join the campaign to defeat him. "Our members are intelligent," Lubin explains. "They don't want to be told what to do, they want to know *why* we ask them to do something. We needed to educate them about D'Amato's record."[28]

The education of teachers, part of what NYSUT called its Reject D'Amato campaign, began on Thursday, November 20, 1997, as NYSUT members showed up at Long Island train stations and at upstate shopping plazas carrying red-and-white signs that said, "Tell the Truth, Al." They handed out leaflets condemning D'Amato's education record.

At a press conference outside New York City's Pennsylvania Station, Sandra Feldman, the president of the UFT, accused the senator of having "one of the worst records in Congress" on education and not "lifting a finger to help our public schools." At Feldman's side were not just teachers, but also Brian M. McLaughlin, president of the New York Central Labor Council, an umbrella group for the city's 1.5 million union members, and Edward J. Cleary, president of the state's 2.3 million-member AFL-CIO.

NYSUT also publicized its campaign against D'Amato at its annual convention in the spring, an event that received wide media coverage. The union invited all three Democratic candidates vying for the Democratic senate nomination—Geraldine Ferraro, the 1984 vice presidential candidate; Mark Green, New York City's public advocate;

and Charles Schumer, the Brooklyn congressman. At one point, three large screens were projected with a long list of D'Amato's votes on education, including his votes to cut student loans, job training funds, Head Start grants, and educational funding in general. "I couldn't believe that he voted against funding for free lunches," said Ferraro at one point. "It boggles my mind."[29]

To get NYSUT members personally involved in the campaign against D'Amato, NYSUT's leaders called upon the union's political action committees (PAC), a local activist network that the union had set up in every state senatorial district in 1995. Lubin told the local PAC members when D'Amato would appear in their district. Their job was to get local members out to demonstrate.

"Every time he stepped out of his car, we had fifteen to fifty NYSUT members meeting him on the sidewalk," Lubin said. "We dogged him all around the state." Sometimes the expected union demonstrations would convince a sponsor to cancel a D'Amato talk. Other times reporters covered the protesters, winning the union free publicity. If nothing else, the protesters always shared their viewpoint with curious onlookers.

At a breakfast forum in New York City sponsored by business groups in December 1997, D'Amato went so far as to blame lagging student scores and a high drop-out rate in the city on the teachers' union. At one point in his speech, D'Amato spotted two tables of teachers and union officials who had all pinned buttons on their lapels that read, "Proud to be a Teacher." The senator stared right at the teachers and said: "Let me suggest to you that those who are in the forefront of opposing changes, those who have come forward with regularity in fighting against the kind of changes that are necessary for education, unfortunately are the teacher unions. That is a fact."

UFT President Sandra Feldman, who was seated at one of the tables, told reporters afterward, "He's got the Big Lie going there, and it's very difficult to counter each and every one of them because these are complex issues about children and education. Now he comes with what he thinks is a convenient target—the teachers' union. But most people knowledgeable about education in New York City know that the UFT has been at the forefront of educational change and reform."[30]

Lubin wrote NYSUT's board members just before Christmas 1997 that the union's highest priority for the first few weeks of the new year was a letter-writing campaign against D'Amato. "So rest up over the holidays if you can," Lubin wrote. "We are preparing for what will shape up to be a year-long battle with an ill-informed, ill-advised individual who just happens to be our own elected U.S. Senator."[31]

On January 22, 1998, Lubin asked local union leaders across the state to organize area teachers in a letter-writing campaign against D'Amato. Lubin knew that union strength is built on the involvement of rank-and-file teachers. "When I speak to a new local president," Lubin explains, "I tell them, 'If you're doing this alone, you're doing this wrong. . . .' When it comes to membership activity, the strongest person in our organization is the building rep, not any local president, not any statewide officer, because the building rep can decide to mobilize or ignore us."

Lubin and others knew that such a campaign was an ambitious proposition, but NYSUT chose to undertake it because they knew that teachers who wrote letters would have to educate themselves about D'Amato's record. One morning in late May 1998, NYSUT members dropped off 25,000 letters packed in mail sacks at D'Amato's Albany office. Few other state organizations anywhere in the country could have mustered such a large mailing, but Lubin was disappointed. "If we have 360,000 members, why can't we get 200,000 of them to write a letter?"[32]

Ultimately, teachers' power would be wielded in the ballot box: about 90 percent of all of NYSUT's members voted, a rate of participation that dwarfed that of almost any other slice of the electorate. A NYSUT poll of its members in early 1998 indicated that D'Amato's attacks had united teachers, as even 39 percent of Republican teachers planned to vote for any Democrat who ran against the senator.[33]

NYSUT didn't endorse any of the three Democratic candidates, but Lubin had a favorite in the campaign: Charles Schumer, the Brooklyn congressman. Lubin had first heard of Schumer from his mother-in-law, Helen Davidoff, who had called him in the fall of 1974, when the twenty-three-year-old Schumer was running in Brooklyn for the New York State Assembly. She said that she had met a "nice young man" at the train station in Flatbush, where she lived, and wanted to know if he was a good candidate. Lubin said he was worth backing. Schumer won, becoming one of the youngest assemblymen ever elected in New York. The day after his election, Lubin's mother-in-law called again to tell him that he had given her good advice because that morning Schumer had returned to the train station to thank her and others for their vote.

During his years working for the UFT in New York City, Lubin had always liked Schumer because he had been a constant friend to public education, the kind of politician that Lubin didn't have to educate on the issues. In his official campaign launch for senator in April 1998, Schumer addressed D'Amato's recent attacks. "Al D'Amato's solution for schools is to bash teachers," the underdog candidate told a small crowd at Brooklyn College. "Al, you cannot improve the schools with a clenched fist. Children need an outstretched hand to learn." His prescription to improve the schools could have been written by NYSUT: to "reduce class size, raise education standards, attract the best new teachers."[34]

Lubin was thrilled when Schumer won the 1998 primary because he believed he was the one candidate who was tough enough to meet D'Amato's expected attacks head-on. "Too many lies for too long" became Schumer's campaign mantra, and Lubin couldn't help notice that it was a variation of the teachers' slogan, "Tell the Truth, Al." As soon as Schumer won the primary, NYSUT endorsed him. The Democratic candidate didn't need money from NYSUT because he was well funded, raising about $15 million to D'Amato's $20 million. A steady stream of money was also coming in from Democratic supporters, mobilized by President and First Lady Clinton.[35]

"Money is the least significant aspect of what we do," Shanker had once told the *New York Times*. "We can never outdo the wealthy in that rat-race. Our real value is the people we put into campaigns."[36] The reason every other serious candidate for statewide office coveted NYSUT's endorsement was because it marked the beginning of a mass mobilization of teachers.

"A NYSUT endorsement brings phone banks, with thousands of phone calls being made on the behalf of a candidate," Lubin said. "It brings literature, it brings presence at community meetings and rallies. . . . We can pack a room. We can get a crowd. We publish articles about a candidate in our newspaper, *New York Teacher*, which probably goes out to half a million people. We also have a political action team that is getting regular information about letter writing, or a quote from the candidate, things to pass around, and to republish at the local level. . . . We also give candidates access to our members. . . . If you are going to be in Oneida County or Albany or Westchester, and you have down time, I'll put a group of retirees together to meet with you or a group of local union presidents. . . . There's a teacher or a school bus driver or a nurse who is going to sign a mailing for you or make a phone call for you."[37]

The 1998 Schumer-D'Amato election marked the first time in NYSUT's history that a phone call was made to every NYSUT member—about 360,000 at the time. Convince a teacher of what was needed, Lubin believed, and a teacher would convince someone else.

On election night 1998, Lubin went out to dinner with his assistant John Costello at Churrascaria Plataforma, a Brazilian restaurant in midtown Manhattan, and the two men bided the time waiting for the polls to close, expecting that a winner wouldn't be declared until the wee hours of the morning. "I put my money on Schumer early," said Lubin, an eternal optimist. "But we thought it was going to be very close." Less than a week before the election, a Mason-Dixon poll showed the two candidates in a statistical tie among likely voters.[38]

As Lubin and Costello waited, teachers all over the state were making last-minute phone calls for Schumer. On Long Island, David Israel, the political action coordinator for Nassau County, D'Amato's home base, listened to a radio ad that predicted another six years for the Republican senator. It made him think philosophically about the election. "Even if we lose," he speculated, "this election has enormously strengthened our base." He figured that nearly twice as many people manned the phone banks for the 1998 campaign as had ever before.

The campaign had brought out teachers that evening who had never before participated in election-night phone banks, including Susan Sparber, from Long Island's south shore. "It's my blind ambition to help retire D'Amato," said Sparber. Maria Loria, a volunteer from Valley Stream, also stopped by the Long Island office. "It's only for a half hour or so," she said, "but I think it can make a difference."[39]

Lubin and Costello got to Schumer's hotel about eight o'clock. They expected they'd be shown to a ballroom where Schumer's supporters were gathering, but they were instead welcomed to the family's personal suite. Lubin felt awkward being there; he knew Schumer, but he wasn't part of his inner circle. The NYSUT officials were about to leave when Schumer's mother invited them to stay and eat, noting how important teachers were to her son's campaign. The men accepted, planning to leave the suite shortly after the polls closed at 9 p.m. But only minutes after that hour, TV anchors began predicting that Schumer would be the next junior senator from New York State. When Schumer made his victory speech later that evening, he called

NYSUT President Tom Hobart, Lubin, and UFT President Sandra Feldman to the stage and thanked them.

You guys did this, he told them.[40]

It might have sounded like just another politic thank you, but it wasn't far from the truth. Schumer had won handily, taking 54 percent of the vote to D'Amato's 46 percent. Twenty-eight percent of those who voted for Schumer said that education was their number one issue.[41] It was true that D'Amato had faced his toughest challenger to date in Schumer and that D'Amato had hurt himself with years of questionable ethics. But it was also true that Schumer's margin of victory over D'Amato—432,000 votes—was roughly the same as the number of teachers and others who belonged to NYSUT at the time. The attack on teachers that D'Amato hoped would ride him into a fourth term had backfired: teachers had taken their revenge at the voting booth.

The day after the election Schumer spoke in New York City, thanking the people who had voted for him. He said he doubted there would ever be another statewide candidate who tried to bash teachers and their union in order to win an election.

"We taught them a lesson," Schumer said. "You did. I did. Together we did."[42]

The next major political campaign that Lubin was involved in lacked the glamour of the Schumer-D'Amato battle, but it involved an issue with greater bearing on the everyday lives of New York's teachers. The issue was pension reform. New York teachers had always had to fight for pensions adequate enough to support them once they retired. New York State Teachers Association (NYSTA), a predecessor of NYSUT, helped establish the New York State Teachers' Retirement System in 1921. Those first pensions ranged from $400 to $800 a year—the equivalent of $3,700 to $7,500 in 2005 dollars—and were offered to people over sixty years old and who had taught for thirty-five years. In 1985, NYSUT led the effort to pass what was called the "30-55" bill, which reduced the age for retirement to age 55 if a teacher had thirty years of service.

A persistent issue that troubled all teacher retirees—and other state retirees as well—was the steady erosion of their pensions to inflation. Lubin often heard about this issue from his father. Irving Lubin had worked as a postal clerk and a junior high teacher in Brooklyn and had been a member of the Teachers Guild, the predecessor to the UFT.

His father's teacher pension, paid to him after he retired in the 1970s after teaching about twenty years, amounted to $3,000 in the late 1990s. At that time, Irving lived in Florida, and when he talked to his son on Sundays, he would often bring up teachers' pensions. Did you get me a raise yet? the father would ask his son. The answer had been a perpetual "No."[43]

NYSUT and other unions that represented state workers would occasionally convince legislators to release supplemental funds to increase pensions. But the groups had to fight the battle for supplemental funds over and over again and those that were passed never kept pace with inflation. To solve this problem, NYSUT had been fighting for about twenty-five years for what was called a cost-of-living adjustment, or COLA, which would automatically increase their pensions each year. At a private meeting of about a dozen AFL-CIO representatives in New York City to discuss Cuomo's final reelection campaign in 1994, Lubin asked the governor to push for the COLA. Cuomo responded bluntly: You will never get a cost-of-living increase.[44] Lubin was angered, but he found that many NYSUT leaders agreed with Cuomo: Legislators didn't want funds dispensed automatically; they wanted credit whenever they doled out dollars.

But some of the blame for the failure to pass a retiree COLA rested with the disorganization of its proponents. Instead of working together, different organizations representing different retirees often proposed their pet COLA bills. When Denis Hughes became president of New York's AFL-CIO in 1999, though, he pushed the state's labor unions to work more closely together, and one of the partnerships he encouraged was between NYSUT and the New York State Civil Service Employees Association (CSEA). Lubin and Danny Donohue, president of CSEA, brought together all those who wanted a COLA bill, and they drafted legislation they could all get behind: A-8516.[45]

On May 9, 2000, NYSUT took the lead in organizing a rally at the Empire State Plaza that drew ten thousand people from twenty different labor unions, the largest rally for pension reform in the state's history. The coalition of unions chartered 125 buses to bring members in from all over the state; 84 of them were filled with NYSUT members, a good number of them retirees who withstood the ninety-degree heat that day. NYSUT provided eight thousand water bottles, eleven thousand boxed lunches, and five thousand snacks to those who attended.

"I'm as proud of our political solidarity as I am of this huge turnout," Lubin said to the gathered crowd as state office workers and officials watched from the office buildings surrounding the plaza. Following the rally, Governor George Pataki gave word that he would sign a COLA bill and he made good on his promise in July 2000. The bill was significant: estimates were that it would initially add $260 million a year to retirees' pensions. The COLA provided annual increases that were the equivalent of 50 percent of the Consumer Price Index (CPI) to the first $18,000 of a pension, with increases of no less than 1 percent and no more than 3 percent of their incomes annually. The bill wasn't perfect, but Lubin believed it opened the door to more generous COLAs that would apply to incomes over $18,000 and keep pace with the CPI.

One other improvement the bill made was to give lump sum pension increases to those who had been retired the longest, for their incomes had eroded the most to inflation. Lubin's father finally got his raise: His annual pension went from $3,000 to $10,000.

But NYSUT's leaders have faced educational issues that are not as straightforward as pensions. For example, NYSUT has wrestled with what to do with charter schools, a reform that Shanker is often given credit for proposing. He imagined charter schools as small, innovative, publicly funded schools created by teachers that would be autonomous from educational bureaucracies and from many state and local laws. These teachers and their schools would explore new technologies, teaching strategies, and time allocation in public schools, looking for ways to produce more learning for more students. "If schools are to improve," Shanker wrote in 1988, "they'll have to support a constant inquiry and search for new and better ways to reach youngsters. If they don't, the public will look for something other than the public schools to educate our children." From these experiments, limited in their duration, Shanker believed educators would discover what worked—and what didn't work.

As the charter movement gained momentum in New York State, though, they were largely commandeered by right-wing educational critics who wanted to use them to show that public schools were dysfunctional—and that the public school bureaucracy and unions were to blame. Shanker, well aware of this development, cooled his enthusiasm for them well before his death in 1997. Just before Christmas in 1998, New York State Governor George Pataki and conservative groups, such as CHANGE-New York, proposed legislation that would fund charter schools that could be established by teachers, par-

ents, administrators, and community residents. Public school advocates and NYSUT were wary of the measure because it opened the
door to schools-for-profit and also siphoned money from public
schools. But when the governor tied the bill to a long overdue pay hike
for state legislators, NYSUT leaders were placed in a difficult position: Should they try to kill the bill and alienate the entire senate and
assembly, which they depended on for important legislation? Or
should they step aside and let it pass?

"You don't win friends in the legislature by constantly saying 'no,'"
Lubin explained. "You have to be flexible and political. Besides, legislators needed and deserved a raise and I'm not so sure we could have
stopped the bill."[46]

NYSUT leaders took a practical middle path, agreeing to let a charter schools bill pass, but only if certain conditions, rare in other states,
were placed on them. NYSUT succeeded in capping the number of
charter schools at one hundred. No religious charters were permitted—
what NYSUT believed was a violation of the constitutional separation
of church and state—and students in the charter schools also had to
take state tests so they could be evaluated. The union also preserved the
right of teachers in all charter schools to unionize, and teachers in
schools that had over 250 students automatically belonged to the union.
While charter schools have drained money from public schools, Lubin
has seen one clear benefit from the bill's passage: it has taken the wind
out of the state's school voucher movement, which calls for public funding of private schools, an anathema to the union. "This governor has
rarely even mentioned vouchers," Lubin says of Pataki. "That's because
he's got his charters and that's satisfied his constituency."

But in early 2006, Pataki and anti-public school forces were pushing hard to increase the cap on charter schools and to provide tax credits for families who send their children to private schools. Once again,
NYSUT found itself leading the defense of public education, perhaps
the battle that has most defined the union during its first three
decades.

In early 2003, Governor George Pataki threatened to cut $1.1 billion
dollars in state aid to education, and NYSUT and a coalition of twenty-
seven other groups, including those who represented teachers, professors, administrators, parents, and anyone else affiliated with the schools,
responded with what they called the March for Public Education. It
was scheduled for May 3, with the goal of convincing the legislature to

override the governor's veto of education funds. The last time the legislature asserted its fiscal independence from the governor had been in 1982, when legislators overrode vetoes by then-governor Hugh Carey, including $311 million in K-12 school aid and $30 million for the state and city university systems.[47]

"The state did not want this to be successful," said Tony Bifaro, the assistant to NYSUT President Tom Hobart and one of the organizers of the rally. "Everything we wanted to do, politically, we had to negotiate with the state, and at every instance a roadblock was thrown up."[48] In the three weeks before the event, the alliance unfurled an advertising campaign of unprecedented proportions. Virtually every movie theater from Albany to Buffalo—and some two hundred screens statewide—ran thirty-second preview ads pumping the rally. The event was advertised on seven billboards in greater Albany. Nearly 1,100 radio spots aired on stations in Buffalo, Rochester, Syracuse, Albany, and the mid-Hudson area.[49] The Benchmark Polling Group, NYSUT's in-house polling center, made fifty thousand calls to union members over a three-week period to encourage them to come out for the march. On May 3, forty thousand New Yorkers filled the vast white marble-and-concrete Empire State Plaza to show their support for public education.

On May 5, 2003, just forty-eight hours after the rally, the legislature overrode the governor's veto on 119 education and health bills. It was no easy feat: to override a veto takes a two-thirds majority in both the New York Assembly and the Senate. They restored educational funding that Pataki had proposed to cut, including money to establish pre-K classrooms, to rebuild schools, to reduce class sizes, and to fund teacher centers dedicated to improving the quality of teaching. In the Senate, the vote to override the governor's budget was unanimous. From the day NYSUT was founded, the union's leaders had prided themselves on the bridges they had built to both Republicans and Democrats and on this day those connections bore fruit: In the Assembly, a dozen key Republicans broke with the Republican governor to vote for the override. With this legislative success, many districts reduced their proposed property tax hikes by as much as half and avoided severe cuts in their school budgets.

Part of what had convinced legislators to buck the governor was the forty thousand people who turned up on the plaza on May 3, the largest crowd that had ever assembled in Albany history. Lubin was the master of ceremonies that day, and he kept calling people to the speakers' stage so they could get a sense of the rally's size. Most who gathered, though, were unaware that the event's organizers had brought along a medical device to protect them: a portable defibrillator.

After Lubin had spoken with Rachel Moyer in February 2002, he considered a response to the New York School Boards Association, which had denounced any law that would bring defibrillators to schools if they weren't funded by the state. The vice president usually didn't write NYSUT press releases, but in this case, Lubin was moved to write the opening line of this one. "What price should we put on a student's life?" he began. "The New York State School Boards Association apparently thinks $3,000 is too much." NYSUT's position was that the state should pay for the machines, but that if it wouldn't, schools should still be required to purchase them. "If the choice is between spending money and saving kids' lives, that choice is a no-brainer," the press release continued. "Teachers and school professionals know that." The press release mentioned the two boys—Louis Acompora and Gregory Moyer—who had most likely lost their lives because no portable defibrillators were on hand when their hearts stopped beating.[50]

NYSUT's lobbyists, including staffers and the Committee of 100, which consisted of teacher volunteers, put the defibrillator bill in the educational lobbying packet that NYSUT discussed with legislators each spring. Paul Hartman, director of advocacy for the New York American Heart Association, and one of the biggest public health proponents of the bill, credits NYSUT with getting it passed. "Whenever we met with a legislator, they asked, 'Where are the teachers on this?' To go in with the union's memo of support made it easier to get past that stumbling block."[51]

The Assembly and the Senate passed the bill, which became law when Governor Pataki signed it in early May. As of December 1, 2002, every school in New York was required to purchase their own defibrillator and to have one staff person trained in its use at all school-sponsored events. It was the first such law in the nation.

At 2:35 in the afternoon on December 16, 2002, a little over two weeks after the defibrillator bill went into effect, Andrea LaFleur, a sixteen-year-old student, suddenly felt faint in one of her classes at the Career and Technical Education Center in Goshen, New York. "I need to sit down," she said to a classmate, before collapsing with a seizure. CPR was administered, but her pulse was weak, and she slowly turned blue.

A student ran to get one of the school's defibrillators, and two of the school's instructors attached the pads from the AED to LaFleur. The machine analyzed LaFleur's condition and gave an audible instruction: "Shock Advised." The girl's condition didn't improve after the first shock. The machine advised another shock, and then another. After the third, LaFleur's heart finally started beating again and she started breathing, making her the first student in the state who was saved by the defibrillator law.

Rachel had envisioned that defibrillators would save students like Andrea, but she and many other backers were surprised to find how many non-students the defibrillators revived. On January 11, 2003, Judy Schneider, a chemistry professor at SUNY Oswego, was saved by an AED after she collapsed at her ten-year-old daughter's swim meet at a high school near Rochester. In March 2003, Dexter Grady, a custodian for the East Hampton Middle School, collapsed during an after-hours pick-up basketball game. Two teachers playing basketball with him, Claude Beudert and Charlie Batemen, gave Grady three shocks with a defibrillator, which got his heart beating again. "If it had happened a few months earlier or my district ignored the law," Grady said, "I'd be dead. There's no question in my mind: That law saved my life."[52]

In April 2003 a defibrillator that Rachel Moyer had donated to NYSUT was taken to the union's annual convention in Washington, D.C. Upon leaving the event, Herb Yules, a UFT delegate and retiree whom Lubin had known for decades, collapsed. Aaron Bifaro, a NYSUT employee, ran and got the defibrillator. "Can you use this?" he asked the nurses huddled over Yules. Nancy Barth Miller, an RN at Staten Island University Hospital, said she "almost passed out" when the AED arrived.

"When he went from gray to pink," Miller said. "I burst into tears."[53]

New York State schools have bought five thousand AEDs, many of them for as little as $2,000 because of the deals Rachel had struck with the machine's manufacturers. In 2004, the legislature passed two more bills that required defibrillators at fitness centers, health clubs, and in state buildings. The law has saved a dozen people in its first two years. Rachel has been able to convince legislators to pass defibrillator bills similar to New York's in thirteen other states.

In 2004, Rachel Moyer addressed over one thousand teachers, custodians, bus drivers, nurses, professors, and retirees who were gathered at NYSUT's annual convention. "I think this union has represented that great things can be done if you are as determined as I have been in my effort, but they can't be done alone. One voice doesn't do it. I don't think in my life I've ever felt more of a kinship with an organization as I do with you."

The phone call she made to Alan Lubin two years earlier, she said later, was the most important phone call she had ever made in her life. Rachel had lost her son, but she had managed to save teachers, retirees, custodians, and a sixteen-year-old girl, Andrea LaFleur, who listened as Rachel spoke that day. When Rachel finished, LaFleur and NYSUT's members stood and cheered for the mother who had devoted herself to saving the lives of others. But the crowd of unionists might as well have been cheering for themselves, because they, as Rachel Moyer and Alan Lubin well knew, were the source of the union's success.

A Legacy of Success[54]

Some of the most important political victories that NYSUT has won over the past three decades include:

- The passage of tenure laws in 1975 that provided tenure transfer rights for teachers who moved into new districts. It also set a two-year probation for those who switched districts;
- The 1976 override of Governor Carey's veto of the Stavisky-Goodman Bill, which required New York City to fund schools at no less than the past three years' average. It was the first override of a governor's veto in 104 years;
- The passage of the Public Employment Relations Board powers bill in 1977, which put teeth into enforcement of PERB orders correcting improper practices;
- The successful lobbying of Governor Hugh Carey in 1978 to repeal the Taylor Law's one-year probation penalty against striking public employees;
- The extension of tenure rights in 1980 to teachers in districts with fewer than eight employees;
- The passage of a 1981 law that gave substitute teachers the right to bargain collectively;
- The passage of the 1982 Triborough Amendment to the Taylor Law, requiring that terms of an expired contract continue until a successor agreement is reached;

- The securing of Excellence in Teaching funding in 1986 to boost teachers' salaries;
- The passage of the "12-for-10" law in 1989 that granted school-related personnel a full year's retirement credit for each school year worked;
- The passage of a half-dozen early retirement incentives; pension supplements; and health insurance protections for retirees;
- The passage of an automatic cost-of-living adjustment (COLA) for state pensioners, including teachers, in 2000; and
- A legislative override of the governor's veto of education funding, which restored over $1 billion in educational spending in 2003.

CHAPTER 10

Educational Reform

Jean Lux, a friendly fifty-one-year-old teacher, remembers what it was like to enter her profession thirty years ago. She was hired fresh out of college in 1975 to teach her first class, a mix of rural and suburban students in an elementary school in Owego, a village about twenty miles west of Binghamton near the Pennsylvania border. A few days before she was to start, a teacher in her school, who acted as an assistant to the principal, approached her.

"She handed me a pile of manuals a few feet high and said, 'This is what you'll teach,'" Lux remembers.[1] That's what passed as on-the-job training. Her principal, who cared more about order than education, was little help. He visited her class a few times that autumn, but his observations disturbed more than they enlightened her. After one visit to her classroom, the stern-faced administrator noted the pieces of Scotch tape she had left on the walls. Another time he wrote, "Worksheets left on windowsills will fade."

"I never went to him for help," Lux remembers. "I was afraid I'd ask the wrong question."

Yet she had endless questions—her formal schooling had hardly prepared her for the real-life demands of teaching twenty-seven young children. To get answers, Lux intercepted more experienced teachers before and after the school day. "Teachers always helped each other," she says. But most of the time, she admits, "I was winging it." Lux's experience was typical of a profession that had a long tradition of abandoning its professionals in the classroom. Collegiality was not encouraged; structured mentoring was nonexistent; and on-the-job training consisted of one or two professional days that administrators scheduled each school year, with perhaps a lecture by an "educational expert." Lux spent a good part of her first year overwhelmed. "I was the one I had to rely on," the Owego teacher says. "Trial and error was the way I learned."

Like all American teachers, Lux had no say in her own training. Al Shanker, the New York City teacher leader, believed this was indicative of the lack of respect many American administrators had for teachers. To make that point, Shanker would tell the story of the day he took his teacher exam to become a math teacher:

> Several thousand of us assembled promptly at 9 a.m. in the cafeteria of a high school. A few minutes later someone in charge appeared, blew a whistle, ordered the applicants to stand and form a double line. We were marched down a hall, and as we were to approach a stairwell we were to use, we heard shouts ordering that our double line become a "single file." Throughout this march from the cafeteria to the classrooms in which we were to take the tests, we continued to receive instructions. "Keep in single file." "Hurry up." "No Talking." "Stop whispering." It was clear from the start that we were back in school. Even though we had gone to college and received our degrees, we were being treated very much like children again.[2]

Even after NYSUT was created in 1972, the state's education leaders, including the State Commissioner of Education and the Board of Regents, which oversaw education in the state, continued to treat teachers, including NYSUT's leaders, like children. "We were to be seen and not heard," says Antonia Cortese, who oversaw the union's educational policy at the time. "It was a little like an afternoon tea, always polite," Cortese said of occasional meetings between teachers and state officials. "It would be, 'What do you think?' and 'What do you think?' But the issue in question had probably already been decided. There was no shared decision-making. It was, 'I'll make the decision and then I'll share it with you.'"[3] Chuck Santelli, then NYSUT's director of research and educational services, said that when asked about their positions in issues, the Regents often concurred with NYSUT's views—until they voted.

"They yessed us to death," Santelli says.[4]

State officials also dismissed NYSUT because it had become a union. "We had merged, we were much larger, we brought in the UFT [United Federation of Teachers] and Al Shanker, so let's face it, they were quite wary," Cortese said. She learned just how wary state officials were of NYSUT when she was nominated to the Teacher Education, Certification, and Practice Board, the professional board for teachers in the state. One of the Regents, Emlyn Griffith, blocked her appointment. He, like Cortese, was from Rome, New York, and was well aware that she had led a teachers' strike there in 1971. In Griffith's mind, she was a militant leader unfit to serve on the state's teacher professional board.[5] Such dismissals made it clear to Cortese and others that the state's educational leaders wouldn't hand them respect or power. Teachers would have to earn it, and the chance to do so came in a battle in the mid-1970s over a proposed change in teacher training known as competency-based teacher education.

Competency-based teacher education (CBTE) was an attempt by state educational leaders to reform teacher training by creating a checklist of skills that teachers would need to have before they could graduate from an education school and become a teacher. The proposed change, mandated by the Board of Regents in 1972, was like most educational reforms that washed over schools before teachers had a say: it was designed by nonteachers, it was imposed from above, and it was untested.

NYSUT's leaders were opposed to the new evaluation scheme. "Our feeling was that a checklist was mechanistic and wouldn't be a good way to prepare candidates to become good teachers," Cortese explained. The union was also opposed to the change because the Regents asked that the teacher competencies be established locally, meaning that no statewide standard would exist, something the union supported. State educational leaders also expected that teachers would rewrite the CBTE requirement, but teachers weren't paid or given release time to do so. Despite NYSUT's opposition, the Board of Regents and the State Education Department steamed ahead with the reform.

Cortese and other teacher leaders were annoyed and bewildered: The state was imposing a new way of evaluating teachers without considering the view of the union that represented New York's teachers. Cortese and other union leaders finally decided to take drastic action. On January 10, 1975, NYSUT sent Western Union mailgrams overnight to all NYSUT teacher leaders who were working with colleges and universities to determine the competency checklists for CBTE. "NYSUT locals participating in CBTE projects are requested to postpone signing CBTE consortial agreements with colleges and universities until further notice," said the short statement, which was sent out less than a month before CBTE guidelines were to be established. The mailgram was signed by NYSUT President Thomas Hobart.[6]

"We had exhausted all the other possibilities," Cortese remembers. "Reason and good arguments hadn't prevailed." The union's refusal to sign off on CBTE convinced state education officials that the union was serious—and well organized. "That night letter just stunned the Regents and the Department of Education," Cortese remembers. "No one had ever fathomed that an entire state of teachers could act in unison." The mailgram proved the arrow that mortally wounded the CBTE reform, which died a slow death. In an effort to hold the Regents accountable, NYSUT also began grading the performances of the Regents. In the union's first Regents Report Card, no Regents received better than a C+. The union also started publishing Regents' comments, which were often anti-teacher, in *New York Teacher*, NYSUT's statewide member newspaper.[7] It wasn't long afterward that Regent Griffith finally nominated Cortese to the Teacher Education, Certification, and Practice Board, and she was appointed.

Union leaders had exerted their power to kill a bad reform, but what it wanted to do was to promote tested reforms that would improve the quality of the schools. The best way they believed to do so was to nurture the talents of teachers. "There was an early recognition that it was the role of the union to improve the skills of our members," Cortese says. "That was a seminal decision, because if you improve instruction, nine times out of ten you're going to have a better performing school." Better the teachers, and you'll better the schools—that became the educational mantra that guided the reforms that NYSUT pushed over the next thirty years. It was also a principle that Al Shanker would speak to often in what would become his bully pulpit, a weekly column in the *New York Times* that would appear for twenty-six years.

"Conflict, strikes, violence, threats and confrontations make news," Shanker wrote in his first column, published on December 13, 1970, "but the more numerous and more time-consuming efforts to improve the schools, reform teacher preparation, integrate faculties, increase state and federal support for public education, expand job training and higher education opportunities, and develop standards of professional accountability are largely ignored by the media. This column is our way of telling the parents and the public where we stand on the important educational issues."

Where We Stand was the column's name. Eight hundred words long, it was filled with plainspoken language and the bold ideas meant for "parents and the public," rather than for school administrators, academics, or politicians. "It's dangerous to let a lot of ideas out of the bag, some of which may be bad," Shanker would say later. "But there's something that's more dangerous, and that's not having any new ideas at all at a time when the world is closing in on you."[8] He used his column to endorse pedagogical experiments that were at first pooh-poohed by the educational establishment, including higher academic standards, the testing of teachers, educational partnerships with the business community, and even charter schools.

Shanker's public ruminations on educational reform and his activism led Sara Mosle, writing in *The New Republic*, to call him "our Dewey, the most important American educator in half a century." Mosle was comparing Shanker to John Dewey, the American philosopher, educator, and writer who, like Shanker, had fought for social justice and for the unionization of teachers, a role that earned him the American Federation of Teachers' (AFT) first membership card in 1916. Along with many teachers, Daniel Patrick Moynihan, the former senator from New York State, was also a fan of Shanker's column. "The impact [of the columns] was extraordinary," he said. "Union leaders in those days rarely wrote essays, still less felicitous, thoughtful analysis of public policies."[9] Teachers pinned his columns to bulletin boards in school offices, and on weekends their friends and family would read it as well. Once Shanker was in Thailand on a humanitarian mission and the Thai prime minister invited the American delegation, including Shanker, to a dinner party. While cocktails were being served, the prime minister walked past members of the United States Congress and approached the New York City teacher leader. "Mr. Shanker?" he said.

"Yes," Shanker replied.

"I usually agree with your columns," said the prime minister, "but the one you wrote two weeks ago was just terrible."[10]

One of Shanker's most popular columns was inspired by an article in the *New York Times* about how to make a perfect loaf of French bread quickly. It was something that the New York City leader, who was a bread baker himself, doubted was possible. He was even more skeptical when he heard that the flawless French loaf was made in a food processor. "I had no trouble believing that the bread would be quick and easy. But delicious?" Shanker wrote. "Nevertheless, I tried the recipe for Thanksgiving. It was terrific!"

The chef had apparently worked on the recipe for years, Shanker explained. He had experimented with different types of yeast, flour, water, water temperature, and even the best type of blade to use. What would have happened if the chef, instead of using trial and error to perfect his bread, had proceeded as many school reformers proceeded in their recipes for change? "He might have rejected the idea of adapting French bread for a food processor in the first place," he said. "Too traditional. Not innovative enough. And not American, anyway. Never mind the fact that French people have been enjoying it for years, and it is admired as a standard all over the world." Shanker was poking fun at school reformers, often content with the "general idea of what they want," he said, but unwilling to perfect the details of their reforms.[11]

The New Yorker, like the French bread chef, was a man willing to experiment. In the mid-1960s, when the United Federation of Teachers (UFT) gained political clout, Shanker and the union tried their own recipe for educational reform. The results failed, but it was a failure that would shape Shanker's thinking about educational reform—and shape the direction of all school reform undertaken by New York's teachers.

When the UFT's first contract expired, they wanted to expand their demands to include professional and educational issues as well as bread-and-butter ones. They pushed hard to establish an experimental educational program in the city called More Effective Schools, the union's first major foray into educational reform. The program, tried in twenty-one of the city's poorest performing schools, established small schools with smaller classes—no class was to exceed twenty-two students in a city school system in which thirty or forty was commonplace.[72] The schools also included other innovations, such as longer school days, preschool classes, team teaching, expanded psychiatric and social services, and special opportunities for both underachieving and gifted students. Shanker believed enough in the program to send his eldest son, Adam, to one of the experimental schools in Bedford-Stuyvesant, Brooklyn.

The experiment was short-lived, however, because the city's Board of Education, unhappy with the program's expense and its control by the union, eventually killed it. A postmortem showed mixed results. Teachers, parents, and students liked the intimate schools far more than traditional public schools. But the analysis also revealed a glaring failure: the students in the smaller classrooms hadn't performed better academically than students in the larger classrooms in traditional city public schools.

Years after the program was scrapped, Chuck Santelli, then NYSUT's director of research and educational services, asked Shanker why he thought the experiment had failed to produce tangible academic results. Shanker admitted that he found the results deeply disappointing, but he believed he knew the cause: teachers taught students in small classrooms the same way they taught those in larger ones.[13]

"Guess what a teacher does with twelve kids in a class?" is the way Shanker once explained the problem. "Exactly the same thing she used to do with thirty. Stand up there and give the same lecture."[14] Shanker took a lesson from the failure: If you wanted students to learn better, you had to train teachers to teach better. But how to retrain teachers? Shanker didn't find an answer in New York City or anywhere else in the United States. He found it in England.

What Shanker found across the sea was a radical alternative to the American way of training teachers. In the United States, teachers traditionally attended college and university to get their degrees before they entered the profession, something that Shanker approved of. Once on the job, though, training was left to administrators and was scant.

In England, Shanker discovered that teachers weren't treated like children; they were treated like creative and responsible professionals. In the 1960s and early 1970s, the English had established and funded over five hundred teacher centers that offered courses taught and taken by mostly primary and secondary school teachers. They received no formal degree or diploma for these courses, which were free and ran anywhere from a few hours to a few weeks. They attended them because they believed that courses taught by experienced teachers who had tested their lessons in their own classrooms would help them teach better.[15]

The centers became learning laboratories. Many collected audiotapes, videos, textbooks, and lesson plans that were donated by teachers. And teachers often talked shop before and after classes over a pint of beer or a cup of coffee. British teachers had broken down the four walls and the closed doors that had isolated Lux and so many other American teachers.

Shanker first wrote about teacher centers in December 1971, and as he often did in his Where We Stand columns, he quoted other educational experts to make his point. In this case, he cited Stephen K. Bailey, chairman of the Policy Institute of the Syracuse University Research Corporation: "In spite of the fact that [teachers] are the ones who work day in and day out on the firing line, the definition of their problems, of their roles, of their goals, always seems to be someone else's responsibility: supervisors, parents, college professors, textbook publishers, self-styled reformers, boards of education, state and national education officials. What the teachers' center idea does is to put the monkey of educational reform on the teacher's own back."[16]

For Shanker and other New York teacher unionists, the teacher centers were not a monkey on their backs, but a welcomed opportunity for professional growth. Shanker lobbied hard to have the centers brought to the United States; they appealed to his love of the practical. "Whatever way the centers are established here," he wrote in the summer of 1973, "the important point is that they would constitute a concrete, realistic, intelligent response to a particular problem. It is precisely because the teachers' center is a practical concept—not a utopian concoction or political expedient—that it has so good a chance of succeeding."[17]

In a rare collaboration, the AFT and the National Education Association (NEA) lobbied the Carter administration for federal money for teacher centers in 1977–1978. The legislation passed; eight centers came to New York State.

"Like most teachers, I was very skeptical about the teacher centers," Marion Donovan, a sixth-grade teacher at PS 261 in the Bronx explained in 1980. "But I found out that the teacher center was the greatest thing that happened to me. It was the first time in my teaching experience that I had a person I could go talk to, who could give me feedback on my ideas, to whom I could explain my problems." Donovan was also impressed how practical the learning was at the teachers' center. "I found myself trying things in the class I had never attempted before and when my students said, 'I never knew learning could be so much fun,' you can imagine how high that made me feel. So the real beneficiaries are the children."[18]

After President Reagan eliminated federal funding for the centers in 1982, NYSUT's leaders lobbied the New York State legislature for funding to resurrect them. In 1984, lawmakers made New York the first state in the country to fund teacher centers, granting $3.5 million to establish forty-four teacher centers across the state. One of the key features of the legislation—pushed hard by NYSUT—was that the majority of each center's board consist of teachers, with the rest consisting of parents, administrators, or community members. Moreover, the law granted local teacher unions the right to appoint these teachers. It was landmark legislation: state legislators had handed control over professional development to teachers. The unofficial motto for centers is now, "Professional development for teachers, by teachers."

In 2004–2005, New York had 126 centers funded with $31 million from the state, which was leveraged to bring in double that amount from nonprofit groups, such as museums, that often cosponsor courses. The classes are no longer voluntary: As of February 2004, all new teachers have to take 175 hours of courses—including those at teacher centers—every five years to keep their teaching licenses. The summer 2005 course brochure for the Greater Capital Region Teacher Center is forty-six pages long and the courses are as diverse as a teacher's life: Teacher Renewal; US History Advanced Placement Summer Institute; Bullying Prevention in a Culture of Cruelty; Effective Rehearsal Techniques for the School Band; The Social, Environmental and Economic Impact of What We Eat Everyday; Criminalistics & Forensic Biology; and The Iroquois Longhouse Workshop.

On one steamy morning in July 2005, about a dozen teachers went down to the shores of the Hudson River in Albany to take a tour of the USS Slater, the last escort ship afloat that protected American soldiers and supplies from Nazi U-boats on the North Atlantic. This teacher center class consists of mostly social studies and history teachers, but there's also a home economics, foreign language, and math teacher. Penny Welbourn, a retired science teacher, gives the tour, sprinkling it with information that teachers can use in their classrooms. Did the teachers know that soldiers manning artillery guns in the Second World War never used earplugs—one of the reasons that many World War II veterans are now deaf? She also recommends movies about war at sea that teachers might show in class, including *The Caine Mutiny*, *The Fighting Sullivans*, and *The Enemy Below*.

"You might want to talk about how communications have changed," Welbourn says, when she talks about the Morse code. "Kids are always amazed. No cell phones, no computers, not everyone had telephones." And when Welbourn points out the radio operators' room below deck, she points out another piece of social history. "Who made all these radios?" she asks. "Women on the home front."

In the ship's galley, Welbourn says to the home economics teacher, "If you're interested, we have recipes that they used for the two hundred men on board that you can break down into recipes for a family of four." The math teacher, Judy Porter, who has been attending teacher center courses for twenty years, comes alive when she sits in a gunner's seat on the deck that controls the 40-millimeter gun used to shoot down enemy aircraft. She cranks a small gray wheel that pivots the gun's barrel up-and-down and side-to-side. Welbourn discusses the variables the gunners had to consider to hit an airplane going by, including a plane's flight direction, its distance from the ship, and even the speed and direction of the wind. "It's all math," Porter says, pleased. "A lot of math formulas use distance, rate, and time."

The teachers here prefer teacher center classes to college ones. "There's no homework or all those papers and it's just as educational," says Mary Flanagan, the foreign language teacher, who thinks she might take her French students here on a class trip next year. "You're also taking a course with people who are interested. Have you ever taken a course with college students?" Teacher center courses are also far more affordable. This one costs just $5.

"A dozen years ago, when I started here, a lot of teachers hadn't heard of teacher centers," says Rosemary Harrigan, director of the Capital Region Teacher Center. "But now I find it hard to find a teacher who hasn't heard of the centers or taken a course with us."[19]

In New York City, the UFT, which has the largest teacher center in the state, went so far as to bring mini-teacher centers right into the city's most troubled schools to turn them around. In 1995, newly appointed Chancellor Rudy Crew knew he needed dramatic changes to improve the city's thirty-two worst schools, where many of the students could not read, write, or do simple math. He also knew he'd need the support of teachers to make fundamental changes, so he consulted with then UFT President Sandra Feldman and UFT Vice President David Sherman. These leaders hammered out dramatic changes: in a newly established Chancellor's district, each school got a strong principal; classes were kept small; curriculum focused on literacy and math; and qualified teachers were brought in. The schools saw progress, but it was slow. In 1999, wanting to speed up the improvements, leaders agreed to pay teachers an extra 15 percent for a school day that was extended by forty minutes. Three days a week, that time was devoted to student instruction. But two days a week, the extra time was devoted to in-school professional development led by the principal, an instructional specialist, the UFT chapter leader, and a person from the UFT Teacher Center.

The training was different than usual, in that it was embedded in the school day. And it was practical. Instead of hearing a general lecture about a new way to approach elementary school mathematics, third-grade teachers learned techniques to teach multiplication. Trainings also became small-scale, grade-specific and followed up with classroom observations and feedback.[20]

Teachers were asked to support the changes—or transfer out of the school. "We needed to know that people who stayed were committed to the plan," says Maria Neira, a UFT official involved in the program who was later elected NYSUT's first vice president. "Anyone who could not live with this model could go elsewhere."

The reforms worked. "The real story is that there is a model that is research-based that can turn around schools," says Neira, "but it comes with a price tag."[21]

As NYSUT pushed for teacher centers in the 1970s, it also worked closely with colleges and universities to add practical courses to their curriculum that would help teachers in the classroom. "Teachers knew how important professional development was," Cortese says. "So we thought, 'Why don't we, the union, do what management should be doing: provide courses to help teachers with classroom management."

In January 1979, NYSUT launched twenty-three classes in a program called Project TEACH, the forerunner of what became its Effective Teaching Program (ETP), which is still in place. "Teachers teaching teachers" became the motto for the program, which provides practical courses at colleges that are taught not by professors, but by working teachers trained by the union. The courses, offered at affordable prices, can provide those who take them with credit toward their teacher certification or a master's degree. Now ETP has a cadre of about 250 trained instructors who teach six undergraduate courses and fifty graduate ones—all approved by the colleges where they're taught—to about nine thousand teachers and paraprofessionals annually. Courses offered in 2006, designed in response to specific classroom needs, include: Cooperative Learning; Developing Multiple Intelligences; Teaching Literacy; and Inclusion: Education for All.

Despite this improved teacher training, NYSUT's leaders were aware that they often lost young teachers who were overwhelmed by their job. In Owego, Jean Lux survived her first few bruising years—but many new teachers don't. A first-year teacher, often plagued by anxiety and feelings of incompetence, is two-and-a-half times more likely to leave the profession than a more experienced colleague. About one-third of all teachers leave the profession within their first five years; in urban schools, as many as half leave. This attrition rate, which dwarfs most other professions, is one reason for the perpetual shortage of teachers—especially experienced ones—in public schools. The flight from the profession is exacerbated because female teachers can pursue opportunities in many other professions now open to them. In the 1990s, NYSUT pushed for a solution for this steady drain of young teachers, and in 1999, Jean Lux's school district was among the first in the state to try it.

In 1997, George Thearle, an approachable former art teacher was appointed principal at the Owego Elementary School, where Lux taught. He knew that an impending crisis threatened his school: a mass exodus of retiring teachers. "We've had to hire seventy-five percent of the teachers we now have," explains Thearle. "We knew their replacements were going to make new teacher mistakes. It was inevitable. They learn from the school of hard knocks, like we all did."[22]

In 1999, Thearle—a former NYSUT building rep—worked with other administrators and NYSUT union leaders in the district to establish a program that would help these teachers succeed. The program they adopted was a reform that NYSUT, urged on by teachers, had been clamoring for since the 1980s: a teacher mentoring program. The program was a response to the common complaint among teachers that they stepped into their first jobs with the same duties as a veteran teacher—to run a classroom—but were given no real-world training about how to succeed. NYSUT won state funding for a mentoring program for new teachers in 1986, the first of its kind in the country. "Mentoring helps teachers become better teachers more quickly because they have a veteran working with them," says Cortese. "And it helps in the retention of teachers. With mentoring programs, we don't see as many people dropping out—especially in our big cities."

Some teachers in Owego were skeptical of the program at first. They feared that administrators would play favorites picking mentors and would use them to spy on teachers in the classroom. To nurture trust, teachers and administrators decided that mentors in their school would only *assist* new teachers, not *evaluate* them, a task that would be left to administrators. They also decided that everything that transpires between mentor and the intern would be confidential and off-limits to administrators. To prevent favoritism, teachers and administrators agreed to work together to select mentors.

As soon as the program was instituted in 1999, Lux, now a confident, experienced teacher, was selected as a mentor. She didn't agree to the job for the money—the school gave only $500 extra to mentors in the 2004–2005 school year. "I don't talk about the stipends because it's not enough to convince people to be mentors," Thearle says. "I tell them that mentoring is good for our teachers and our learning environment."

By 1999, Lux had worked twenty-four years in the elementary school teaching the lower grades. She teaches fewer students now—a result of union efforts to reduce class sizes. Instead of twenty-seven students, she usually teaches about twenty, a size she feels enables her to "reach out and touch every kid." Lux's first surprise was how much work the mentoring job was: she meets with two beginning teachers at the end of each day for about forty-five minutes, and she often leaves the sessions with work to do to help them. In 2004–2005, she mentored Jessica Cornick, a twenty-six-year-old in her first year as a second grade teacher. At the end of a day late in June, the two met in Cornick's classroom after the young teacher had had a particularly difficult time getting her students to sit still for a lesson on local geography— all her students seemed to have something to say. Lux reassures her intern—that's a big part of her job—reminding her what all experienced teachers know: teaching a formal lesson is difficult in the heat of late June. She also reminds her that her teaching style encourages participation rather than silent obedience.

"You walk into your classroom or mine and there's always a buzz," says Lux. Then she passes on a trick of the trade: "Sometimes," she says, "when all the kids have something they want to say, I have them all tell the person next to them. Then we move on." It's a small thing, but it registers. "That's a good idea," Cornick says.

During the school year, Cornick would sometimes visit her mentor's class to see how she taught a particular subject, such as the addition of large numbers, for example, or how to spell. The benefits to Cornick were clear and immediate; Lux has been pleasantly surprised, though, that the give-and-take of mentoring has invigorated her teaching.

"If I knew Jessica was coming in to watch me teach, I wanted my lesson to be wonderful," Lux says. "And when we talk about student behavior, classroom organization, or lesson plans, it makes me evaluate what I've been doing. They're teaching me the newest practices." Perhaps the best part of working with new teachers, Lux finds, is what she calls that "spark" they bring to the job.

"It's given me a new energy and makes me want to try new things," she says.

Because of NYSUT's lobbying, the state Board of Regents, which oversees education in the state, approved a regulation that required all new teachers hired after 2004 to receive mentoring. But Owego has gone beyond the law and will provide a mentor in Cornick's second year, if she stays, and even her third. The district will also continue to offer seminars for new teachers on topics such as grading, stress management, and student discipline.

"The biggest thing that mentoring does is provide a comfort level for teachers that wasn't here before," says Thearle, who is convinced that six years of the mentoring program has transformed his school. "We no longer have the isolation of the classroom that was so prevalent twenty or thirty years ago. We're bringing teachers into a culture of teaching and learning."

This collegiality is a staple of other professions, such as medicine and law, and teachers also practice it in some foreign education systems, such as in China, Taiwan, and Japan, which have had great success turning out high-achieving students. In these Asian countries, teachers at the same grade level routinely work together to perfect lesson plans.[23]

As NYSUT research predicted, the addition of the mentoring program at the Owego Elementary School has helped teachers to embrace their profession and succeed in it. Of the forty-four hires that Thearle has made over the last five years, not one has left the profession. And only two new hires have left his school—and they were experienced teachers who didn't adapt well to the cooperative environment.

Thearle also credits the mentoring program with another profound, yet unexpected, change in the school. "I had to deal with only twenty-three discipline issues last year," Thearle says. "But the year I started I had over four hundred. Mentors have helped new teachers figure out how to handle behavioral issues, one of the parts of the job that they struggle with most. That's given me more time to work on areas like curriculum and raising test scores."[24]

Establishing mentoring and teacher centers can be seen as a reform that has made schools better and teachers' lives easier. But NYSUT has also pushed for reforms that have made teachers' lives more difficult, such as creating some of the highest teacher standards in the nation. New York is one of seven states in the country that require teachers to pass a state test. And only New York and six other states require teachers to earn a master's degree before they receive permanent certification—a requirement NYSUT pushed for in the 1970s and that went into effect in 1978. Seventy percent of teachers in the state have earned master's or doctorate degrees—the nationwide average is only 43 percent—which puts New York teachers first among the fifty states. The 175 hours of coursework that new teachers are now required to take every five years in order to keep their certification is among the highest requirements in the nation.[25]

Educating teachers not only improves teaching, it helps keep educators in the profession. After five years, only one-third of teachers who had received a conditional teaching license, such as that received after a summer's training, were still teaching. But among teachers who complete five years of training—a BA in a subject field and then an MA in education—84 percent are still teaching in five years.[26]

Shanker, though, wanted more than a patchwork of teacher certification protocols that differed wildly from one state to another. "Teachers will be able to assume fully professional roles," wrote Shanker in a Where We Stand column in 1986, "only if we get rid of the factory-like setup in schools where teachers are treated like mere hired hands required to follow orders from above and develop schools in which teachers can exercise judgment and creativity." Just as doctors, lawyers, and accountants had created their own national standards, Shanker wanted teachers to establish theirs—a reform that the NEA initially resisted. Shanker believed national certification would ensure that teachers would not be excluded from teaching if they moved to states with different certification requirements. Besides, he argued, "citizens and students in our highly mobile society need to know that, wherever they choose to live, teachers in the local schools will have met high national standards." A federal rather than a state exam is also less vulnerable to politicians who want to water down licensing standards in times of acute teacher shortages. "Ever hear of a substitute surgeon or a temporary attorney?" asked Shanker.[27]

In 1985, Shanker called for a national examination for teachers, well aware that the public historically paid more to professionals who met high standards. "Most educators and an increasing number of political leaders agree that teaching should be a profession, by which they mean that teachers should be well paid and have high status," Shanker wrote. "But the high pay and status of the most highly respected professions do not come through mere exhortation, but mainly as a result of long and difficult training and the acquisition of expertise."[28]

When a national board was established, Shanker was delighted. "When Americans look back 50 or 100 years from now, they may well find that May 15, 1987 was a major turning point in the history of our system of education," he wrote in his Where We Stand column on May 17, 1987. "On that day, the National Board for Professional Teaching Standards was established." The board was run by a majority of teachers and was independent of the government. It set clear and high standards for what teachers should know and be able to do. While fewer than five hundred New York teachers have received national certification, the numbers around the country are growing steadily.

Teacher mentoring, teacher centers, and higher professional standards—all reforms championed by NYSUT—have managed to achieve what educational writer Linda Darling-Hammond has called a "quiet revolution in teaching." Until the 1980s, she wrote, "the idea that teacher knowledge was critical for educational improvement had little currency. Continuing a tradition begun at the turn of the twentieth century, policymakers searched for the right set of test prescriptions, textbook adoptions, and curriculum directive to be packaged and mandated to guide practice. Educational reform was 'teacher-proofed' with hundreds of pieces of legislation and thousands of discrete regulations prescribing what educators should do. . . . Policymakers increasingly realize that regulations cannot transform schools; only teachers, in collaboration with parents and administrators, can do that."[29] And one of the ways that all involved wanted to transform schools was to raise academic standards.

In April 1983, during President Reagan's first term, the National Commission on Excellence in Education released a report called "A Nation at Risk," which education writer and historian Diane Ravitch would call "the most important education reform document of the twentieth century."[30] The study's authors warned that the American education system was "being eroded by a rising tide of mediocrity that threatens our very future as a nation and a people. . . . If an unfriendly foreign power had attempted to impose on America the mediocre educational performance that exists today, we might well have viewed it as an act of war. As it stands, we have allowed this to happen to ourselves. . . . We have, in effect, been committing an act of unthinking, educational disarmament."[31]

Many teacher unionists in New York and across the country winced at the alarm sounded by the report and argued that its authors had depicted public education as in far worse condition than it was. The report had, after all, come during the presidency of Ronald Reagan—a man who had advocated abolishing the Department of Education. When advance copies were circulated prior to the NYSUT convention in April 1983, Sandra Feldman, the future president of the UFT and the AFT, said that union leaders cringed while reading it together. "We all had this visceral reaction to it," she told a reporter for the *New York Times* in 1996. "You know, 'This is horrible. They're attacking teachers.'"[32]

But Shanker, who trusted his own counsel more than any other, read the report through. He liked the title "A Nation at Risk," for it implied that the nation needed a strong educational system to protect itself, just as it needed a strong national defense. He didn't find an ideological attack against public education in the text. For example, he found the authors had not recommended the usual litany of Reagan reforms, such as school prayer, tuition tax credits for families using private schools, vouchers, and the elimination of the Department of Education (although Reagan had directed the panel to make those recommendations).[33] And instead of recommending that the federal government leave public education to states and local governments—another Reagan position—the study's authors called for citizens to "hold educators and elected officials responsible for providing the leadership necessary to achieve these reforms" and to "provide the fiscal support and stability."

Shanker also saw that the study's authors had reviewed national and international test data and found that America's students were fading against foreign competition. If the trend continued, other better-educated populations and their economies would pass Americans by. The authors of "A Nation at Risk" prescribed a general lifting of academic standards—something that Shanker had long been preaching. They recommended that high schools beef up their academic course offerings, especially in English, math, science, social studies, foreign languages, and computer sciences. They also thought standards in colleges were too low and they urged that "schools, colleges, and universities adopt more rigorous and measurable standards, and higher expectations, for academic performance and student conduct, and that 4-year colleges and universities raise their requirements for admission." The report also recommended making teaching more professional with better pay and training, a goal shared by all teacher unionists.

Feldman remembers that the New York teacher unionists reviewed the report around a table prior to NYSUT's April 1983 convention with one eye on Shanker, waiting for his response. "When Al finished reading the report," Feldman remembers, "he closed the book and looked up at all of us and said, 'The report is right, and not only that, we should say that before our members.'"[34] Cortese remembers that a vigorous debate followed within NYSUT about how to respond to the report. The vast majority of NYSUT's board members who met shortly before the annual convention wanted to condemn it, and they were angry with Shanker's contrary position. "[He didn't say] that the schools are all fine, teachers are all doing well, and the students are all learning," Cortese remembers. "He had a knack for always surprising people, which didn't bother me, but it bothered other people."[35]

A few days later, on April 30, 1983, Shanker stood up before two thousand attendees at NYSUT's annual convention and made his case. Shanker began by putting the report in historical context. The authors of "A Nation at Risk" were unlike the education critics of the 1950s, 1960s, and 1970s. "For a long time we had a lot of people who hated teachers or they didn't like public schools and they put out reports all the time saying that teachers are lousy, they're incompetent, they should be paid less or they shouldn't have tenure and so forth." The authors of "A Nation at Risk," he argued, were potential allies of teachers. Still, he predicted that many educators would assail the report and he was right: The NEA soon denounced it as alarmist and anti-teacher. Next, Shanker led his teachers through what would happen if all teachers decided to reject these reform efforts.

> If that happens, if all we do is send back that kind of a strong negative message to leaders of commerce and industry who would like school improvement, then I think several things will happen. One is that the same leaders are going to say, "Well, if that's the reaction, we're not in favor of putting more money there." And there might even be a further reaction on the part of these leaders to say public schools are hopeless, maybe we do have to shake the whole thing up, that maybe we do have to pin our hopes on the non-public schools and move in another direction. . . .
>
> And what I'm saying is we absolutely should not just reject what they have to say and turn them away, which would be an opportunity to increase what we could get in education, an opportunity lost. . . . They want to bring billions of dollars into education. They are not anti-teacher. They are not anti-teacher unions. They are also not always as knowledgeable as they should be about how public schools function and how they should work. They have some ideas. Some of these ideas are not very good. Some of them are good. Some of them

can be shaped up, if we engage in a discussion. I would strongly urge that . . . we view these reports and the people who are making them not as enemies, but as potential allies and as potential friends and potential supporters of education. . . .

There are billions and billions of dollars sitting there which weren't there yesterday and which we can get for public education if we rise to the challenge of sitting down with top leaders in our country who will talk to us as equals and we will talk to them as equals. . . . We have an opportunity now to bring status to American teachers and money to American education, an opportunity which we never had before, and I am sure we won't miss it.[36]

Chuck Santelli, NYSUT's educational policy aide, had heard Shanker speak at each year's convention since the union was founded in 1973. Inevitably, NYSUT's members would interrupt Shanker's speeches with cheers, and each year delegates inevitably rose to their feet at the end of the speech to give their leader a standing ovation. Not this year. Santelli, like other NYSUT members, was shocked by Shanker's endorsement of "A Nation at Risk." Applause was feeble. Yet Cortese and others supported the stand Shanker had taken. "I thought Al's response was brilliant," she said. "By not coming out against it and basically agreeing with it, he made us a player at the table."[37] Paul Cole, a longtime NYSUT activist, put it this way: "We had a choice of being the caboose or the engine of school improvement—and we chose the latter."

Shanker pushed the entire membership of the AFT to support reform. Milton Goldberg, the executive director of the commission that wrote "A Nation at Risk," believed that if Shanker had opposed the report, it might have been dismissed, its fate to be buried in a library. "It was vital that someone with stature step up," Goldberg said. "Al Shanker never wavered on that issue and the rest of the education community and public finally caught up to him."[38]

A few months after "A Nation at Risk" was released, delegates at the AFT's 1983 convention, which was dominated by NYSUT members, passed a resolution supporting tougher high school graduation requirements and testing that would gauge whether students were learning. In the late 1980s, Shanker and the AFT joined the push to have state and federal legislators raise academic standards and institute tests to see if schools were achieving them. In 1994, when Congress was in the middle of reauthorizing federal education legislation,

Shanker fought to add tough academic standards. President Bill Clinton, who often consulted with Shanker on educational issues, pushed in 1997 to do what "Al Shanker wanted us to do all along," which was to establish national standards that would include the testing of all children in fourth and eighth grade. After Clinton's State of the Union address in February 1997, in which Clinton unveiled his plan, he called Shanker, who was dying from cancer. "You know, I hope you feel good now," Clinton told him, "because you've been telling us to do this for years and years and years, and finally your crusade will be America's crusade."[39]

Many credited Shanker with the legislative success. "If any single person could be said to be responsible for the astonishing shift in public sentiment that recently prompted the president of the United States to call for national educational standards—a proposal that would have been unthinkable a few years back," said E. D. Hirsch Jr., the education writer, in 1997, "that person would be Al Shanker."[40] In 1995, the AFT produced a series of reports called "Making Standards Matter," that evaluated which states were producing rigorous standards and assessments. They followed that up with "Defining World Class Standards," which compared the standards and assessments in the United States to those in other countries.

In New York State, NYSUT steadily pushed for some of the toughest standards in the nation—which "wasn't something that was popular among all our members," Cortese notes.[41] The union worked with Thomas Sobol, New York's education commissioner, to create a New Compact for Learning, passed in 1991. The legislation strove to raise standards that all students would have to meet, and called for intervention when schools did not improve.

In 2002, *Education Week* ranked New York's standards as the highest in the nation, and in January 2004, it gave the state "A" grades for its standards and accountability.[42] But pushing for such high standards "has been a tough road for teachers," Cortese says. "They don't get enough resources, enough professional development, and they're constantly blamed, but Shanker said we should do it anyway, and that was a courageous position. He didn't just influence me and NYSUT and the AFT; he influenced the entire country."[43]

If Shanker were alive today—he died in February 1997—he would undoubtedly ask, Have the reforms in New York State—mentoring, teacher centers, and higher standards—produced quantifiable achievements for New York's students?

The results are promising. A *Newsweek* magazine survey of high schools in 2003 concluded that New York State was home to twenty-eight of the top one hundred public high schools in the United States. Other, more quantifiable measures of student success have shown that expecting more of New York's students has produced better students. In 1986, only 36 percent of high school graduates passed Regents exams, the gold standard of achievement in New York State high schools. In 2002, the percentage of students passing them had risen to 55 percent.[44] And from 1997 to 2003, the number of New York's high school students taking Advanced Placement courses—one of the few measurable standards used across the nation—has risen more than 50 percent.[45] Another national measure—the number of college-bound students who received SAT scores over 600—increased 22 percent in New York between 2000 and 2004.

The success also extends to younger children: the number of fourth graders who met all the state standards on the English Language Arts test increased from 48 percent in 1999, the first year it was given, to 64 percent in 2003. On the National Assessment of Educational Progress (NAEP), often called the Nation's Report Card and one of the most reliable measures of student learning, the percentage of public school fourth graders in the top two categories (proficient and advanced) in reading increased by 30 percent from 1992 to 2002. In math, this same test found that the percentage of fourth graders in New York who attained those top two levels rose by 29 percent over the same period. Among eighth graders, the percentage of students in the proficient and advanced categories in math rose 73 percent from 1990 to 2000.[46] The union had pushed for tougher standards for both students and teachers, and had achieved them. But while they were working to raise educational standards in their state's schools, NYSUT's members were engaged in another endeavor that most of its members weren't aware of: defending teachers, trade unionists, and democracy all over the world.

NYSUT Educational Achievements[47]

NYSUT has been involved in educational reform since its founding. Some of its major achievements include:

- Participating in State Education Commissioner Ewald Nyquist's Task Force on Teacher Education and Certification from 1975–1977;

- Creating the Dial-a-Teacher program, which gives students telephone access to help with homework. The program was begun by the UFT in New York City in the 1970s, and now is common throughout the state;
- Supporting the Regents Action Plan in 1984 that, while modest by today's efforts, raised the bar for graduation by requiring passage of minimum competency tests;
- Taking a leading role in Commissioner Thomas Sobol's 1988 Task Force on the Teaching Profession, which recommended raising standards for teacher preparation;
- Sponsoring numerous programs for students, such as Regents Review Live, a thrice-a-year exam review broadcast by SUNY Satellite, and cosponsored by NYSUT, State Education Department and the New York State Teacher Center Consortium;
- Putting teachers in the majority of the Teacher Education Certification and Practices Board in 1987, which oversees teacher centers, discipline, and licensing cases;
- Helping establish in 1987 the National Board for Professional Teaching Standards, an independent, nonprofit, nongovernmental agency, to encourage teacher excellence;
- Working with State Education Commissioner Richard Mills, hired in 1996, to push for higher standards for all students.

CHAPTER 11

International Solidarity

It was Saturday, April 10, the last day of NYSUT's 2005 convention in New York City, and many of the state's dignitaries had already paid their respects to NYSUT's members. U.S. Senators Charles Schumer and Hillary Clinton had spoken. So had Denis Hughes, the president of New York's AFL-CIO and Eliot Spitzer, the man who would become New York's next governor. But the black-haired Mexican woman who took the stage just before the delegates broke for lunch lacked such stature. She was unknown to nearly all the convention delegates; this was her first trip to New York and her first sojourn to the United States. At the podium this morning, she lowered the mike, raised her head, and began to speak in her native Spanish.

"Good morning," she began. "My name is Monserrat Banda Arteaga and I am a teacher in the province of Guanajuato in Mexico. I have come with five of my colleagues to thank you and speak to you about our struggle."[1]

A good number of the delegates, listening through an interpreter, must have wondered: Why had this woman journeyed two thousand miles to speak to them—and for what was she thanking them? Why had she been given one of the coveted spots at the podium? Wasn't their union's interest local—to win sound teacher contracts in their schools, to improve education in their districts, and to elect pro-education politicians in their state? These questions were all part of a larger one, which teachers and other workers have asked for as long as labor unions have existed: Why should we here care about the concerns of people so far away?

The answers have everything to do with the decision that New York's teachers made in 1972 to create not just a teachers' association, but a statewide teachers' *union* affiliated with organized labor. Before this decision, the majority of New York's teachers belonged to the New York State Teachers Association (NYSTA), affiliated with the National Education Association (NEA). The NEA did have an international group, the World Confederation of Organizations of the Teaching Profession, but the group did little. Its most publicized event was an annual meeting held each year in a foreign city, which provided excursions for state presidents approaching retirement. Few of the rank-and-file had even heard of the group or its annual event.[2]

When New York's teachers decided to join the American Federation of Teachers (AFT), part of the AFL-CIO, they joined America's labor movement, which had long supported workers abroad who were struggling for justice and influence. Tom Hobart, NYSUT's president for thirty-two years, would travel to over forty countries during his tenure, visiting unionists and teachers all over the world. The aid American workers gave to those in other countries was principled—at its best, unionism has supported democracy and human rights—but it also was, and still is, a matter of self-interest: the stronger unions everywhere are, the stronger each union is.

New York City teachers learned that when they went out on strike in 1960 to win the right to form a teachers' union. The strike might have very well been lost—and the modern teachers' movement crushed before it was born—if not for the crucial support of New York's unionists.

"The very idea of unionism is solidarity," said AFT President Al Shanker in 1990. "It means, 'I'm not strong enough to do it alone. I need to band together with brothers and sisters.' And then you realize, well it's not just enough to do it in one city, you have to do it in a state, in a country, because there are problems that you can't solve locally. Then you realize that you can't just do that with teachers. You're not strong enough. And so you are in a general labor movement with other workers. Then, pretty soon, you find the same is true on a worldwide basis."[3]

"I'm not strong enough to do it alone"—that's what Arteaga learned when she started teaching in 1996 in the poor, rural community of Dolores Hidalgo in Guanajuato, Mexico. She taught from fifty to seventy-five students each day, as part of a program called SABES, which was designed to educate and teach job skills to poor Mexican youth. The hope was that this education would provide the skills they needed to find good work in Mexico, an alternative to the dangerous trek many make across the border to find work in the United States. Most of Arteaga's students were the poorest in the region, the sons and daughters of farmers, rarely provided an education. Her classroom floor was the dry, pink-gray dirt of the village; her roof was an old, billowing oak tree that provided shade from the equatorial sun. Arteaga's vocation consumed her: She went door-to-door to recruit students.

She scrounged pencils, paper, and books. She even solicited donations from local families to build three one-room schoolhouses to shelter her students from wind, rain, and heat. When the materials were secured, she worked with students and volunteers from the village to build the schoolhouses cinderblock by cinderblock, holding them together with mortar mixed with the water they had to carry a few hundred yards, bucket by bucket.

The government treated the SABES educators shabbily. The law provides Mexican workers with more rights than American ones—they are granted the right to organize and are guaranteed maternity leave and severance pay, for example. But in reality, Mexican authorities routinely disregard workers and their rights. "I was paid a salary of eight hundred dollars a month with no paid vacation, no sick days, and no medical insurance," Arteaga explained to NYSUT's delegates. "I was also required to sign an undated letter of resignation in the event of my becoming pregnant while in the employ of SABES." She and the Mexican teachers were treated in the same way New York's teachers were treated—before they had unionized.

When their teaching contract came up for renewal, Arteaga and other SABES teachers made a list of changes they wanted. But the program's administrators told them that a contract had already been signed by a union—one administrators had formed. Angered, Arteaga and other teacher leaders organized an independent teachers' union in January 2003, called the Independent Union of Workers and Employees of SABES, known by its Spanish acronym, SITESABES. Knowing they could not succeed alone, they sought assistance from the Frente Autentico del Trabajo (FAT), an independent labor federation that has been fighting to establish independent unions in Mexico for twenty-five years.

But on December 9, 2003, twenty-six of the SITESABES teachers, including Arteaga, were called into the SABES office in the city of Leon and fired. Those who returned to their schools the next day were met by policemen. If they entered their classrooms again, the teachers were told, they'd be imprisoned. In the following weeks, students protested the wholesale firings and asked for the return of their teachers. Instead, Arteaga and other activist teachers were blacklisted.

NYSUT leaders learned of Arteaga and the SITESABES story through the Labor-Religion Coalition, a group of unions, religious institutions, and students founded in 1997 by Hobart and Howard Hubbard, the bishop of the Catholic Diocese of Albany. The group fights for economic justice at home and abroad, and when they learned what had happened to these Guanajuato teacher unionists, they organized a delegation of seven NYSUT members who flew to central Mexico to meet them. Nancy Close, president of the East Islip Teachers Association on Long Island, said she was "inspired and humbled" by the resolve of the Mexican teacher organizers, and she and the other delegates convinced NYSUT to bring them to the convention. The conventioneers who heard Arteaga describe her struggle were also moved, and after she spoke, they stood and applauded. Arteaga had to hold back tears, in part because "I feel there's more support here than in my own country."

Buckets were passed and NYSUT's delegates filled them with $6,500 to support the Mexican teachers while they continued organizing. NYSUT members also signed letters that were sent to Guanajuato officials—and to Mexican President Vincente Fox—demanding that Guanajuato officials hold secret ballot union elections—a rarity in Mexico. As NYSUT's delegates filed out of the main hall for lunch, Arteaga crossed paths with Antonia Cortese, a NYSUT founder and an executive vice president of the AFT.

"We're afraid what's going to happen to us when we return," Arteaga confided in Cortese. She feared the authorities in Guanajuato would find out they had come to ask for NYSUT's help and that there would be retaliations, perhaps even jailings or physical assaults. "You stay in touch with us," said Cortese, speaking while surrounded by a river of NYSUT unionists. "And if anything happens, there will be half a million letters sent on your behalf."

The Mexican unionists were buoyed by their trip to New York City, and went back to finish their campaign to have SITESABES recognized. In May 2005, an election was held, but SITESABES lost to the government union, in large part because the workers who were hired to replace SITESABES supporters—scabs, in union parlance—had been allowed to vote in the union election, in violation of Mexican law. But good had also come from the elections. In a rare occurrence, the region's labor board allowed international observers to watch the vote and one of them, Maureen Casey, from the Labor-Religion Coalition, believes the votes were counted fairly, a success in itself. The election also marked a first in Mexican labor union elections: workers were allowed to cast their ballots in secret.

"We've lost the battle," said one Mexican teacher after the election, "but not the war."[4]

As well as battling to help unions such as SITESABES take root, NYSUT has battled to support democracy around the world. The AFT—whose motto is "Democracy in Education and Education for Democracy"—has long fought authoritarian governments abroad, whether in Chile, South Africa, and Argentina, or in China, Russia, or Poland. NYSUT members have contributed to these efforts, living up to the part of their mission statement that asks them to "further the cause of social justice." One reason New York and national teacher unionists have taken up these battles abroad against tyranny of the Left or Right is because they know dictatorial governments never tolerate free trade unions.

"One cannot have a trade union or a democratic election without freedom of speech, freedom of association, and assembly," AFL-CIO President George Meany said at the 1979 AFL-CIO convention. "Without a democratic election, whereby people choose and remove their rulers, there is no method of securing human rights against the state—no democracy without human rights, no human rights without democracy, and no trade union rights without either." Shanker, who headed the AFL-CIO's International Affairs Committee for many years, made the connection between democracy and trade unionism more bluntly: "The first thing the dictator does," he said, "is get rid of the trade unions."[5]

That's what happened in Poland during the 1980s. After food prices rose dramatically, seventeen thousand workers at the Lenin Shipyards, led by Lech Walesa, an electrician, staged a strike, barricading themselves inside the shipyard. Sympathy strikes erupted throughout the country. These workers organized themselves into an independent labor union called Solidarity, which by 1981 had a membership of about ten million Poles, most of the country's workforce. Solidarity pushed the Polish military leader General Wojciech Jaruzelski to reform the economy and conduct free elections, but the Soviet Union pressured the general to crack down on the union. On December 13, 1981, Jaruzelski imposed martial law in Poland in an attempt to crush the union that he would attempt to outlaw the following October. Some leaders were arrested; others went underground. During what would be a dark seven years in Poland, Solidarity looked for people abroad to sustain them.

Many considered Solidarity a lost cause, "as Don Quixotes pursuing unrealistic goals," Walesa would later say.[6] But working people across the world, including unionists in Japan and Western Europe, and those in the AFL–CIO in the United States, refused to abandon the Polish workers. Lane Kirkland, AFL–CIO president at the time and a friend and ally of Shanker's, believed that the millions of workers in Solidarity were a potent force for change across the Soviet empire because they could not all be dragged to prison, as intellectual dissidents in the Soviet Union often were.[7] Shanker shared that vision, and he sounded the alarm the week after Polish authorities tried to destroy Solidarity. He criticized President Ronald Reagan for responding weakly to the crackdown. "This is clearly one of the historic moments of the Twentieth Century," he wrote. "Fortunately, the American people know what to do."[8]

After Solidarity went underground, NYSUT immediately provided an office for Polish exiles in the United Federation of Teachers (UFT) building in New York City, and paid for equipment and supplies. In October 1982, the UFT helped the Committee in Support of Solidarity to organize a concert by Polish violinist Wanda Wilkomirska, which raised $10,000 for the Polish dissidents. NYSUT members contributed upwards of $200,000 during the 1980s, much of it through the AFL–CIO Polish Workers Aid Fund, which supported Polish activists in hiding and their families, and also helped pay for computers and presses. Teachers also kept the plight of Polish workers in the public eye through the 1980s by attending numerous demonstrations in New York City. "When other people got tired of the cause, UFT teachers kept on showing up," says Eric Chenoweth, who was the executive secretary of the Committee in Support of Solidarity. "They never tired."[9]

In 1988, while Solidarity was still illegal, Adam Urbanski, the Rochester Teachers Association president, traveled to Poland with Shanker and UFT President Sandra Feldman to attend a human rights conference organized by Solidarity. On a train ride from Warsaw to Krakow, Urbanski and Shanker debated the prospects of a political revolution in Poland and throughout the Soviet empire. "I told him I did not believe that the Communists could be overthrown," Urbanski said. "'With all due respect,' Al said, 'I believe they can.'"[10]

Soon after the visit, Solidarity launched a series of strikes that forced Jaruzelski to legalize the union. An open election was held in April 1989 and the Polish people voted overwhelmingly for Solidarity candidates. The Communists had been rejected, and by the end of the year, Communist regimes had crumbled in nearly every Soviet bloc country of Eastern Europe. Ronald Reagan is usually credited with the fall of the Soviet empire; often overlooked, though, is the crucial role played by labor—including teachers—during that historic change.

Walesa came to the AFL-CIO convention in November 1989, just months after Solidarity's historic victory. "Dear brothers and sisters," Walesa said. "You have proven to be our most steadfast allies in the trade union struggle for human freedom. . . . A vast movement for democracy and freedom is developing in my country. It is changing the political face of Poland and of the world. And that movement has been made possible only through the peaceful struggle of working people, of trade unionists like you and me."[11]

That same month, Shanker thanked Walesa and others in the Polish resistance for inspiring unionists in the West to remember their mission.

> You and the other brave people in Solidarity gave us an unforgettable lesson in the preciousness of democratic institutions. You showed us that democracy and all that goes with it are just as important to [you] as they are to people living in democracies—maybe even more important. People believe these things are worth fighting for, worth risking everything, including their lives, for. And Solidarity's struggle to get these precious rights has since been echoed by the Chinese students and workers calling for democracy in Tiananmen Square, the Hungarian people's rejection of communism and the thousands of East Germans who continue to flee to the democratic West. . . .
>
> And we thank you for demonstrating so powerfully that free trade unions are essential to a democratic society. Many people here and in other industrialized nations have forgotten that. They think of unions merely as economic interest groups and even wonder why unions need to exist at all now that there's bread and butter on the table; shouldn't individual workers strive for the additional crumbs on their own? And when unions get involved in politics, many people cry foul; shouldn't unions mind their own business and stick to the economic conditions of the workplace? But Solidarity's struggle reminded the world that you can't separate economic conditions from political conditions, that demands for bread and butter and for a voice in how the loaf is distributed are expressions of human rights and of the desire to secure and protect those rights. You reminded us that individual workers who criticize their bosses and government can lose their livelihood and are silenced with official lies, but an independent union of workers can fight economic oppression and unleash the demand for truth. . . .
>
> I wish I could also thank you for demonstrating that trade unions are necessary to preserve a democracy, but we must establish

that for ourselves. Some people think trade unions are no longer needed. They've done their job—and thanks. But as long as our society lasts, there will be issues and struggles in which the organized voice of workers will be vital. Human rights are not won once and for all, and neither is democracy.[12]

When Communism crumbled in Poland, Herb Magidson, NYSUT's vice president and chair of the AFT's Teachers Under Dictatorship Committee, proposed that a group of New York's teachers visit Poland to share techniques about how to teach in a democracy. Solidarity's education leaders accepted the offer, and NYSUT sent a delegation of ten teachers from the state in the summer of 1990. "Those teachers who are going will not only have an unforgettable learning experience themselves," said Urbanski, the Rochester teacher, "but they will make a historic and meaningful contribution to the establishment of democracy in a country that is yearning for it. The popular saying in Poland is, 'Freedom can be won, and democracy can only be learned.' They want to learn democracy from Americans."[13]

Carol Slotkin, a high school social studies teacher from Sullivan County, was disturbed by the uniformed Russian soldiers who still walked the streets of Polish cities. Kathleen Donahue, a social studies teacher from Hilton and NYSUT's future vice president, felt as if she was stepping back in time. Families still tilled small family farms with horses, and women from the countryside sold hand-knit sweaters and other crafts, such as hand-carved figurines or leather boxes. It wasn't a comfortable trip: the food was dreary, the rain was constant, and few Poles spoke English.

Still, the American teachers were excited to be part of rebuilding democracy. Donahue quickly learned that the exchange of ideas was not part of the Polish educational system, as almost all Polish teachers relied on lectures in the classroom. "It was an entirely different school structure and they were told what to teach," Donahue said. She and the other New York teachers demonstrated teaching styles that encouraged free thinking among students, such as breaking students into small groups so they could explore ideas.

One day, a Polish teacher asked Slotkin: How do you teach kids to live in a democracy? "That's when I realized that teaching in a democracy is teaching children to be good citizens," Slotkin says. "That's the goal of everything we do in a public school. We want to foster students who can read and write and who understand the importance of voting and running for public office, and who know how to think critically and analyze information so you can make sound political decisions."[14]

Slotkin, Donahue, and the others also taught their Polish counterparts how to participate in a free independent union, something that was new in a country where union organizers were spied on and sometimes jailed. Donahue packed her local teachers' contract on the trip, and would pull it out to show Polish teachers what a union contract looked like. The New York teachers shared what a grievance was, how the union was structured, how officers were elected, and how conflicts with administrators at the bargaining table were resolved—the kinds of union issues "we took for granted," Slotkin says. Again and again, Donahue repeated the three W's of union advocacy: fight for better wages, welfare, and working conditions. "One voice doesn't get you those things," she told them. "You achieve them through a union."[15]

Magidson became friends with Wiktor Kulerski, who became a minister in Poland's Ministry of Education and then the president of the Institute for Democracy in Poland, which worked to spread democracy at home and in other Eastern European countries. A member of Solidarity once asked Kulerski: Why are we spending so much time and money on developing workshops on civics and democracy abroad? Kulerski's answer: for the same reason that Al Shanker and the AFT supported those ideals in our country.[16]

Union rights had been taken for granted in Chile, a country that had been ruled democratically for 150 years. But that long period of political openness ended in 1973, when General Augusto Pinochet launched a violent coup d'état to overthrow the democratically elected government of Salvador Allende. Once in power, Pinochet and his military jailed, exiled, and "disappeared" people who opposed him, including unionists. Independent unions, including the Colegio de Profesores, a national teachers' union, were outlawed and replaced with government ones. Chile's national public education system was dismantled. Public education was "municipalized," and control was turned over to mayors, hand-picked by Pinochet, who slashed education funding. Nearly twenty thousand teachers were fired in one month alone—and teacher activists were the first to go.

In 1985, though, the government-sponsored teachers' union had become so discredited that new elections were held and a coalition of democratic teachers regained control of Colegio de Profesores.[17] When Oswaldo Verdugo, president of the union, was arrested for opposing the Pinochet government, Shanker and other AFT officials pressured the American government to send a representative to meet him in jail. When Verdugo was released, Sandra Feldman, the president of the UFT, Herb Magidson, and others traveled to Chile to lead a demonstration to support the teacher union activists.

Democratic forces inside and outside the country pressured Pinochet to hold a national plebiscite in 1988 on a constitution that would keep Pinochet in power for another eight years. Chileans organized a movement called the Coalition for the NO to defeat Pinochet, which included independent political parties, human rights organizations, church groups, women's organizations, and labor unions, including the Colegio de Profesores. The plebiscite was scheduled for October 5, 1988, and anti-Pinochet forces, fearful that the election would be stolen by the dictatorship, called upon teachers and other unionists the world over to come and observe the election.

A few days before the plebiscite, Walter Dunn and other longtime NYSUT activists—including Hobart, Magidson, Fred Nauman, and Paul Cole—flew into Santiago and boarded a bus to their hotel. This was the first time that Dunn, NYSUT's even-keeled second vice president, had ever traveled to a foreign country as an election observer. On the drive over, the bus hit thick traffic. Dunn and the others peered out the bus windows and saw crowds of Chileans gathered on the street. The teacher unionists had run smack into an anti-Pinochet demonstration. Dunn noticed that the roads were wet, although it wasn't raining. Then he glimpsed a tank-like vehicle that was shooting bursts of water into the demonstrators to disperse them. It was on that ride that Dunn first smelled tear gas, which the military used to break up the demonstration. The unionists were getting a drive-by education about what life was like under the Pinochet regime.

One of the first stops the American teachers made in Santiago was to the United States Embassy, where the U.S. ambassador told them that on the day of the vote they should expect to see lots of soldiers, who would be deployed to keep order at the polls. But the ambassador warned the unionists that they should return to their hotels immediately if they saw soldiers who had smeared their faces with charcoal. That meant they were about to commit acts they didn't want to be recognized for. For the next few days, whenever a military jeep or truck rolled by on the street, Dunn peered into it to look at the faces of the young soldiers.

On the day of the plebiscite, Dunn traveled alone to a polling place in the city of Los Andes. When he arrived, he was pulled aside by armed soldiers until one of the civilians in charge of the polling station had him released. After the polls closed at the school, Dunn watched the election workers count the ballots. "Yes" votes to give Pinochet another eight years in power were stacked in one pile; the other pile, stacked with the "No" votes, slowly overtook the "yes" stack. Dunn couldn't cheer—he was supposed to be a neutral observer—but he felt deeply satisfied. That night, Pinochet's inner circle debated whether to squelch the results. They might have if international observers such as Dunn had not traveled to Chile as witnesses for democracy.

In April 1994, Dunn traveled with Hobart and other NYSUT members to South Africa to observe the election that marked the end of apartheid, the system that for forty-six years had brutally segregated the races and discriminated against nonwhites. Before the election, Dunn heard Nelson Mandela speak at an historic rally at Soweto Stadium, replete with local dancers and exultant singing. During the vote, Dunn saw an old black man carry his wife to a polling place in a wheelbarrow. The next day he watched a South African reporter on TV ask how long she had to wait to cast her ballot on election day. I've waited my entire lifetime, she told him.

South Africans voted for a coalition government with a black majority. On his last night in South Africa, Dunn went out to dinner at a Johannesburg steakhouse with the other twelve AFT colleagues who had come to watch the election. As he ate, a middle-aged white man walked over to the table. Thank you, the man said, for giving up your time. Thank you, he said, for traveling all the way to South Africa. And thank you, he said, for helping us have democracy.[18]

NYSUT's members have worked to build unions and democracy around the world. It has also provided its members a place where they can express themselves as caring neighbors and responsible citizens. NYSUT members have raised money for breast cancer research, for aid to victims of the World Trade Center attacks, and for relief after natural disasters, such as the 2004 tsunami in Southeast Asia, which Hobart visited, and Hurricane Katrina in 2005.

Frances L. Brown, the former paraprofessional who taught for twenty-one years in the South Bronx ("I'm training you so you can take care of me in my old age," she had told her students), has found another way to give. After retiring, she became chair of the AFT-Africa AIDS Campaign for the AFT's Black Caucus in New York. To publicize the campaign, she has passed out brochures at NYSUT conferences and stepped up to podiums at public schools and churches. She's spoken to college sororities and fraternities about the program and made a presentation to the Museum of Natural History during its Black History Program.

"I tell people that in Nigeria we are losing ten to fifteen teachers every week," Brown says. "I tell them, 'Did you know that twelve-year-olds are now heads of households because their parents, who are teachers, are dying? We've lost an entire generation to this pandemic disease.' I also say to them that I know we can't help everyone, there are hundreds of thousands who are dying. That's why we focus on educators. Without them, whole societies are destroyed."

Wherever she goes to round up support, Brown takes one of the $10 pins that the AFT-Africa AIDS Campaign sells to raise funds. "Every time somebody opens their mouth, I say, 'Here's a pin. Ten dollars please.' People see me coming and they start feeling their chest for their pin. We've been nickel-and-diming it ever since. We've raised about $25,000 in New York City." AFT members have given over $170,000 to the program, which has leveraged another $4 million from the president's Emergency Program for AIDS Relief, launched in 2003.

In 2004, Brown went to Nigeria with a delegation from the AIDS Campaign. She stuffed her suitcase with whatever the union would give her—pencils, notepaper, T-shirts, hats—to give to African teachers. She wanted to if the dollars she raised were getting through, so whenever she met with an African teacher she'd make sure they had received the AIDS teaching kit from the AFT. The kit is part of a program designed to train African teachers to teach their peers how to prevent HIV and provide quality care to those with AIDS.

"For me, the union means unity," Brown says. "My mother and father were unionists. A union means you watch out for each other. That's what I know. And if our fellow teachers are in need, we should be there for them. And vice versa. This is why we are in a union. No matter where you are or what continent you live on, we care. It's solidarity, all around the world. It's a global thing, and let me tell you, it's a good thing, and I'm proud, very proud, to be part of it."[19]

CONCLUSION

March 2005 saw the retirement of Tom Hobart, New York State United Teacher's first and only president for the union's first thirty-two years. When asked about his proudest achievement during his tenure, Hobart said it was his first: helping broker the state teachers' merger in 1972. "We were two small organizations," Hobart said of NYSUT's predecessors, the New York State Teachers Association (NYSTA) and United Teachers of New York (UTNY), "and we became a powerhouse of 540,000 people. That's the reason we were able to do so much."

If there are lessons that the union movement can learn from NYSUT's success, that's the first: If a union doesn't grow, it shrinks, and if it shrinks, it often withers away. The percentage of unionized workers in the United States peaked at 35 percent in the early 1950s, and has shrunk to 13 percent today. The great exception to this decline is the rising number of public sector workers who have unionized, and New York teachers have been at the forefront of that wave. In the mid-1950s, only a few thousand of New York City's teachers were unionized. In 1960, the tiny Teachers Guild brought all the city's teachers together under the umbrella of the United Federation of Teachers (UFT), and the number soon leaped to seventy thousand. When Al Shanker realized that the UFT had little clout in Albany, he courted upstate teachers, and the state's two teacher groups became NYSUT in 1973, with two hundred thousand members. Since that year, NYSUT's embrace has grown so much that its name—New York State United *Teachers*—has become a misnomer. Elementary and high school teachers have welcomed college professors and assistant teachers into the union; educators have welcomed bus drivers and secretaries; school employees have welcomed health care workers; and all the union's employees have let retirees remain in NYSUT. As of 2005, New York's teachers' union has over a half-million members, and it's still growing.

This success has echoed across the country. The American Federation of Teachers had only 40,000 members in 1955, but membership is now 1.4 million, a third of them from New York. The AFT's vigorous expansion has spurred its once placid rival, the National Education

215

Association (NEA), to adopt union tactics it once condemned, such as collective bargaining and strikes. Now the NEA is also a strong advocate for teachers.

Another lesson is that leaders with vision are necessary to build unions. Forging teacher unity in New York was not inevitable. If Al Shanker and Tom Hobart hadn't stepped outside the fraternal warfare that had plagued teachers in America for half a century, New York's two teacher groups—NYSTA and the UFT—might still be fighting for turf and teachers rather than advocating for teachers and education. Shanker had to convince unionists that upstate teachers were not all rube Republicans; Hobart had to convince upstate teachers that New Yorkers were not union stooges. Both men showed that perceived enemies were potential allies, and because of their leadership, teachers discovered the power of unity. New York's teachers continue to work for unity: in 2005, NEA/New York, which split from NYSUT in 1976, agreed to return to the fold, and all of New York's teachers united again in 2006. Today, NYSUT nurtures future leaders by recruiting them for its Committee of 100, the phalanx of NYSUT activists who routinely invade Albany to lobby legislators, and by cultivating promising leaders at its summer Leadership Institute.

Shanker also showed bold leadership when he decided to embrace the educational reform document "A Nation at Risk" in 1983, and the educational standards movement that followed its release. At first, Shanker was nearly alone in his support. The NEA's leaders condemned it and many of NYSUT's leaders wanted to, but Shanker was able to convince the AFT and NYSUT that the fight for higher standards was an essential teachers' fight, and by doing so he gained teachers a seat at the table of educational reform. NYSUT has subsequently embraced the standards and accountability movement, pushing for high achievement goals.

Shanker's decision ensured that the union would remain a key player in educational policy. But he had another motive as well. He knew that when a union can inspire rather than just deliver, it can unleash a power far greater than the sum of its individuals. "It's as much your duty to preserve public education," Shanker told teachers, "as it is to negotiate a good contract." Today, the duty to preserve public education includes the fight against vouchers, which would drain funding from public schools and leave them as second-class institutions. The duty also includes the fight to boost education dollars to the state's woefully underfunded poorer urban schools, part of the long-standing Campaign for Fiscal Equity. Shanker's assumption that it is the duty of teachers to preserve our public schools taps into the idealism that lives in the heart of every teacher. They know that teaching isn't just a job—it's a calling. NYSUT protects that calling from faddish educational fixes and authoritarian administrators; it also nurtures that calling with mentors and teacher centers.

But NYSUT's circle of influence now extends to other states and even other countries. That's because they made the crucial decision in 1972 to create a union aligned with organized labor. The importance of that decision is a lesson for all American workers, who often divide their power by seeing themselves as only working class or middle class, immigrant or native, rural or urban. New York's teachers abandoned the conceit that they were superior to other working Americans when they joined America's labor movement. In doing so, they've learned that their need for decent wages, good health care, and a quality education for their children is not any different from the needs of plumbers, carpenters, and nurses.

NYSUT's link to organized labor has led New York teachers to places many never expected to go. They have helped teachers organize unions in Mexico, and to build democracy in countries such as Poland, South Africa, and Chile. NYSUT has become a trusted place from which New York's teachers can work to make their classrooms, their schools, and the world a better place, something far more difficult to achieve alone. "The very idea of unionism is solidarity," said Al Shanker in 1990. He was talking about unionism all around the world—but he might as well have been talking about NYSUT.

APPENDIX

TEACHER GROUPS AND THEIR ACRONYMS

AFT (American Federation of Teachers) Founded in 1916 in Chicago, the AFT was a national union of teachers that immediately affiliated with other workers through the American Federation of Labor (AFL). The original union, which included a New York City local, was formed as a more militant alternative to the NEA. It now includes the teachers of most large American cities and the teachers of New York State.

ESFT (Empire State Federation of Teachers) See UTNY.

NEA (National Education Association) The NEA was the first nationwide organization of teachers and was founded in 1857 to "elevate the character and advance the interests of the profession of teaching and to promote the cause of education in the United States." The NEA still includes the large majority of American teachers, and is particularly strong in suburban and rural areas.

NYCT (New York Congress of Teachers) See NYSUT.

NYSFT (New York State Federation of Teachers) See UTNY.

NYSTA (New York State Teachers Association) NYSTA was the association of upstate teachers founded in 1845 that represented most upstate and Long Island teachers prior to the state teachers' merger in 1973. For nearly all its history, NYSTA was the New York affiliate of the National Education Association (NEA).

NYSUT (New York State United Teachers) NYSUT is the name of New York's statewide union that was formed in 1973 from the merger of NYSTA and UTNY. NYSUT's original name was the New York Congress of Teachers (NYCT), which was revised because a parent-teacher group with a similar name petitioned the state to have it changed.

TG (Teachers Guild) The Teachers Guild was formed in 1935 by New York City teachers who, wanting to separate themselves from

Communist teachers, broke off from the Teachers Union, then the New York affiliate of the American Federation of Teachers (AFT). The Teachers Guild later became the New York affiliate of the AFT. In 1960, the guild, which represented New York City's elementary and junior high school teachers, merged with high school teachers to form the United Federation of Teachers (UFT).

TU (Teachers Union) The Teachers Union, formed in 1916, was the first teachers' union in New York City. That year, teachers in the TU met in Chicago with those from other urban areas to form the American Federation of Teachers (AFT). The TU survived even after many of its members, who complained Communists had undue influence in the group's proceedings, broke away to form the Teachers Guild in 1935. The TU was active until the formation of the United Federation of Teachers (UFT) in 1960.

UFT (United Federation of Teachers) The UFT formed in New York City in 1960 as a result of the merger between the Teachers Guild, which was the American Federation of Teachers' affiliate in New York City, and the High School Teachers Association (HSTA). After teachers voted in 1961 to have the UFT represent all teachers in New York City, it became the largest affiliate in the AFT.

UTNY (United Teachers of New York) UTNY was the third and last name for the statewide teachers union that was an offshoot of New York City's United Federation of Teachers (UFT). UTNY was affiliated with the American Federation of Teachers and challenged NYSTA in the late 1960s and 1970s for the leadership of New York State's teachers. In the 1960s, UTNY was named the Empire State Federation of Teachers (ESFT). Its name was changed to the New York State Federation of Teachers (NYSFT) before it became UTNY. UTNY was formed in 1971and merged with the NEA-affiliated New York State Teachers Association (NYSTA) in 1973 to form New York State United Teachers (NYSUT).

NYSUT OFFICERS, 2006

Richard C. Ianuzzi, President

Richard Ianuzzi was elected NYSUT president in April 2005 after serving as a NYSUT vice president and on the NYSUT Board of

Directors. He succeeded Tom Hobart Jr., who retired after leading the union since its formation in 1973. Ianuzzi also serves as a vice president of the American Federation of Teachers and vice president of the New York State AFL-CIO.

Ianuzzi comes from Smithtown, Long Island, where he taught elementary school in Central Islip public schools for thirty-four years, including fourth grade for the last twenty years. Raised in a union household, Iannuzzi was active in his local union from the beginning of his career, joining his local on strike in November 1970, his first year on the job. He was vice president of the Central Islip Teachers Association from 1976 to 1996 and president from 1996 to 2004.

Alan Lubin, Executive Vice President

Alan Lubin was elected executive vice president in 1993, after serving twenty-six years as an elected leader in the United Federation of Teachers, NYSUT's New York City affiliate. On NYSUT's Board of Directors since 1973, he serves as a vice president of the American Federation of Teachers and of the New York State AFL-CIO, where he is on the executive committee. Lubin's job is to oversee NYSUT's legislative and political action programs and is secretary/treasurer of VOTE-COPE, the union's political action fund. Lubin spearheaded the permanent cost-of-living adjustment law for retired public employees (COLA), Schools Against Violence in Education (SAVE), and the law mandating that a defibrillator be placed in every New York school.

Lubin has won numerous awards, including the Carolyn Holmes Humanitarian Award from the Coalition of Black Trade Unionists in 2004; the Champion of Labor Award from the New York State Democratic Party in 2004; and the prestigious UFT Charles Cogen Teacher Union Award in 1999.

Maria Neira, First Vice President

Maria Neira, an elementary school bilingual teacher who rose through the ranks of union leadership to become a nationally recognized expert on educational issues, was elected first vice president of NYSUT in April 2005 after serving as second vice president for six months.

Neira, a longtime member of NYSUT's Board of Directors, oversees the union's research and educational services department. In that role, she is NYSUT's advocate to the Board of Regents and to the State Education Department. Neira previously served as assistant to the president on education issues for the UFT, NYSUT's New York City affiliate, where she helped promote education reform. She also served as director of the UFT's Special Educator Support Program. Elected an American Federation of Teachers vice president in July 2004, she sits on the AFT's K-12 program and policy council.

Neira began teaching in New York City in 1977 and later served as a fourth-grade bilingual teacher at the Bilingual Bicultural Minischool in Manhattan, where she developed and implemented a schoolwide, hands-on science program for children in grades K-6. She has served on more than a dozen New York State Education Department committees and task forces. She is also a member of several professional organizations, including the National Staff Development Council, National Science Teachers Association, and Puerto Rican Educators Association. In 2005, she was honored for her leadership by the UFT's Hispanic Affairs Committee and by Somos El Futuro, an annual state legislative conference. Neira also received the 2005 Ellis Island Medal of Honor from the National Ethnic Coalition of Organizations.

Neira coordinates NYSUT's fundraising activities for American Cancer Society programs, including the Making Strides Against Breast Cancer annual walks. She also is a member of the New York State United Way Board of Directors.

Kathleen M. Donahue, Second Vice President

Kathleen M. Donahue, a veteran teacher with more than twenty-four years experience as president of the 400-member Hilton Teachers Association, was elected second vice president of New York State United Teachers in April 2005. Donahue has served twenty-one years as president of the Monroe County Federation of Teachers, comprising twenty-two NYSUT local unions, and the Monroe County Education Coalition Steering Committee, a group of educational stakeholders who have worked to provide quality education in the public schools. She served on NYSUT's Board of Directors for eight years as an at-large director and on the executive committee for six years.

Donahue taught for twelve years at the elementary level and eighteen years at the middle level in social studies and interdisciplinary English/social studies. She also taught for five years as an adjunct professor at the State University of New York at Brockport. Outside the classroom, Donahue launched the Democracy in Education Program in Poland, twice accompanying a NYSUT delegation to Poland to work with members of the Solidarity union in the fledgling democracy. Her international labor work has also taken her to Israel.

Ivan Tiger, Secretary-Treasurer

Ivan Tiger, a veteran activist, was an English teacher at Julia Richman High School in Manhattan for nearly all his teaching career. He was elected NYSUT's secretary-treasurer in 2000.

Since the 1970s, Tiger served on the UFT's negotiating team and executive board and has served on numerous committees working to improve education. He chaired a special effort to deliver educational services to homeless schoolchildren in New York City, and he has also worked with the UFT's Asian Heritage Committee and on numerous educational panels for the American Federation of Teachers.

A native of New York City, Tiger became active in the UFT as a young teacher and was recruited in the UFT's 1962 strike to organize pickets. Tiger quickly rose through the UFT's ranks and often worked for education reforms that brought higher standards to the classroom. He has served on the NYSUT Board of Directors since 1993 and has been active in VOTE-COPE, the union's voluntary political action effort.

FORMER NYSUT OFFICERS

Thomas Y. Hobart Jr., President, 1973–2005

Tom Hobart was NYSUT's first president and held that post until he retired in 2005. He was first elected president of NYSUT's predecessor, the New York State Teachers Association (NYSTA), in 1971. From that position, he led the negotiations with Al Shanker, then president of the United Federation of Teachers (UFT), that resulted in the merger of the two groups into NYSUT. Hobart first served as a building rep in 1964 in Buffalo and was elected president of the Buffalo Teachers Federation in 1969. Hobart was one of the founders of the Labor-Religion Coalition and served as an international ambassador for NYSUT, representing New York's teachers on trips to over forty countries during his tenure.

Albert Shanker, Executive Vice President, 1973–1978

Al Shanker was America's most famous teacher leader from the 1960s—when he led the launch of the modern teachers' movement in

New York City—until his death in 1997, at age 68. He was the president of the United Federation of Teachers (UFT) from 1964 until 1985. He was also the president of the American Federation of Teachers, the national union of teachers, from 1974 until his death in 1997. Shanker educated Americans with his weekly *New York Times* column Where We Stand and was the prime mover behind the New York State merger of teachers in 1973 that created NYSUT. After serving as copresident of the union for one year with Tom Hobart, Shanker became NYSUT executive vice president, a post he held in the union until 1978.

Dan Sanders, Executive Vice President, 1978–1987,
First Vice President, 1973–1978

Dan Sanders, a confidante of Al Shanker's, served as NYSUT's executive vice president from 1978 to 1986. Prior to his election to that post, he served as first vice president of NYSUT for five years. Sanders was a social studies teacher and one of the core group of teachers at Junior High School 126 in Queens who helped launch the modern teachers' movement during the late 1950s. From 1966 to 1972, he served as the assistant to Shanker, then UFT president. He was also a key figure in the negotiations leading to the merger that created NYSUT. Sanders died in 1999 at age 69.

Herb Magidson, Executive Vice President, 1987–1993,
Secretary-Treasurer, 1978–1987

Herb Magidson served as NYSUT's executive vice president from 1987 to 1993. Prior to that post, Magidson served as secretary-treasurer of NYSUT for eight years. He had been a member of NYSUT's Board of Directors since 1972. Magidson, who rose up the ranks of the United Federation of Teachers in the late 1960s, also served as a vice president of NYSUT's national affiliate, the AFT, and served as chairman of the AFT's Political Action Committee and its Teachers Under Dictatorship Committee. He often represented the union abroad, including trips to Poland and Hungary in 1989. Magidson is a trustee of the AFL-CIO Benefit Trust and chair of the AFT Disaster Relief Fund, which uses donations from AFT members to help others in the union who have suffered from disasters such as Hurricane Katrina.

Ken Deedy, First Vice President, 1978–1985

Ken Deedy was elected first vice president of NYSUT in 1978, a post he held until 1985. Deedy was one of the key negotiators for United Teachers of New York (UTNY), the group of unionized teachers that merged with the New York State Teachers Association (NYSTA) in 1973 to form NYSUT. Deedy was a science teacher in the Farmingdale school district and a president of the Farmingdale Classroom Teachers Association.

Antonia Cortese, First Vice President, 1985–2004,
Second Vice President, 1973–1985

Antonia Cortese was one of the original officers of NYSUT, elected second vice president in 1973, a position she held until 1985, when she was elected first vice president, a post she held until 2004. Cortese oversaw NYSUT's newspaper and was responsible for NYSUT's nationally respected Division of Research and Educational Services. Cortese also was a vice president of the New York State AFL-CIO. Cortese began her education career as a fourth-grade teacher and school social worker in her hometown of Rome, New York. Her teacher union involvement started with the Rome Teachers' Association, and she was the leader of the Rome teachers' strike in 1971. In 2004, Cortese left NYSUT to become executive vice president of the American Federation of Teachers.

Walter Dunn, Second Vice President, 1985–2004

Walter Dunn served as NYSUT's second vice president from 1985 until his retirement in 2004. He served on NYSUT's Board of Directors beginning in 1972 and on its Executive Committee from 1978. Dunn began his teaching career in 1962 in the East Islip School District in Suffolk County on Long Island. Dunn was elected president of the East Islip Teachers Association in 1971 and served in that capacity for twenty-five years. In 1985, he was elected a vice president of the American Federation of Teachers and oversaw the extensive expansion of membership services in the union.

Fred Nauman, Secretary-Treasurer, 1987–2000

Fred Nauman, a veteran teacher and union leader in New York City, was NYSUT's secretary-treasurer from 1987 until 2000 and served on

NYSUT's Board of Directors since 1972. Nauman began his career as a junior high school science teacher in Brooklyn. He was one of nineteen teachers fired during the 1968 Ocean Hill–Brownsville controversy in New York City. Nauman also served as director of the college scholarship fund of the United Federation of Teachers and as special assistant to Al Shanker. He currently serves as president of the New York State Alliance for Retired Americans.

Edward Rodgers, Secretary-Treasurer, 1973–1978

Edward Rodgers was elected NYSUT's first secretary-treasurer, a post he held from 1973 until 1978. Before he held that position, Rodgers was a teacher and a truant officer in the North Babylon school district on Long Island and served as the vice president of the New York State Teachers Association (NYSTA), the NEA group that merged with the United Federation of Teachers (UFT) to become NYSUT in 1973. Rodgers was a key member of the NYSTA team that negotiated the teachers' merger with the UFT.

NYSUT BOARD OF DIRECTORS, 1973–2005

Shelvy Young Abrams
Edward J. Alfonson
George E. Altamore
Carmen Alvares
Michael Andrews
Robert Astrowsky
Esther M. Aswad
Allene Ayling
Michael R. Barbera
LeRoy Barr
Allen Benezra
Donald Benker
Patricia Bentley
Anthony Bifaro
Rowena Blackman-Stroud
William P. Blanchard
Sandra Bliss
Michelle Bodden
Annette Bonder

Richard Boris
Barbara Bowen
Carol Linda Brandon
Grace Brindley
Peter Burke
John Burns
Constance Cabell
Claude Campbell
Arthur Cardinali
Mary Anne Cariello
Robert Carillo
Sandra Carner-Shafran
Frank Carucci
Stacey Caruso-Sharpe
James Cast
William G. Cea
Robert Cherrington
Stephen Clements
Paul Cole

Jane Conetta
John Connolly
Thomas A. Corigliano
Michael Corn
Antonia Cortese
Glenda Cowen
Lee Cutler
Kenneth Deedy
David DeFelice
Vito DeLeonardis
Iris DeLutro
Kathleen Donahue
Loretta Donlon
Nuala Drescher
Gary J. Duesberg
Walter Dunn
Selina Durio
Ruth Dworkin
Edwin Espaillat
Louis Fabiano
Paul Farfaglia
Richard Farkas
Sandra Feldman
George Fesko
Ray Frankel
Ronald Frantz
Steven Frey
Barry Friedman
Benjamin Frisbie
Harolyn Fritz
Marcella Fugle
Kathleen Fuller
Vincent Gaglione
Robert A. Galusha
Aminda Gentile
Janet Goddard
Robert L. Goldfarb
Anne Goldman
David I. Goldman
Jerome Goldman

Robert Gordon
Barbara Governale
JoAnn Graham
Robert Granger
Edward J. Greene Sr.
Joanne Hannon
Carlos L. Hargraves
Barbara Harms
Arthur Hartman
Dane Helt
Dianne Hettrich
Velma Hill
Ponsie B. Hillman
Thomas Y. Hobart Jr.
Stuart Horn
Eileen R. Hotaling
Richard Ianuzzi
David Israel
Harvey Iventasch
Howard Jones
Ronald Jones
M. Jane Kauffman
Carol A. Keefe
Ann Kessler
Peter S. Kilcommons
Carolyn King
Pauline Kinsella
Nancy E. Kleintop
Doris Knudsen
Susan Kressler
Joseph N. Lamendola
Elizabeth Langiulli
Abe Levine
Solomon Levine
Robert F. Lewis
Barbara Lipski
Steven London
Alan Lubin
Glenn Lucas
Edward J. Luksik

Herbert M. Magidson
Nicholas Maletta
Richard F. Mann
Alice Marsh
Ida Massaro
Ciro Matarazzo
Sylvia Matousek
Thomas Matthews
Ellen Schuler Mauk
George Mayer
Anthony McCann
Daniel G. McConnell
Katherine McKenna
Robert McKenzie
Carla McLaud
Joseph McLaughlin
Dorothea Meinecke
Michael Mendel
Harriet Merchant
David Miller
Richard Miller
Thomas Murphy
Fred Nauman
Maria Neira
Malcolm Nelson
Thomas Pappas
Carol Parker
Joseph A. Pasquarella
Deborah Paulin
Paul Pecorale
Jeannette M. Pietrantoni
Arthur Pepper
Thomas Pisa
Irwin H. Polishook
Maria Portalatin
Mario Raimo
Stephen Rechner
Timothy Reilly
Nadia Resnikoff
Thomas E. Rivers

Edwin Robisch
John F. Roden
Frances J. Rodgers
Stanley Rosengarten
Jeffrey Rozran
Abraham Ruda
Judith Rudman
Elaine Sanders
William Scheuerman
Simon Schwartz
Joseph Shannon
Barbara Shapiro
James J. Sheedy Jr.
David Sherman
Roderick Sherman
Milton Silverstein
Barbara Silverstone
Carol Slotkin
James Smith
Ronald Smith
John Soldini
Neal B. Sorkin
Jeanett Stapley
Henry J. Steck
Kristin Sterling
Mel Stern
Louis Stollar
Maurice Sussman
Joseph Sweeny
Robert Sympson
James Tabert
Richard C. Teevan
Gary Terwilliger
Walter Tice
Ivan Tiger
Dennis Tracey
Kenneth Ulric
Adam Urbanski
Dona Vermilya
Emil Voigt

Frank Volpicella
Samuel J. Wakshall
Randi Weingarten
Gloria Weinman
Minnie Wheeler
David L. Whitelaw

Josephine D. Wise
James Wood
Eileen M. Wrightsman
Irwin Yellowitz
Jeffrey Zahler
Jack Zuckerman

NOTES

CHAPTER 1. RADICAL ROOTS: THE RISE OF THE UNITED FEDERATION OF TEACHERS

1. Fred Nauman, Interview with author, 13 November 2003 and follow-up phone call.

2. George Altomare, *UFT Oral History Collection*, Tape 1, Side 1.

3. Schierenbeck, "Al Shanker's Rise to Power," in *Class Struggles: The UFT Story*.

4. Albert Shanker, Anonymous Audiotape Interview, Tape 1.

5. Jack Schierenbeck, "Al Shanker's Rise to Power," in *Class Struggles: The UFT Story*.

6. George Altomare, *UFT Oral History Collection*, Tape 1, Side 1.

7. Albert Shanker, Interview, by Marcia Reccer. AFT President's Collection, 31.

8. Ibid., 45.

9. "Albert Shanker = Teacher Power," *Bill Moyers' Journal*, 16 April 1974.

10. David Selden, *The Teacher Rebellion*, 25.

11. Elaine Sanders, Interview with author, 10 January 2006.

12. Jack Schierenbeck, "UFT and the Strike of 1960," in *Class Struggles: The UFT Story*.

13. Albert Shanker, "Reflections," 22.

14. Thomas Brooks, *Towards Dignity*, 15.

15. Dan Sanders, *UFT Oral History Collection*, 6.

16. Albert Shanker, Interview, by Marcia Reccer. AFT President's Collection, 47.

17. Jack Schierenbeck, "The Struggle Continues," in *Class Struggles: The UFT Story*.

18. Selden, *The Teacher Rebellion*, 9.

19. George Altomare, *UFT Oral History Collection*, Tape 1, Side 1.

20. Elaine Sanders, Interview with author. 10 January 2006.

21. Jack Schierenbeck, "The Struggle Continues," in *Class Struggles: The UFT Story*.

22. George Altomare, Interview with author, 9 April 2005.

23. Albert Shanker, Interview, by Marcia Reecer. AFT President's Collection, 45.

24. Jack Schierenbeck, "Al Shanker's Rise to Power," in *Class Struggles: The UFT Story*.

25. Fred Nauman, Interview with author, 13 November 2003.

26. Quoted in Thomas Brooks, *Towards Dignity*, 77.

27. Stephen Cole, *The Unionization of Teachers*, 16–17.

28. David Selden, *The Teacher Rebellion*, 18–20.

29. David Selden, *The Teacher Rebellion*, 21.

30. George Altomare, *UFT Oral History Collection*, Tape 1, Side 1.

31. Thomas Brooks, *Towards Dignity*, 61–62.

32. George Altomare, *UFT Oral History Collection*, Tape 1, Side 1.

33. By this time, Sanders had gone north to live in Putnam Valley, a town in Westchester County, and taught social studies in the Lakeland School District, which he would soon help organize. Sanders remained in close contact with Selden and Shanker, and would work as an aide to Shanker in 1966. In 1973, he would become a vice president of NYSUT, the statewide union, a post he would hold until 1987 (see his biography in the appendix).

34. David Selden, *The Teacher Rebellion*, 30.

35. Stephen Cole, *The Unionization of Teachers*, 59.

36. David Selden, *The Teacher Rebellion*, 31.

37. Stephen Cole, *The Unionization of Teachers*, 57.

38. George Altomare, *UFT Oral History Collection*, Tape 1, Side 1.

39. George Altomare, *UFT Oral History Collection*, Tape 2, Side 1.

40. Roger Parente, *UFT Oral History Collection*, Tape 1, Side 2.

41. George Altomare, *UFT Oral History Collection*, Tape 2, Side 1.

42. Thomas Brooks, *Towards Dignity*, 67.

43. George Altomare, *UFT Oral History Collection*, Tape 2, Side 1.

44. Ibid.

45. David Selden, *The Teacher Rebellion*, 37.

46. George Altomare, *UFT Oral History Collection*, Tape 2, Side 2.

47. Leonard Buder, "Teachers Strike Is Set for Today; Schools to Open," *New York Times*, 7 November 1960.

48. Jack Schierenbeck, "UFT and the Strike of 1960," in *Class Struggles: The UFT Story*.

49. Ibid.

50. George Altomare, Interview with author, 10 December 2003.

51. Claudia Levin Productions, "Episode 2: Those Who Can Teach," *Only a Teacher*.

52. Jack Schierenbeck, "UFT and the Strike of 1960," in *Class Struggles: The UFT Story*.

53. Ibid.

54. David Selden, *The Teacher Rebellion*, 48.

55. Thomas Brooks, *Towards Dignity*, 75–76.

56. Robert H. Chanin, Interview for the American Century Project.

57. Thomas Brooks, *Towards Dignity*, 76.

58. David Selden, *The Teacher Rebellion*, 63–64.

59. Thomas Brooks, *Towards Dignity*, 78.

60. Jack Schierenbeck, "UFT and the Strike of 1960," in *Class Struggles: The UFT Story*.

61. Jack Schierenbeck, "Establishing Leadership," in *Class Struggles: The UFT Story*.

62. Thomas Brooks, *Towards Dignity*, 83.

CHAPTER 2. TEACHER MILITANCY IN THE 1960S

1. Robert Allen, Interview with author, 24 September 2004, 24.

2. Ibid., 34.

3. Thomas Y. Hobart, Interview, *NYSUT Oral History Project Interviews*, Volume 2, 10 December 1990, 2.

4. Sylvia Matousek, Interview, *NYSUT Oral History Project Interviews*, Volume 2, 7 April 2000, 9–10.

5. Robert Allen, Interview with author, 24 September 2004, 24.

6. Ibid., 40.

7. Thomas Brooks, *Towards Dignity*, 81.

8. William Edward Eaton, *The American Federation of Teachers*, 150.

9. Quoted in the *New York Times*, 13 February 1941, in Eaton, 146.

10. Albert Schiff, "Teachers' Strikes in the United States," *Phi Delta Kappan*, January 1953, 133–35, quoted in Eaton, 149.

11. John DeGregorio, Interview with author, 26 January 2005.

12. Robert E. Doherty, "A Short and Not Entirely Unbiased History of the First Fifteen Years of New York's Taylor Law," *J. Collective Negotiations*, 364.

13. "How Teacher Strikes Became Illegal," *New York Teacher*, 9 June 2005.

14. Robert Allen, *NYSUT Oral History Project Interviews*, 15 June 2000, 4.

15. Robert Allen, Interview with author, 24 September 2004, 73–74, 83.

16. "Governor Signs New State Law to Curb Public Employee Strikes," *New York Times*, 22 April 1967. In 1969, the cap on fines was lifted and the eighteen months that a union could be denied check-off privileges was lifted as well.

17. "Extermination Threat," *New York Times*, 26 May 1967.

18. Albert Shanker Memorial Service Transcript, 3.

19. Jack Schierenbeck, "Al Shanker's Rise to Power," in *Class Struggles: The UFT Story*.

20. Bernard Bard, "Albert Shanker: A Portrait in Power," 472.

21. Ibid., 469.

22. Jack Schierenbeck, "Al Shanker's Rise to Power," in *Class Struggles: The UFT Story*.

23. Bernard Bard, "Albert Shanker: A Portrait in Power," 468.

24. Jack Schierenbeck, "Al Shanker's Rise to Power," in *Class Struggles: The UFT Story.*

25. Robert J. Braun, *Teachers and Power: The Story of the American Federation of Teachers*, 151–53.

26. Albert Shanker Memorial Service Transcript, 12.

27. Fred Nauman, Interview with author, 13 November 2003.

28. Philip Taft, *United They Teach: The Story of the United Federation of Teachers*, 233.

29. "Shanker to Dear Parent," 6 September 1968, quoted in Taft, 189.

30. Elaine Woo, "Al Shanker's Last Stand."

31. Tony Bifaro, *NYSUT Oral History Project Interviews*, Volume 1, 4 January 2002, 1.

32. "All Strikes Justified, State Teachers Told," *NYSTA Guidelines*, 18 June 1971.

33. "Lindenhurst Teachers Jailed," *Challenger*, 3 September 1971, NYSUT Research Library, Latham, New York.

34. "Strikes Hit Two More NYS School Districts; 1 Ends," *Hudson Register*, 11 September 1970, NYSTA Collection, Volume II, Boxes 407–411, News Clippings (1970–1972), Kheel Center for Labor-Management Documentation and Archives, Catherwood Library, Cornell University, Ithaca, New York.

35. "1971—Tough Year for Teacher Bargaining," *Challenger*, 28 January 1972.

36. Emanuel Kafka testimony before the New York State Commission on the Quality, Cost and Financing of Public Education (the Fleischmann Commission), 15 January 1971.

37. Press Release, National Education Association, 30 June 1971, Kheel Center, Cornell University, Ithaca, New York.

CHAPTER 3. ENTERING THE POLITICAL FRAY: THE JERABEK ATTACK

1. Lynn Costell, Interview with author, 7 June 2004. All quotes in the chapter by Costello come from this interview or follow-up conversations with the author.

2. "Budget: Unwanted Baby Spanked to Life," *Albany Times-Union*, 4 April 1971.

3. "How Could They Do It?" *NYSTA Legislative Bulletin*, 3 April 1971.

4. "Sordid Friday—The Bagman Collects," *NYSTA Legislative Bulletin*, 3 April 1971.

5. *The New York Red Book*, 197.

6. Marcella Fugle, Telephone interview with author, 15 September 2004.

7. Fred Lambert, quoted in Claudia Shacter-de Chabert, "A History of the New York State United Teachers," 50.

8. Deedy, Interview with author, 12 May 2004.

9. Emanuel Kafka, *NYSUT Oral History Project Interviews*, Volume 2, 1 February 1992, 5.

10. Memorandum from Emanuel Kafka, NYSTA President to Board of Directors, 7 April 1971, Kheel Center, Cornell University, Ithaca, New York.

11. Lynn Costello, Interview with author, 7 June 2004.

12. Memorandum from Ned Hopkins to Frank White, 14 February 1972, Series VI B., Hopkins Subject Files, Kheel Center, Cornell University, Ithaca, New York.

13. Harry Wilson, Interview, in quoted in Claudia Shacter-de Chabert, "A History of the New York State United Teachers," 49.

14. Charles Jerabek, Interview with author, 11 November 2004.

15. Emanuel Kafka address to Long Island VOTE Rally, 14 May 1971, Kheel Center, Cornell University, Ithaca, New York.

16. *NYSTA News Trends*, June 1971, Kheel Center, Cornell University, Ithaca, New York.

17. Emanuel Kafka, *NYSUT Oral History Project Interviews*, 4.

18. Untitled article, 29 April 1971, the files of Lynn Costello.

19. "Guidelines for Local Leaders," 29 May 1971, the files of Lynn Costello.

20. "Guidelines for Local Leaders," 11 May 1971, the files of Lynn Costello.

21. *NYSTA Legislative Bulletin*, No. 1, September 1971, in Shacter, 52.

22. "Guidelines for Local Leaders," 29 May 1971, the files of Lynn Costello.

23. "Streamlining Marks New VOTE Thrust," *Challenger*, 7 January 1972.

24. Ed Rodgers Comment column, *Challenger*, 7 April 1972.

25. Lynn Costello, Interview with author, 7 June 2004.

26. "Teachers Pledge Political Funds," 29 April 1971, the files of Lynn Costello.

27. Nick Maletta, Interview with author, 28 September 2004.

28. Lynn Costello, Interview with author, 7 June 2004.

29. Ibid.

30. "Political Gifts by Teachers," *Newsday*, August 1971, the files of Lynn Costello.

31. Lynn Costello, Interview with author, 7 June 2004.

32. Nick Maletta, Interview with author, 28 September 2004.

33. Dan Sanders, elected NYSUT's first vice president in 1973, would develop this lobbying effort into NYSUT's Committee of 100, a small army

of volunteer teachers who lobby state politicians' for pro-education legislation each year. "The legislature used to say to us, 'This is what the union wants, but what do teachers want?'" Hobart explained. "This was our way of telling them." Author interview with Thomas Hobart, 23 December 2005.

34. Quoted in "Teacher Lobbying Day," *Challenger*, 24 March 1972.

35. Walter Dunn, Interview with author, 22 October 2004.

36. Lynn Costello, Interview with author, 7 June 2004.

37. Lynn Costello, Interview with author, 7 June 2004.

38. "Islip GOP Rejects Jerabek Bid," undated *Newsday*, the files of Lynn Costello.

39. "Annual Dinner in Honor of Anthony Pace" program, files of Lynn Costello, and Lynn Costello, Interview with author, 7 June 2004.

40. Lynn Costello, Interview with author, 7 June 2004.

CHAPTER 4. PLANTING THE SEEDS OF UNITY

1. Walter Tice, Interview with author, 13 March 2004.

2. Ibid.

3. A. H. Raskin, "Shanker's Great Leap," *New York Times Magazine*, 9 September 1973.

4. Walter Tice, Interview with author, 13 March 2004.

5. "Teacher Power," Interview with Albert Shanker and Emanuel Kafka, *Inside Education*, April 1971.

6. Emanuel Kafka, *NYSUT Oral History Project Interviews*, Volume 2, 1 February 1992.

7. Ibid.

8. "Teacher Unity in New York State: A Position Paper by NYSUT," 13.

9. "Shanker Elected by Teacher Group," *New York Times*, 24 October 1971.

10. Ibid.

11. Ken Deedy, Interview with author, 1 June 2005.

12. Quoted in "Delegates Vote for New NYSTA President," *Oswego NY Palladium-Times*, 8 November 1971.

13. House of Delegates Transcript, 7–9 November 1971, Syracuse, New York. NYSUT Research Library, Latham, New York.

14. David Rossie, "NYSTA Discovers a Strange Bedfellow," *Evening Press*, Binghamton, New York, 9 November 1971, NYSTA Collection, Volume II, Boxes 407–411, News Clippings (1970–1972), Kheel Center, Cornell University, Ithaca, New York.

15. New York State Teachers Association, afternoon session, 8 November 1971, 42, NYSUT Research Library, Latham, New York.

16. "A Message from Al Shanker," 5 November 1971, UFT archives.

17. "NYSTA Discovers a Strange Bedfellow," *Evening Press*, Binghamton, New York. NYSTA Collection, Volume II, Boxes 407–411, News Clippings (1970–1972), Kheel Center, Cornell University, Ithaca, New York.

18. "All Offices Contested By Teachers," Syracuse, NY, Associated Press, 8 November 1971, NYSTA Collection, Volume II, Boxes 407–411, News Clippings (1970–1972), Kheel Center, Cornell University, Ithaca, New York.

19. Thomas Hobart, Interview with author, 1 July 2004.

20. "Hobart, Rodgers, Cortese elected," *Challenger*, 19 November 1971.

21. Thomas Hobart, Interview with author, April 2004.

CHAPTER 5. MERGER NEGOTIATIONS BEGIN

1. Thomas Hobart, *NYSUT Oral History Project Interviews*, 24 March 1992, 1; follow-up conversations with the author, 2005.

2. "Proposal for Joint NEA-NYSTA Projects," Collection S293, Box 395, file folder: Shanker-NYSTA-UTNY Unite, Kheel Center, Cornell University, Ithaca, New York.

3. "Everything You Always Wanted to Know about Merger . . . but Didn't Know Whom to Ask," Collection S293, Box 394, file folder 2, Kheel Center, Cornell University, Ithaca, New York.

4. Thomas Hobart, *NYSUT Oral History Project Interviews*, Volume 2, 66.

5. "Total Teacher Unity NYSTA's Aim," *Challenger*, 19 November 1971. NYSUT Research Library, Latham, New York.

6. Thomas Hobart, Interview with author. 4 April 2004. Many years later, Hobart says he apologized to Shanker for making these comments. Shanker told the NYSUT president that he didn't remember Hobart making them.

7. "Teacher Unity in New York State: A Position Paper by NYSUT."

8. Thomas Hobart, Interview with author, March 2004.

9. Transcript of NYSTA's Delegate Assembly, Saturday afternoon session, 22 April 1972, NYSUT Research Library, 4.

10. Antonia Cortese, Interview with author, March 2004.

11. "Shanker Urges Teachers Unit to Defend Schools," *Niagara Falls Gazette*, 1 December 1971.

12. "NYSTA Leads Coalition Conference . . . and Meets with UFT's Shanker," *Challenger*, 3 December 1971.

13. "Text for Teachers: In Unity, Strength," *Newsday*, 17 November 1971.

14. "Shanker Bids LI Teachers," *Long Island Press*, 17 December 1971.

15. "Levittown Teachers Union Ousts Association in Election," 23 January 1972, NYSTA Collection, Volume II, Boxes 407–411, News Clippings (1970–1972), Kheel Center, Cornell University, Ithaca, New York.

16. Telegram to Albert Shanker from Martin Collinan, President AFT Local 1382, 14 January 1972. Kheel Center for Labor-Management Docu-

mentation and Archives, Catherwood Library, Cornell University, Ithaca, New York, in Shacter, 75.

17. "Teachers Seek Peace with Shanker's Union," *Dunkirk Observer*, 25 January 1972, NYSTA Collection, Volume II, Boxes 407–411, News Clippings (1970–1972), Kheel Center, Cornell University, Ithaca, New York.

18. "'Let's Talk Unity' Says Faculty Group," *Beacon News*, 11 December 1971, quoted in Shacter, 75.

19. Thomas Hobart, Interview with author, 1 July 2004.

20. Myron Lieberman, "The Union Merger Movement: Will 3,500,000 Teachers Put It All Together?" 53.

21. Thomas Hobart, Comment column, *Challenger*, 14 April 1972.

22. Antonia Cortese, Interview with author, 2 March 2004.

23. Walter Tice, Telephone interview with author, 30 July 2004.

24. Thomas Hobart, Interview with author, 6 April 2004.

25. Thomas Hobart, Interview with author, 6 April 2004.

26. Walter Tice, Telephone interview with author, 30 July 2004.

27. Antonia Cortese, Telephone interview with author, March 2004.

28. Thomas Hobart, Interview with author, 12 April 2004.

29. Thomas Hobart, *NYSUT Oral History Project Interviews*, Volume 2, 10 December 1990, and Interview with author, 4 April 2004.

30. Quoted in "Text for Teachers: In Unity, Strength," *Newsday*, 17 November 1971.

31. Ken Deedy, Interview with author, 12 April 2004, and by telephone, 2004.

32. Robert Allen, Interview with author, 24 September 2004, 105–07.

33. Thomas Hobart, Interview with author, March 2004.

34. Thomas Hobart, Interview by Claudia Shacter-de Chabert, 10 June 1989, in Shacter, 77.

35. Antonia Cortese, *NYSUT Oral History Project Interviews*, Volume 1, 1 February 1992, 4.

36. Thomas Hobart, Interview by Claudia Shacter-de Chabert, 10 June 1989, in Shacter, 38.

37. Thomas Hobart, Interview with author, March 2004.

38. Thomas Hobart, Comment column, *Challenger*, 14 April 1972.

39. "Joint Statement of Thomas Y. Hobart, Jr., president of the New York State Teachers Association, and Albert Shanker, president of the United Teachers/New York, AFL-CIO," NYSUT merger file, Latham, New York.

40. Official minutes of the Board of Directors Meeting, 14–15 April 1972, NYSUT Research Library, Latham, New York.

41. These questions and comments were taken from the notes of Ned Hopkins, for the 14 April 1972 NYSTA Board of Directors meeting. NYSTA Collection, 1969–1972, Volume II, Series VI, Hopkins Subject Files,

1969–1972, Box 386, File Folder 2, Board of Directors Meeting, April 1972, Kheel Center, Cornell University, Ithaca, New York.

42. Ned Hopkins notes for April 1972 Board of Directors meeting. NYSTA Collection, Volume II, Series VI B., Hopkins Subject Files, Box 386, Folder 2, Board of Directors Meeting, April 1972, Kheel Center, Cornell University, Ithaca, New York.

43. Official Minutes of the Board of Directors Meeting, 14–15 April 1972, NYSUT files.

CHAPTER 6. THE CONCORD CONVENTION: FROM TWO ENEMIES, ONE UNION

1. Doug Matousek, *NYSUT Oral History Project Interviews*, Volume 2, 18 February 1992.

2. Thomas Hobart, Interview with author, 12 April 2004.

3. Ibid.

4. Doug Matousek, Interview with author, 12 April 2004.

5. Antonia Cortese, Interview with author, March 2004.

6. *NYSTA 1972 House of Delegates*, Saturday, April 22, morning session, 38.

7. "Teachers Group Approves Merger," *New York Times*, 23 April 1972.

8. *NYSTA 1972 House of Delegates*, Saturday, April 22, morning session, 41–42.

9. Ibid., 46.

10. *NYSTA 1972 House of Delegates*, Saturday, April 22, morning session, 44–45.

11. Ibid., 66.

12. Ibid., 69.

13. Ibid., 70.

14. Paul Cole, Interview with author, March 2004.

15. "Catharine Gets the Nod at Convention," *Challenger*, 3 September 1971.

16. "Congressional Record Shows Barrett Praise," *Challenger*, 24 September 1971.

17. Doug Matousek, Interview with author, 12 April 2004.

18. *NYSTA 1972 House of Delegates*, Saturday, April 22, afternoon session, 68.

19. Dan McKillip, Interview with author, 19 April 2005.

20. At that time, officers traditionally held office for two consecutive one-year terms before stepping down.

21. *NYSTA 1972 House of Delegates*, Saturday, April 22, afternoon session, 47–52.

22. Thomas Hobart, *NYSUT Oral History Project Interviews*, Volume 24, March 1992, 4.

23. Ibid., 4.

24. "House on Merger: Overwhelming OK," *Challenger*, 28 April 1972.

25. "Teachers-Union Merger Advances Another Step," UPI report in *Newsday*, 23 April 1972.

26. Jeanette DiLorenzo, *NYSUT Oral History Project Interviews*, 27 April 1992, Volume 2, 3.

27. *NYSTA 1972 House of Delegates*, Sunday, 23 April 1972, 158–163.

28. Claudia Shacter-de Chabert, "A History of the New York State United Teachers," 99.

29. Thomas Hobart, *NYSUT Oral History Project Interviews*, 75.

30. "Teacher Unity-Year One: A Report to the Delegates, 1974," New York State United Teachers files.

CHAPTER 7. A NATIONAL MERGER?

1. "Merger Rumblings Heard Around the Nation," *Challenger*, 3 March 1972, and Myron Lieberman, "The Union Merger Movement: Will 3,500,000 Teachers Put It All Together?" *Saturday Review*, 24 June 1972.

2. "Teachers' Unions in State to Merge," *New York Times*, 1 April 1972.

3. David Selden, *The Teacher Rebellion*, 189.

4. Walter Tice, Telephone interview with author, spring 2005.

5. "Teacher Unity in New York State: A Position Paper by NYSUT," 27.

6. Address by Sam M. Lambert, *National Education Association, Addresses and Proceedings of the 110th Annual Meeting* held at Atlantic City, New Jersey, 24–30 June 1972, Volume 110.

7. "The New York Disaffiliation: A History of Underlying Factors," *Common Sense*, a special publication for NEA members in New York, published by the National Education Association, files of Dan McKillip.

8. Antonia Cortese, *NYSUT Oral History Project Interviews*, 15 June 2000, 35–36.

9. "Blacks Rebuff Shanker at N.E.A. Parley," *New York Times*, 29 June 1972.

10. Antonia Cortese, Telephone interview with author, March 2004.

11. *Addresses and Proceedings of the 110th Annual Meeting* held at Atlantic City, New Jersey, 24–30 June 1972, Volume 110, 243.

12. Verbatim Transcript of November 21–22, 1975 NYSUT Board of Directors meeting, NYSUT files, 29.

13. Walter Tice, Telephone interview with author, 25 April 2005.

14. "NYCT Will Be 'Model' for Nation's 3 Million Teachers," *New York Teacher*, September 1972.

15. David Selden, 130–31.

16. "Teacher Unity in New York State: A Position Paper by NYSUT," 43–44.

17. Teacher Unity/No. 1, 15 December 1972, UFT Files.

18. "NEA Unit in Coalition with AFT to Build Merger," *New York Teacher*, December 1972.

19. "Merger Question Dominated NEA Convention," *New York Teacher*, July 1973.

20. "Toni Cortese Running for President-Elect of NEA," press release, NYSUT files.

21. "Cortese, Tice Backed by NYSUT Board for Top NEA Posts," *New York Teacher*, 13 May 1973.

22. Robert Paliwodzinski, *NYSUT Oral History Project Interviews*, Volume 2, 25.

23. Walter Tice, Telephone inverview with author, 25 April 2005.

24. "NEA Convention Tackles Merger, Governance," *New York Teacher*, July 1973.

25. David Selden, *The Teacher Rebellion*, 204.

26. David Selden, "Questions and Answers about the AFT: A Handbook for Leaders and Staff," *Labor Today*, June 1979, Dan McKillip's files. Optional membership in the AFL-CIO was an offer that Selden said he had discussed with Shanker and Lane Kirkland, the AFL-CIO's secretary-treasurer at the time and the future president of the AFL-CIO. Shanker, though, later said he had never agreed to such a proposal.

27. David Selden, *The Teacher Rebellion*, 205.

28. *Proceedings of the 111th Annual Meeting* held at Portland, Oregon, 3–6 July 1973 Representative Assembly, National Education Association, Washington, D.C., 1973, 10.

29. Ken Melley, Telephone interview with author, 4 November 2005.

30. "Merger Question Dominated NEA convention," *New York Teacher*, July 1973, 14.

31. "Selden Views NEA Merger Talks as 'Most Significant Event' in AFT history," *New York Teacher*, 26 August 1973.

32. Eadie Shanker, Interview with author, 19 May 2004.

33. Alden Whitman, "The Rise and Rise of Albert Shanker," *New York Times*, 15 January 1975.

34. David Selden, *The Teacher Rebellion*, 161.

35. "Shanker Confirms Report He Will Be Candidate for AFT Presidency," *New York Teacher*, 4 November 1973.

36. George Altomare, Interview with author, April 2005.

37. David Selden, *The Teacher Rebellion*, 204.

38. "Selden and Shanker Differ on Outlook for Merger," *New York Times*, 24 August 1973.

39. David Selden, *The Teacher Rebellion*, 209.

40. "The Rise and Rise of Albert Shanker," *New York Times*, 15 January 1975.

41. "The New York Disaffiliation: A History of Underlying Factors," 4–5, the files of Dan McKillipo.

42. "Teacher Unity: Present Hopes Dashed . . . But the Need Persists," *New York Teacher*, 3 March 1974.

43. Ibid.

44. "NEA Breaks Off Teacher Unity Talks," *New York Teacher*, 3 March 1974.

45. "An Open Letter to NEA Leaders from Thomas Y. Hobart, President, NYSUT," 6 June 1974, 7, NYSUT Research Library, Latham, New York.

46. "NEA Terminates Merger Discussions," from the Kheel Center, Cornell University, Ithaca, New York.

47. "NEA + AFT = Big-Time Labor," *Learning Magazine*, September 1973.

48. "Teacher Unity: Present Hopes Dashed . . . But the Need Persists," *New York Teacher*, 3 March 1974.

49. "Teacher Unity-Year One: A Report to the Delegates," 1974, NYSUT files.

50. "Dade County, Florida, Teachers in First Merger since New York's," *New York Teacher*, 6 January 1974.

51. Robert Paliwodzinski, *NYSUT Oral History Project Interviews*, Volume 3, 22 July 2001, 31.

52. "Insight . . . into the Teacher Movement in Florida," FEA publication, April 18, 1974, UFT files.

53. "An Open Letter to NEA Leaders," from NEA President Helen Wise, May, 1974, UFT files, 3.

54. The AFT and the NEA affiliates in Florida did eventually merge into the Florida Education Association in 2000. "'New York Will Not Be Balkanized,'" *New York Teacher*, 30 November 1975.

55. "The Fight with NEA—Not of Our Choosing," *New York Teacher*, 30 November 1975.

56. "Teacher Unity in New York State: A Position Paper by NYSUT," 33.

57. Thomas Hobart, *NYSUT Oral History Project Interviews*, 4 January 2002.

58. "Teacher Unity—Year One: A Report to the Delegates," 1974, NYSUT files.

59. "NEA Board Element Seeks Lid on AFL-CIO Affiliation Advocacy," *New York Teacher*, 24 February 1974.

60. "NEA Board Moves to Punish Directors Who Dissent," *New York Teacher*, 12 May 1974.

CHAPTER 8. COMING APART

1. Don Cameron, *The Inside Story of the Teacher Revolution in America* (Lanham, Maryland Scarecrow Education, 2005), 120–21.

2. "NEA Scores NYSUT," *Albany Times-Union*, 22 March 1975.

3. Thomas Hobart, Interview with author, 15 May 2005.

4. Thomas Hobart Interview, *NYSUT Oral History Project Interviews*, Volume 2, 24 March 1992, 12.

5. "NEA Ultimatum Rejected," a reprint of Thomas Hobart's letter to NEA President John Ryor of November 12, in *New York Teacher*, 16 November 1975, 2–3.

6. Verbatim transcript November 21–22, 1975 NYSUT Board meeting, NYSUT disaffiliation file, 2–4.

7. "Board Moves to Cut NEA Ties," *New York Teacher*, 30 November 1975.

8. Antonia Cortese, *NYSUT Oral History Project Interviews*, Volume 1, 1 February 1992, 7.

9. "NEA Board Crushes Compromise Plan," *New York Teacher*, 21 December 1975, 5.

10. "One Helluve Time for NEA Wedge," *New York Teacher*, 21 December 1975, 8.

11. "Letters on NEA Intervention," *New York Teacher*, 21 December 1975, 10.

12. "Preliminary Report on the Issues Dividing NYSUT and NEA," *New York Teacher*, 15 February 1976, 19.

13. Robert Paliwodzinski, *NYSUT Oral History Project Interviews*, Volume 3, 22 July 2001, 35–36.

14. *NYSUT Fourth Annual Representative Assembly*, 4–7 March 1976, New York City, NYSUT offices, Latham, New York, 53–54.

15. Thomas Hobart, Telephone interview with author, 23 September 2005.

16. Robert Allen, *NYSUT Oral History Project Interviews*, 7.

17. "NYEA's Executive Director [Dan McKillip] Talks of His Years at NYSUT and the Future of NYEA," *NYEA Advocate*, 8 October 1976, files of Dan McKillip, 22.

18. Edwin Robisch, *NYSUT Oral History Project Interviews*, 5 January 2002, 33.

19. "Area NYSUT Staff Out—Quit, Was Fired, or Both," Binghamton Press, 27 February 1976, NYSUT Research Library, Latham, New York.

20. Robert Allen, *NYSUT Oral History Project Interviews*, Volume 1, 1 February 1992, 6.

21. Robert Allen, Interview with author, 24 September 2004, 120.

22. Robert Paliwodzinski, *NYSUT Oral History Project Interviews*, Volume 3, 43.

23. Robert Paliwodzinski, Telephone interview with author, 26 October 2005.

24. Antonia Cortese, *NYSUT Oral History Project Interviews*, Volume 1, 1 February 1992, 12.

25. "Two Unions Vie for Teacher Loyalties," *Knickerbocker News*, disaffiliation file, NYSUT Research Library, Latham, New York.

26. Antonia Cortese, *NYSUT Oral History Project Interviews*, Volume 1, 33.

27. Antonia Cortese, Interview with author, 16 March 2005.

28. *NYSUT Fourth Annual Representative Assembly*, 1976, 113–15.

29. Ibid., 117.

30. Ibid., 210.

31. "The New York Disaffiliation: A History of Underlying Factors," 16.

32. Robert Paliwodzinski, *NYSUT Oral History Project Interviews*, Volume 3, 42–44.

33. Thomas Pisa, *NYSUT Oral History Project Interviews*, Volume 3, 3 January 2002, 22.

34. Dan McKillip, Interview with author, 19 April 2005.

35. *NYSUT Fourth Annual Representative Assembly*, 67.

36. "Keep the Clock," the address of Executive Vice President Albert Shanker to the *Fourth Annual Representative Assembly* of the New York State United Teachers, March 6, 1976, NYSUT's disaffiliation file, 315ff.

37. "Shanker: Will You Let NYSUT be Destroyed?" *New York Teacher*, 14 March 1976, 9.

38. "Keep the Clock," *New York Teacher*, 14 March 1976, 9.

39. *Proceedings of the Representative Assembly of the 114th Annual Meeting* held at Miami Beach, Florida, June 27–July 1, 1976, National Education Association, Washington, D.C., 1976.

40. "N.E.A. in Welcome to New Yorkers," *New York Times*, 4 July 1976, 34. Despite Hopkins's harsh words against the NEA, he would later leave NYSUT and the AFT and join that organization.

41. "New York Educators Association 1976–77 Status Report," prepared by Dan McKillip, 26 October 1977, files of Dan McKillip.

42. Dan McKillip, Interview with author, 19 April 2005.

43. "An Analysis of the NYEA Effort," 1, files of Dan McKillip.

44. "Board Votes Economies to Mold Balanced Budget," *New York Teacher*, 2 May 1977, 3.

45. Thomas Hobart's opening address to *NYSUT's Fifth Annual Representative Assembly*, March 24–27, 1977, Niagara Falls, NY, NYSUT Research Library, Latham, New York.

46. Phil Kugler, Telephone interview with author, 3 June 2005.

47. Robert Paliwodzinski, *NYSUT Oral History Project Interviews*, 47.

48. "An Analysis of NEA Effort," files of Dan McKillip.

49. Antonia Cortese, *NYSUT Oral History Project Interviews*, Volume 1, 33.

50. Ken Deedy, Telephone interview with author, 30 September 2006.

51. Thomas Hobart, *NYSUT Oral History Project Interviews*, 4 January 2002, 5.

52. Ibid., 13.

53. James Wood, Interview with author, 3 January 2005.

54. The decision Magidson and other NYSUT leaders made in the early 1980s to return all the money earned from its benefit trust back into the trust, rather than divert some for union expenses, has served its members well. In 2004, the union's 403(b) employee retirement program had fifty thousand participants and a portfolio of $2 billion.

CHAPTER 9. WIELDING POLITICAL POWER

1. Rachel Moyer, Telephone interview with author, 28 February 2005.

2. Ibid.

3. Alan Lubin, Interview with author, 2 December 2004.

4. Ibid.

5. Rachel Moyer, Telephone interview with author, 28 February 2005.

6. Myron Lieberman, *The Teacher Unions*, 195.

7. Alan Lubin, Interview with author, 2 December 2004.

8. Quoted in ibid.

9. Bayard Rustin, "Decency and Dignity," *United Teacher*, 30 August 1970, UFT files.

10. "By Overwhelming Margin, 1,461–42 Paras Accept 'Landmark' First Pact," *United Teacher*, 30 August 1970, UFT Files.

11. Frances Brown, Telephone Interview with author, 1 August 2005.

12. "Albert Shanker = Teacher Power," *Bill Moyers' Journal*, PBS, 16 April 1974.

13. *NYSUT 25th Anniversary Booklet*, NYSUT Research Library, Latham, New York, 30.

14. Albert Shanker Memorial Service Transcript, 9 April 1997, 18.

15. Herb Magidson, Interview with author, 28 December 2005.

16. "Teacher Unionism: A Quiet Revolution . . . Now Enters a Wider Arena," *New York Times*, 28 October 1973.

17. Claudia Shacter-de Chabert, "A History of the New York State United Teachers," 10.

18. "Albert Shanker: A Portrait in Power," *Phi Delta Kappan*, March 1975, 471.

19. "Carey Wins Endorsement of A.F.L.-C.I.O. by 90%," *New York Times*, 5 October 1974.

20. Thomas Hobart, Interview with author, 22 October 2003.

21. "Shanker's Group Endorses Carter," *New York Times*, 19 August 1976.

22. *Diaries of Mario M. Cuomo*, quoted in Myron Lieberman, *The NEA and AFT: Teacher Unions in Power and Politics*, 84.

23. Thomas Hobart, Email correspondence with the author, 28 March 2005.

24. "Members Urged to Work for Cuomo Victory on Election Day," *New York Teacher*, 3 October 1982.

25. Alan Lubin, Interview with author, 2 December 2004.

26. "Response to Alfonse," *The Bottom Line*, 14 November 1997, files of Alan Lubin, NYSUT offices, Latham, New York.

27. "D'Amato Ad Spurs Teachers to Start a Yearlong Response," files of Alan Lubin, *Rochester Democrat and Chronicle*, 14 November 1997.

28. Alan Lubin, Interview with author, 2 December 2004.

29. "Teachers Cheer as Democratic Candidates Denounce D'Amato," *New York Times*, 3 May 1998.

30. Adam Nagourney, "With No Challengers Handy, D'Amato Steps Up Attack on Teachers," *New York Times*, 2 December 1997.

31. "January Letter Writing Campaign," memorandum from Alan Lubin to NYSUT Board of Directors, Alan Lubin's files, NYSUT offices.

32. Alan Lubin, Interview with author, 2 December 2004.

33. "Just the Facts!" *New York Teacher*, 25 May 1998.

34. "Schumer Enters Race for Senate Saying He Can Unseat D'Amato," *New York Times*, 9 April 1998.

35. "Schumer, D'Amato Carry Attacks into Campaign's Final Weekend," *Buffalo News*, 1 November 1998.

36. A. H. Raskin, "Teachers Now Lions in Political Arena," *New York Times*, 15 January 1975.

37. Alan Lubin, Interview with author, 2 December 2004.

38. "Survey Puts Schumer Ahead of D'Amato," *Buffalo News*, 31 October 1998, files of Alan Lubin.

39. Betsy Sandberg, "Election Night: How Sweet It Was," *New York Teacher*, 18 November 1998.

40. Alan Lubin, Interview with author, 9 December 2004.

41. "New York Voters," *New York Times*, 4 November 1998.

42. "The Senator-Elect Discusses Education, Health, Jobs and Why His Kids Go to Public Schools," *New York Teacher*, 2 December 1998.

43. Alan Lubin, Telephone interview with author, March 2005.

44. Alan Lubin, Interview with author, 2 December 2004.

45. Ibid.

46. Alan Lubin, Telephone interview with author, 27 October 2005.

47. "Historic Override Is Great News for Public Ed and Health Care," *New York Teacher*, 21 May 2003.

48. "May 3, 2003," video, NYSUT Research Library, Latham, New York.

49. "Making the May 3 March Magnificent," *New York Teacher*, 7 May 2003.

50. "Statement by New York State United Teachers on Passage of School Defibrillator Legislation," Press Release, 27 February 2002, NYSUT Research Library, Latham, New York.

51. Paul Hartman, Telephone interview with author, March 2004.

52. Sylvia Sanders, "Saving Lives," *New York Teacher*, 3 December 2003.

53. Liza Frenette, "Sudden Collapse, Amazing Rescue," *New York Teacher*, 23 April 2003.

54. *NYSUT 25th Anniversary, 1973–1998*, 16.

CHAPTER 10. EDUCATIONAL REFORM

1. All quotes and other information from Jean Lux come from the author's visit to Owego Elementary School, June 2004.

2. Albert Shanker, "Supervisors' Rigidity Angers Teachers," Where We Stand column, *New York Times*, 6 February 1983.

3. Antonia Cortese, Telephone interview with author, 11 May 2006. Cortese said she became the NYSUT official who oversaw educational policy because the rest of NYSUT's leaders, all men, were more interested in overt political policy, such as lobbying the legislature or strategizing over teacher strikes.

4. Chuck Santelli, Interview with author, 14 March 2006.

5. Antonia Cortese, Telephone Interview with the author, 16 March 2006.

6. CBTE Programs Mailgram, 10 January 1975, from the files of Chuck Santelli.

7. Chuck Santelli, Interview with author, 14 March 2006.

8. Albert Shanker speech to the AFT QuEST (Quality Educational Standards in Teaching) Conference, Washington, D.C., July 1985, quoted in *The Power of Ideas, American Education*, 2.

9. Daniel Patrick Moynihan, quoted in Albert Shanker Memorial Service Transcript, 12.

10. Albert Shanker, Marcia Reecer Interview, AFT archives, 10.

11. "A Recipe for School Reform," Where We Stand column, *New York Times*, 24 December 1995.

12. Thomas Brooks, *Towards Dignity*, 83–84.

13. Chuck Santelli, Interview with author, 5 Feburary 2005.

14. Albert Shanker, Marcia Reecer Interview, AFT archives, 21.

15. M. Loiretta Petit, "Teacher Centers: Will They 'Sell'? *The Educational Forum*, March 1978, 316. For more on who teachers trust to learn from see

the April 1986 issue of *Phi Delta Kappan*, which was cited by Albert Shanker in his 20 April 1986 column, "Teacher Colleagues #1 Resource."

16. "Teachers' Centers: A British First," *Phi Delta Kappan*, November 1971, quoted by Shanker in "The 'Teacher Center' A Major Educational Advance," *New York Times*, 26 December 1971.

17. Albert Shanker, "Teacher Centers: A Needed Educational Reform," *New York Times*, 22 July 1973.

18. Quoted in Sally Reed, "Teacher Centers Are Becoming New Force," Survey of Continuing Education, *New York Times*, 7 September 1980, Teacher Centers file, NYSUT Research Library, Latham, New York.

19. Rosemary Harrigan, Interview with author, 11 July 2005.

20. Julia E. Koppich, "Using Well Qualified Teachers Well," *American Educator*, Winter 2002.

21. Maria Neira, Telephone interview with author, 6 October 2005.

22. George Thearle, Author's visit to Owego Elementary School in June 2005 and telephone interview, 18 July 2005.

23. Harold Stevenson and James Stigler, authors of *The Learning Gap*, quoted in Albert Shanker, "Working Together," *New York Times*, 2 May 1993.

24. George Thearle, Author's visit, 18 July 2005.

25. National Association of State Directors of Teacher Education and Certification, The NASDTECT Manual on Preparation and Certification of Educational Personnel, 2002, quoted in "Explosion of Excellence," a NYSUT report, March, 2004, 6–7.

26. Linda Darling-Hammond, "Keeping Good Teachers: Why It Matters, What Leaders Can Do."

27. Albert Shanker, "The Case for National Standards," *New York Times*, 1 June 1986.

28. "Raising the Bar for Educators," *American Teacher*, April 2003.

29. Linda Darling-Hammond, "The Quiet Revolution: Rethinking Teacher Development," *Educational Leadership* 53, March 1996, 4–7.

30. Diane Ravitch, "The Test of Time," The Hoover Institution, 2003.

31. National Commission on Excellence in Education (Excellence commission), "A Nation at Risk" (1983), quoted in "A Test of Time," 27–28.

32. Quoted in Sara Mosle, "The Answer Is National Standards," *The New York Times Magazine*, 29 October 1996, 45ff, quoted in Kahlenberg's "Albert Shanker's Legacy."

33. An intriguing account by one of the writers of the report—and how the Reagan administration tried to hijack it—is: "An Insider's View of 'A Nation at Risk' and Why It Still Matters," by Gerald Holton, *Chronicle Review*, 25 April 2003.

34. Quoted in Sara Mosle, "The Answer Is National Standards," *The New York Times Magazine*, 29 October 1996, quoted in Kahlenberg's "Albert Shanker's Legacy," 6.

35. Antonia Cortese, Interview with author, 17 February 2005.

36. Transcript of Albert Shanker speech at the 1983 NYSUT Representative Assembly, 370ff, NYSUT Research Library, Latham, New York.

37. Antonia Cortese, Interview with author, 17 February 2005.

38. Quoted in Thomas Toch, "A Speech That Shook the Field," *Education Week*, 26 March 1997, quoted in Kahlenberg's "Albert Shanker's Legacy."

39. Albert Shanker Memorial Service Transcript. Clinton recounted the conversation at Shanker's memorial service held in Washington, D.C., in April 1997—an event that Vice President Al Gore and New York Senator Daniel Patrick Moynihan also attended.

40. E. D. Hirsch, quoted in "Always Setting the Standard," *American Teacher*, April 1997, 4, quoted in Kahlenberg's "Philosopher or King," 7.

41. Antonia Cortese, Interview with author, 17 February 2005.

42. "Explosion of Excellence," 6.

43. Antonia Cortese, Interview with author, 17 February 2005.

44. "Explosion of Excellence," 10.

45. College Entrance Examination Board and Educational Service, 2004, quoted in "Explosion of Excellence," 11.

46. "Explosion of Excellence," 9.

47. *NYSUT's 25th Anniversary Booklet*, NYSUT Research Library, Latham, New York, 46.

CHAPTER 11. INTERNATIONAL SOLIDARITY

1. Transcript of New York State United Teachers' Representative Assembly, General Session 4 and 5, Saturday, 9 April 2005, NYSUT Research Library, Latham, New York.

2. Thomas Hobart, Interview with author, April 2004.

3. Albert Shanker, quoted in the Introduction to the AFT seminar, "Unionism and Democracy: The Experience, the Legacy, the Future," 19–21 April 2005, AFT.

4. "Report from Guanajuato election," email from Maureen Casey, 2 June 2005.

5. Albert Shanker, from the Introduction to the AFT seminar, "Unionism and Democracy: The Experience, the Legacy, the Future," 19–21 April 2005, sponsored by the Albert Shanker Institute.

6. "A Special Message from Lech Walesa," from the address that Walesa made to the AFL-CIO convention, *New York Teacher*, 25 December 1989.

7. Quoted in Arch Puddington, *Lane Kirkland, Champion of American Labor*, "chapter 7, Solidarity Forever."

8. Albert Shanker, "World Watching Poland and Reagan," *New York Times*, 20 December 1981.

9. Eric Chenoweth, Telephone interview with author, 17 October 2005.

10. Adam Urbanski, Telephone interview with author, 14 October 2005.

11. "A Special Message from Lech Walesa," *New York Teacher*, 25 December 1989.

12. Albert Shanker, "Democracy Owes You," *New York Times*, 21 November 1989.

13. Linda K. Wertheimer, "Democracy in Teacher's Lesson Plan," *Democrat and Chronicle*, Kathleen Donahue's files.

14. Carol Slotkin, Telephone interview with author, 25 July 2005.

15. Kathleen Donahue, Interview with author, 2004.

16. Herb Magidson, Interview with author, 28 October 2005.

17. Oswaldo Verdugo, "Rebuilding After Pinochet," speech to the AFT 1990 convention, *American Educator*, Fall 1990, 21.

18. Walter Dunn, Interview with author, 28 July 2005.

19. Frances Brown, Telephone interview with the author, 29 July 2005.

SELECTED BIBLIOGRAPHY

The Albert Shanker Institute. Washington, D.C., website with links and written materials: www.shankerinstitute.org/aboutal.html

Allen, Robert. Interview with author. 24 September 2004.

"Always Setting the Standard." *American Teacher* (special issue). April 1997.

American Federation of Teachers. "Unionism and Democracy: The Experience, the Legacy, the Future" (seminar). 19–21 April 2005. Sponsored by The Albert Shanker Institute.

AFT. "Raising the Bar for Educators." *American Teacher*. April 2003. www.aft.org/pubs-reports/american_teacher/apr03/raising.html (accessed ???).

Bailey, S. K. "Teachers' Centers: A British First." *Phi Delta Kappan* 53(3). 1971.

Bard, Bernard. "Albert Shanker: A Portrait in Power." *Phi Delta Kappan*. March 1975.

Bernard, Sheila Curran, and Sarah Mondale. *School: The Story of American Public Education*. Boston: Beacon Press, 2001.

Bernhardt, Debra E. and Rachel Bernstein. *Ordinary People, Extraodinary Lives*. New York: New York University Press, 2000.

Bradley, Ann. "The End of an Era." *Education Week*. 5 March 1997.

Braun, Robert J. *Teachers and Power: The Story of the American Federation of Teachers*. New York: Simon and Schuster, 1972.

Brooks, Thomas. *Towards Dignity: A Brief History of the United Federation of Teachers*. New York: United Federation of Teachers, Local 2, American Federation of Teachers, AFL-CIO, 1967.

Brown, Frances L. Telephone interview with author. 1 August 2005.

Cameron, Don. *The Inside Story of the Teacher Revolution in America*. Lanham, Maryland: Scarecrow Education, 2005.

The *Challenger* newspaper, 1971–1972. NYSUT Research Library, Latham, New York.

Chanin, Robert H. Interviewed by E. Heintz for the American Century Project. 1999. Available: www.doingoralhistory.org (e_heintz.pdf) (accessed ???).

Chenoweth, Eric. Telephone interview with author. 17 October 2005.

Claudia Levin Productions. "Episode 2: Those Who Can Teach." *Only a Teacher*, a PBS video series, Films for the Humanities and Sciences, 2000.

Cole, Paul. Interview with author. Albany, New York. March 2004.

Cole, Stephen. *The Unionization of Teachers*. New York: Praeger Publishers, 1969.

Cortese, Antonia. Interviews with author. March 2004, 16 March 2005, 17 February 2005.

Costello, Lynn. Interview with author. East Islip, New York. 7 June 2004.

Cuomo, Mario M. *Diaries of Mario M. Cuomo: The Campaign for Governor*. New York: Random House, 1984.

Darling-Hammond, Linda. "Keeping Good Teachers: Why It Matters, What Leaders Can Do." *Educational Leadership* 60(8). May 2003.

———. "The Quiet Revolution: Rethinking Teacher Development." *Educational Leadership* 53. March 1996.

DeGregorio, John. Telephone interview with author. 26 January 2005.

Deedy, Ken. Interview with author. Latham, New York. 12 May 2004.

Doherty, Robert E. "A Short and Not Entirely Unbiased History of the First Fifteen Years of New York's Taylor Law." *J. Collective Negotiations* 13(4). 1984.

Donahue, Kathleen. Interview with author. Latham, New York. 2004.

Dulles, Foster Rhea and Melvyn Dubofsky. *Labor in America: A History, Fourth Edition*. Arlington Heights, Illinois: Harlan Davidson, 1984.

Eaton, William Edward. *The American Federation of Teachers, 1916–1961*. Carbondale, Illinois: Southern Illinois University Press, 1975.

Fennell, Dorothy. NYSUT Oral History Project Manuscript. NYSUT Research Library, Latham, New York. October 2002.

Freeman, Joshua B. *Working-Class New York*. New York: The New Press, 2000.

Fugle, Marcella. Telephone interview with author. 15 September 2004.

Harrigan, Rosemary. Telephone interview with author. 11 July 2005.

Hartman, Paul. Telephone interview with author. March 2004.

Hobart, Thomas Y. Interviews with author. 1 July 2004, March 2004, 4 April 2004, 12 April 2004.

———. Interview by Claudia Shacter, 10 June 1989, for her master's thesis, "A History of the New York State United Teachers: The Merger Story." NYSUT Research Library, Latham, New York.

Holton, Gerald. "An Insider's View of 'A Nation at Risk' and Why It Still Matters," *Chronicle Review*. 25 April 2003.

Kahlenberg, Richard. "Albert Shanker's Legacy." *Education Next*. 14 January 2003.

———. *All Together Now: Creating Middle-Class Schools Through Public School Choice*. Washington, D.C.: Brookings Institution Press, 2003.

———. "Philosopher or King." *Education Next*. Spring 2003.

———. "Remembering Al Shanker: Five Years After His Death, Al Shanker's Tough Liberalism Looks Better Than Ever." *Education Week*. 27 February 2002.

Kerchner, Charles Taylor, Julia E. Koppich, and Joseph G. Weeres. *United Mind Workers: Unions and Teaching in the Knowledge Society*. Hoboken, New Jersey: Jossey-Bass, 1997.

————. *Taking Charge of Quality: How Teachers and Unions Can Revitalize Schools*. Hoboken, New York: Jossey-Bass, 1998.

Koppich, Julia E. "Using Well-Qualified Teachers Well." *American Educator*. Winter 2002.

Kozol, Jonathan. *The Shame of the Nation: The Restoration of Apartheid Schooling in America*. London: Harper Perennial, 1992.

Lambert, Fred. Interviewed by Claudia Shacter for her thesis, "A History of the New York State United Teachers: The Merger Story." NYSUT Research Library, Latham, New York.

Lambert, Sam M. National Education Association, *Addresses and Proceedings of the 110th Annual Meeting* held at Atlantic City, New Jersey. Volume 110. 24–30 June 1972.

Le Blanc, Paul. *A Short History of the U.S. Working Class*. Amherst, New York: Humanity Books, 1999.

Lieberman, Myron. "The Union Merger Movement: Will 3,500,00 Teachers Put It All Together?" *Saturday Review*. 24 June 1972.

————. *The Teacher Unions: How They Sabotage Educational Reform and Why*. New York: Encounter Books, 2000.

Lieberman, Myron, Charlene Haar, and Leo Troy. *The NEA and AFT: Teacher Unions in Power and Politics*. Rockport, Massachusetts: Pro Active Publications, 1994.

Loveless, Tom, editor. *Conflicting Missions? Teachers Unions and Educational Reform*. Washington, D.C.: Brookings Institution Press, 2000.

Lubin, Alan. Interviews with author. 2, 9 December 2004, March 2005, 27 October 2005.

Magidson, Herb. Interview with author. Washington, D.C. 28 October 2005, 28 December 2005.

Maletta, Nick. Telephone interview with author. 28 September 2004.

Matousek, Doug. Interview with author. New York City. 12 April 2004.

McKillip, Dan. Interview with author. Lake Placid, New York. 19 April 2005.

Mosle, Sara. "The Answer Is National Standards." *New York Times Magazine*. 27 October 1996.

————. "Albert Shanker: Labor's Love Lost." *New York Times Magazine*. 4 January 1998.

Moyer, Rachel. Telephone interview with author. 28 February 2005.

Moyers, Bill. "Albert Shanker = Teacher Power." *Bill Moyers' Journal*. PBS. 1974.

Mungazi, Dickson A. *Where He Stands: Albert Shanker of the American Federation of Teachers*. Westport, Connecticut: Praeger Publishers, 1995.

Murolo, Priscilla, and A. B. Chitty. *From the Folks Who Brought You the Weekend*. New York: The New Press, 2001.

Murphy, Marjorie. *Blackboard Unions: The NEA and the AFT, 1900–1980*. Ithaca, New York: Cornell University Press, 1990.

National Commission on Excellence in Education. "A Nation at Risk." USA Research, 2nd edition, March 1, 1984.

National Education Association. *Addresses and Proceedings of the 110th Annual Meeting* held at Atlantic City, New Jersey. Volume 110. 24–30 June 1972.

——— . *Proceedings of the Representative Assembly of the 114th Annual Meeting* held at Miami Beach, Florida, June 27–July 1, 1976. Washington, D.C., 1976.

Nauman, Fred. Interview with author. Latham, New York. 13 November 2003.

"NEA + AFT = Big-Time Labor." *Learning Magazine*. September 1973.

"The New York Disaffiliation: A History of Underlying Factors." *Common Sense*, a special publication for NEA members in New York, published by the National Education Association, files of Dan McKillip.

The New York Red Book. Eightieth edition. Albany, New York: Williams Press, 1971–1972.

New York State Teachers Association (NYSTA). *House of Delegates Transcripts, 1970–1972*. NYSUT Research Library, Latham, New York.

——— . Records. Kheel Center for Labor-Management Documentation and Archives, Catherwood Library, Cornell University. Ithaca, New York.

New York State United Teachers (NYSUT). Records. Kheel Center for Labor-Management Documentation and Archives, Catherwood Library, Cornell University. Ithaca, New York.

——— . *NYSUT 25th Anniversary, 1973–1998*. NYSUT Research Library, Latham, New York.

——— . *Annual NYSUT Representative Assemblies, 1973–2005*. NYSUT Research Library, Latham, New York.

——— . "Explosion of Excellence: The Education Revolution No One Is Talking About." NYSUT files. Latham, New York. March 2004.

——— . "May 3, 2003." Video, NYSUT files. Latham, New York.

——— . *NYSUT Oral History Project Interviews, 1990–2002*. Volumes 1–3. NYSUT Research Library, Latham, New York. Interviews include: Tony Bifaro, Robert Allen, Bernard Ashe, Esther Aswad, Dan Benker, Bill Cea, Paul Cole, Mike Corn, Antonia Cortese, Vito Deleonardis, Jeanette DiLorenzo, Matthew Doherty, Sandra Feldman, Thomas Y. Hobart, Emanuel Kafka, Ely Kaplan, Leon Lieberman, Herb Magidson, Doug Matousek, Sylvia Matousek, Tony McCann, Fred Nauman, Robert Paliwodzinski, Tom Pisa, Irwin Polishook, Hobie Rhinehart, Ed Robisch, Lucille Swain, Walter Tice, Gloria Weinman, James Wood.

——— . Verbatim Transcript of 21–22 November 1975 Board of Directors meeting. NYSUT files. NYSUT Research Library, Latham, New York.

New York State United Teachers Representative Assembly, 1973–2005. NYSUT Research Library, Latham, New York.

Noah, Timothy. "Albert Shanker, Statesman: The Fiery Unionist as Educational Leader." *New Republic*. 24 June 1985.

Paliwodzinski, Robert. Interview with author. 26 October 2005.

Petit, M. Loiretta. "Teacher Centers: Will They 'Sell?' *The Educational Forum.* March 1978.

Podair, Jerald. *The Strike That Changed New York: Blacks, Whites, and the Ocean Hill–Brownsville Crisis.* New Haven, Connecticut: Yale University Press, 2002.

Puddington, Arch. *Lane Kirkland, Champion of American Labor.* Hoboken, New Jersey: John Wiley & Sons, 2005.

———. "Missing Albert Shanker." *Commentary.* 1 July 1997.

Ravitch, Diane. "In Memoriam: Albert Shanker." *The New Leader.* 24 February 1997.

———. *The Great School Wars: A History of the New York City Public Schools.* New York: Basic Books, 1988.

———. *The Revisionists Revisited: A Critique on the Radical Attack on Schools.* New York: Basic Books, 1978.

———. "The Test of Time." The Hoover Institution. 2003. www.education-next.org/20032/32.html (accessed June 2005).

———. *The Troubled Crusade: American Education, 1945–1980.* New York: Basic Books, 1983.

Ryor, John. Verbatim Transcript of the John Ryor presentation to the NYSUT Board of Directors, *New York Teacher* (special issue). Disaffiliation file, NYSUT offices, Latham, New York.

Santelli, Chuck. Interview with author. NYSUT offices, Latham, New York. 5 February 2005.

Schierenbeck, Jack. *Class Struggles: The UFT Story.* 1996. www.uft.org/about/history/history_uft/ (accessed August 2003).

Schiff, Albert. "Teachers' Strikes in the United States." *Phi Delta Kappan.* January 1953.

Shacter-de Chabert, Claudia. "A History of the New York State United Teachers: The Merger Story." Master's thesis, SUNY, Empire State College, 1989. Provided by NYSUT Research Library.

Selden, David. "Questions and Answers about the AFT: A Handbook for Leaders and Staff." *Labor Today.* June 1979.

———. *The Teacher Rebellion.* Washington, D.C.: Howard University Press, 1985.

Shanker, Albert. Albert Shanker Memorial Service Transcript. American Federation of Teachers, courtesy of Richard Kahlenberg. 9 April 1997.

———. Anonymous Audiotape Interview. Cassette Recording UFT OH1. New York: Robert F. Wagner Labor Archives, New York University, Undated.

———. American Federation of Teachers. *The Power of Ideas: Al in His Own Worlds: A Collection. American Educator* (special issue). Spring/Summer 1997.

————. "Reflections." *Phi Delta Kappan* (1991) reprinted in *American Educator* (special issue *The Power of Ideas*). Spring/Summer 1997.

————. Interview by Marcia Reecer. Transcript from AFT President's Collection, Albert Shanker, Box 66, Folder 53. Detroit, Michigan: Walter P. Reuther Library, Wayne State University.

————. Where We Stand columns. NYSUT online archive. nysut.org/shanker/

————. "A Message from Al Shanker." UFT archives. 5 November 1971.

Shanker, Eadie. Interview with author. New York, New York. 19 May 2004.

Slotkin, Carol. Telephone interview with author. 25 July 2005.

Stevenson, Harold and Stigler, James. *The Learning Gap, Best Ideas From the World's Teachers on Improving Education in the Classroom*. Free Press, 1994.

Stone, Bernice. "Why Beginning Teachers Fail." *Principal*. September 1987.

Taft, Philip. *United They Teach: The Story of the United Federation of Teachers*. Los Angeles: Nash Publishers, 1974.

"Teacher Power." Interview with Albert Shanker and Emanuel Kafka. *Inside Education*. April 1971.

"Teacher Unity in New York State: A Position Paper by NYSUT." Dan McKillip's files.

Tice, Walter. Interviews with author. 2004–2005.

Toch, Thomas. "Tensions of the Shanker Era: A Speech That Shook the Field." *Education Week*. 26 March 1997.

Tyack, David B. and Larry Cuban. *Tinkering Toward Utopia: A Century of Public School Reform*. Cambridge, Massachusetts: Harvard University Press, 1995.

UFT Oral History Collection. New York: Robert F. Wagner Labor Archives, New York University, 1985. Interviews include those of George Altomare, John Bailey, Charles Cogen, Velma Hill, Roger Parente, Dan Sanders, Jeanette DiLorenzo, and others.

Urbanski, Adam. Telephone interview with author. 14 October 2005.

Verdugo, Oswaldo. "Rebuilding After Pinochet." Speech to the AFT 1990 convention. *American Educator*. Fall, 1990.

Woo, Elaine. "Al Shanker's Last Stand." *Los Angeles Times Magazine*. 1 December 1996.

Wood, James. Interview with author. Latham, New York. 3 January 2005.

INDEX

AAA (American Arbitration
Association), 109
Abzug, Bella, 164–65
Acompora, John, 156
Acompora, Karen, 156
Acompora, Louis, 156, 177
AEDs (automatic external defibrilla-
tors): described, 156; early failures
to pass legislation requiring,
156–57; Gregory Moyer's death
and lack of, 155; Moyer's appeal
to Alan Lubin on issue of,
158–59, 177, 179; New York
State school resistance to, 156;
NYSUT's support of bill requiring schools to have, 177–79
AFL (American Federation of
Labor), 11, 27–28
AFL-CIO: Carey endorsement by,
164; international democratic
principles supported by, 207;
Miami convention (1973) of,
127; pension COLA bill supported by, 173; Polish Solidarity supported by, 208; Shanker named to
executive council of, 125–26, 127
AFL-CIO affiliation: international
implications of, 204; Lambert's
attack on, 117; NEA's New
Business Item 20 forbidding,
117, 118–19, 132; NEA's position
against, 121, 123; New York
teachers decision for, 86, 87,
88–89, 110, 112; by United
Teachers of Dade, 130–31

AFL-CIO Polish Workers Aid
Fund, 208
African American community (New
York): Ocean Hill-Brownsville
conflict and, 42–44, 118, 125,
158, 159, 161; Selden and
Shanker's differences on, 125;
UFT September 9, 1968 strike
impact on, 43–44
AFSCME (American Federation of
State, County, and Municipal
Employees), 38, 70–71, 121–22,
159
AFT-Africa AIDS Campaign,
213–14
AFT (American Federation of
Teachers): affiliation between
AFL and, 11; affiliation between
Teachers Guild and, 10; AFT-
Africa AIDS Campaign, 213–14;
convention (1983) held by, 199;
legacy of, 215–16; lobbying for
teaching centers by, 188; "Making
Standards Matter" reports by,
200; membership compared to
NEA, 130; membership resurgence (1960s) of, 32; mergers
between local affiliates of NEA
and, 115; motto of, 207; move to
have NYSTA join, 77; organizing
model of, 159; petition calling for
merger with NEA, 121; prejudices afflicting, 2; "Proposal for
Joint NEA-NYSTA Projects" on,
78–79; teacher membership in

AFT (American Federation of
Teachers) *(continued)*
New York with, 67; Teachers
Under Dictatorship Committee
of, 210; TU's charter revoked by,
12
AFT Emergency Program for
AIDS Relief, 214
AFT's Black Caucus (New York),
213
Albany Times-Union (newspaper),
163
Allende, Salvador, 211
Allen, James E., Jr., 22
Allen, Robert (Bob): becomes
NYSTA teacher organizer,
36–38; concerns on teaching con-
ditions by, 29–31; on Ned
Hopkins, 89; on importance of
Taylor Law, 35–36; during NEA-
NYSTA conflict, 139–40, 141;
Rose-Dominick Bill lobbying
done by, 33–34; union activities
by, 31–32
Allen, Woody, 44, 98
Altomare, George: CATU formation
ad placed by, 20–21; early union
activities of, 13, 14, 23–24; early
union organizing efforts at NYC
high schools, 17–19; preunion
concerns at Astoria Junior High
School, 9, 10; on Shanker-Selden
conflicts, 126
Altomare, Pauline, 8, 25
Amalgamated Clothing Workers
Union, 8, 9, 25, 40
American Arbitration Association
(AAA), 109
American Civil Liberties Union, 43
American Federation of State,
County, and Municipal
Employees (AFSCME), 38,
70–71, 121–22, 159

American Federation of Teachers
(AFT). *See* AFT
American labor movement: achieve-
ments of the, 27–28; militancy
during the 1960s and early
1970s, 34–35; NYC's teachers
role in, 27; Polish group
Solidarity supported by, 207–11
The American Teacher (TU publica-
tion), 11–12
Andersen, Hans Christian, 145
"Annual Dinner Ball" (Islip Town
Republican Committee), 62
anti-teacher bills (1971): Charles
Jerabek's sponsoring of, 51–52;
defeat of, 63–64; description of
four, 49–51; introduction of
Kingston-Jerabek bill, 55;
NYSTA's fundraising for campaigning against, 54, 55–57;
NYSTA's strategy against, 54–55;
passage of original four, 55;
Shanker on successful fight
against, 74
Arteaga, Monserrat Banda, 203,
204–5, 206
Astoria Junior High School: concerns of teachers from, 9, 10, 11;
early union activities by teachers
from, 11, 14
Ast, Raymond, 32
Atlantic City convention (NEA),
115–20

Bailey, John, 18, 20–21
Bailey, Stephen K., 187–88
Baldwin Faculty Association, 146
Barrett, Catharine O'Connell, 74,
80, 90, 105, 106, 107–8, 116,
117, 121
Batemen, Charlie, 178
Bay Ridge High School (Brooklyn),
12

Beach, Marge, 116, 121

Beagle, Si, 23

Beechracft King Air (NYSUT airplane), 147

Belden, Marguerite S., 94

Benchmark Polling Group (NYSUT), 176

Benny, Jack, 98

Bethelehem Central School District, 46

Beudert, Claude, 178

Bifaro, Aaron, 178

Bifaro, Tony, 45, 176

"Big Guild, Little Guild," 16, 19

Binghamton Press, 140

Blank, Doris, 137–38

Blattman, Abel, 81

Board of Regents, 182, 184, 194

Boy Scout Handbook, 41

Brennan, Christine, 63

Bronx High School of Science, 12

Brooklyn School District, 42

Brotherhood of Sleeping Car Porters, 26, 158

Brown, Chad, 161

Brown, Frances L., 161, 213–14

Brown, Robert, 161

Brown, Shep, 161

Brydges, Earl W., 49

Buckley, James, 56, 57–58, 165

Buffalo Evening News, 87, 88, 91

Buffalo Teachers Federation (BTF): disaffiliation from NYSUT by, 142–43; Hobart as president of, 87; NYSTA local affiliate, 30

Buffalo teachers' strike (1947), 32–33

Bukowski, Robert, 45

Campaign for Fiscal Equity, 217

Capasso, Ralph, 83

CAPE (Coalition of American Public Employees), 121

Cardinali, Arthur, 146

Carey, Hugh, 164, 176, 179

Carter, Jimmy, 165

Casey, Maureen, 206

CATU (Committee for Action Through Unity), announcement of founding of, 20–21

CBTE (competency-based teacher education), 183–84

Cea, William, 75

Challenger (NYSUT newspaper): on Hobart attendance at Rockefeller dinner party, 112; on Hobart's critical view of UTNY, 79–80; on increase of serious contract disputes (1971), 46; on NYSUT-UTNY merger negotiations, 82, 84, 88, 90; photo of Hobart, Cortese, and Rodgers in, 75

CHANGE-New York, 174

charter school movement, 174–75

Chenoweth, Eric, 208

Cherrington, Robert B., 93, 137

Chilean Coalition for the NO, 212

Chilean teacher unions, 211–13

City University of New York (CUNY), 78–79

civil rights movement, 157–58

Cleary, Edward J., 167

Clinton, Bill, 157, 170, 200

Clinton, Hillary, 170, 203

Close, Nancy, 206

Cochrane, John, 63

"Coffee Cup Teachers," 75

Cogen, Charlie, 12, 21, 26, 27

COLA (cost-of-living adjustment) bill, 173–74, 180

Colegio de Profesores (Chile), 211, 212

Cole, Paul, 74, 75, 102–3, 104, 105, 108, 137, 138, 212

collective bargaining: advantages of, 16; divisional bargaining compared to, 22; NYSTA efforts to

collective bargaining *(continued)*
win right to, 33; petition calling
for national teacher, 122; Robert
Allen on lack of true, 31; Teacher
Guild's focus on, 17; Wagner Act
permitting, 16–17
Columbia University, 12
Committee in Support of Solidarity,
208
Como, Perry, 98
Competency-based teacher educa-
tion, 183–84
Concord convention. *See* NYSTA
Concord convention (1972)
Condon-Wadlin Act: Buffalo strike
(1947) triggering the, 32–33;
movement to overturn, 32; Rose-
Dominick Bill proposed to
replace, 33–34; strikes forbidden
by, 7, 22, 23, 25
Condon, William F., 32
Congress of Industrial
Organizations (CIO), 28
Conservative Party, 57–58
Cook, Clyde, 77–78, 92
Cornell University, 12
Cornick, Jessica, 193
Cortese, Antonia: during Concord
convention, 99–100, 104, 105;
elected as second vice president,
112; on Guanajuato teachers,
206; on lack of respect given to
teachers, 182; on NEA's attacks
against NYSUT, 138, 141, 142,
149; NYSTA-UTNY merger
negotiation role of, 75, 77, 78, 80,
86–87, 89, 93, 94; on NYSUT
teacher centers, 191; runs for
NEA office, 122
Costello, John, 171
Costello, Lynn: attendance at Islip
Town Republican Committee
"Annual Dinner Ball" by, 62–63;

on campiagn to defeat Jerabek,
57–59, 64; desire to improve
teacher conditions by, 52; lobbying against anti-teacher bills by,
61–62; response to anti-teacher
bills (1971) by, 51–52; teaching
career of, 49; war chest fundraising role by, 53–54, 55–56
Costello, Sharon, 61–62
CPI (Consumer Price Index), 174
Crabbe, Buster, 71
Crawford, Ronald, 140
CSEA (Independent Civil Service
Employees Association), 71
Cuomo, Mario, 165, 166, 173

D'Amato, Alfonse: attacks against
teachers by, 166–67; NYSUT's
successful campaign against elect-
ing, 167–72
Darling-Hammond, Linda, 196
Davidoff, Helen, 169
Davis, Sammy, Jr., 98
Davis, Thelma, 116
Deedy, Ken, 53, 72, 81, 90, 108,
149
democracy: American teachers' role
in rebuilding Polish, 210–11;
labor union commitment to prin-
ciples of, 207; NYSUT contribu-
tions to building, 213–14
Democratic Party, 163. *See also*
Republican Party
Densmore, Constance T., 93
Dewey, John, 185
Dial-a-Teacher program, 202
DiLorenzo, Jeannette, 23, 24, 109,
143
DiLorenzo, John, 24, 25
DiMaggio, Joe, 71
District Council 37 (AFSCME), 38
divisional bargaining strategy, 22
Dole, Bob, 167

Dolores Hidalgo (Guanajato, Mexico), 203, 204
Donahue, Kathleen, 210, 211
Donovan, James B., 42
Donovan, Marion, 188
Dowd, Bernard J., 33
Dubinsky, David, 25
Duesberg, Gary, 93
Dunn, Walter, 3, 55, 61–62, 82, 212–13
Duryea, Perry B., Jr., 60

East Islip high school meeting (1972), 55–56
education reform: achievements of, 200–202; CBTE attempt to reform teacher training, 183–84; Clinton's plan for, 200; French bread article by Shanker on, 185–86; mentoring program (NYSUT) as, 192–94; More Effective Schools (UFT program) on, 186–87; national board established as part of, 196; "A Nation at Risk" report (1983) debate on, 196–99, 216; NYSUT's push for higher standards, 194–96; as "quiet revolution in teaching," 196; Shanker on failure of UFT program, 186–87; summary of NYSUT achievements in, 201–2; teaching centers as, 187–96. *See also* teaching profession
Education Week, 200
EITA (East Islip Teachers Association), 55
Eldred, Arvis, 33
Emergency Coalition of Teacher Organizations, 55
Emergency Program for AIDS Relief (AFT), 214
Empire State Federation of Teachers (NYSFT), 46–47, 71

Empire State Plaza rally (2000), 173
ETP (Effective Teaching Program) [NYSUT], 191
Evening Press (newspaper), 73, 74
Excellence in Teaching funding (1986), 180

Farmingdale Federation of Teachers, 53
FEA (Florida Education Association), 131–32, 136–37
Feldman, Sandra, 41, 81, 167, 168, 172, 190, 197, 208, 212
Female Health Education Teachers of Bensonhurst, 15
Ferraro, Geraldine, 167, 168
Fire Fighters Association, 71
Florida Education Association (FEA), 131–32
Fordham University, 12
Fox, Vincente, 206
Frankel, Ray, 24
Franklin K. Lane High School (Queens), 17–18
French bread/education reform metaphor, 185–86
Fugle, Marcella, 51
Fuller, Paul, 94

Goldberg, Milton, 199
Goodell, Charles, 56–57
Grady, Dexter, 178
"grandmothers-and-apple-pie" respect of teachers, 29
Greater Capital Region Teacher Center, 189
Greenberg, Abe, 10
Green, Mark, 167
Greer, Virginia S., 95
Griffith, Emlyn, 182, 184
Grover Cleveland High School (Queens), 12
Guild Bulletin (AFT newspaper), 14

"Guild Coffeemobiles," 18
Guilderland Central Teachers
    Association, 138
Gumeson, George (Jerry), 116

Hanley, James M., 106
Harriman, E. H., 85
Harris, Jim, 135
Harris poll on possible NYSUT
    split (1976), 139
Hechinger, Fred M., 15
Hedstrom, Carl E., 74, 75
Herndon, Terry, 146
Hickman, Roberta, 116
Hirsch, E. D., Jr., 200
Hobart, Thomas (Tom), Jr.: CBTE
    reform opposed by, 183–84; on
    collapse of NEA-AFT negotia-
    tions, 129; concerns following
    NYSTA-UTNY merger
    approval, 110; during Concord
    convention, 98, 99, 104, 105, 106,
    108; criticism of Shanker during
    merger negotiations by, 79–80;
    early union participation by, 30;
    elected new president, 111–12;
    exploring of merger issue by,
    77–78; friction between Frank
    White and, 80; international
    union activities by, 204, 212, 213;
    legacy of, 216; on NEA's attacks
    against NYSUT, 135, 136–37,
    138, 139, 147–48, 149; New York
    Teacher article on merger by, 132;
    as NYSTA leader, 61, 74–75;
    NYSTA-UTNY merger negoti-
    ating role by, 81, 83–85, 86,
    90–95; response to Riesel's col-
    umn attacking power of NYSUT,
    164; retirement of, 215; role in
    Schumer's election by, 172;
    Sanders' challenge to presidency
    of, 149–50

Hochberg, Samuel, 18, 20
Hofstra University rally (1971), 56
Hopkins, Ned, 81, 88, 89, 102, 146
Horowitz, Seymour R., 93
HSTA (High School Teachers
    Association): higher pay demands
    of, 17–18; proposed merger
    between Teacher Guild and,
    19–21; support of Jamaica High
    School wildcat teachers' strike
    (1959) by, 18–19
Hubbard, Howard, 205
Hughes, Denis, 173, 203

Independent Civil Service
    Employees Association (CSEA),
    71
Inside Education (publication), 69
International Brotherhood of
    Electrical Workers, 25
International Ladies Garment
    Workers Union (ILGWU), 25
international teacher solidarity:
    Chilean union rights and,
    211–13; Mexican teachers and
    and, 204–5; NYSUT's link to,
    203–14, 217; Polish group
    Solidarity as part of, 207–11
Israel, David, 171

J.&J. Clothing, 8
Jamaica High School (Queens), 18
Jaruzelski, Wojciech, 207
Javits, Jacob, 57
Jerabek, Charles A.: anger against
    lobbying teachers by, 61; anti-
    teacher bills (1971) sponsored by,
    2, 51–52; on efficacy of NYSTA's
    strategy, 54–55; election defeat
    of, 63; end of political career of,
    64; NYSTA Concord convention
    award to, 109; professional back-
    ground of, 51; Republican Party

refuses to endorse, 62; Shanker on successful fight against, 74; teacher's campaign to defeat election of, 57–58

Jewish teachers and community (New York), 43–44

JHS 142 (Red Hook), 24

Joan of Arc Junior High School (Manhattan), 19

Junior High School 73 (Bedford-Stuyvesant), 7, 8

Kafka, Emanuel (Manny), 45, 53, 55, 56, 57, 69–70, 71–73, 86, 99

Kennedy, John F., 28

Kerry, John, 157

Kessler, Ann, 158

Kingston-Jerabek bill (1971), 55

Kingston, John, 55

Kirkland, Lane, 208

Koch, Ed, 165

Kolodny, Jules, 21

Kulerski, Wiktor, 211

LaBombard, Donald, 142

Labor-Religion Coalition, 205–6

LaFleur, Andrea, 177–78, 179

Lambert, Fred, 52, 53

Lambert, Sam, 116–17

Legislation. *See* New York state legislation

Lehman, Herbert, 26

LFT (Levittown Federation of Teachers), 83

"lighthouse contracts," 45

Lindsay, John, 34, 35, 57

Lockman, Monroe, 27

Lopez, Ed, 55, 61–62

Loria, Maria, 171

Lubin, Alan: on charter school bill, 175; pension reform activities by, 172–74; Rachel Moyer's appeal to, 158–59, 177, 179; Reject

D'Amato campaign role by, 167–72; Shanker's influence on, 157–58; teaching career and early union activities of, 157–58

Lubin, Irving, 172–73

Lux, Jean, 181, 187, 191, 192, 193

McCoy, Rhody, 42

MacDougal, Roy, 57

McGovern, George, 63, 125

McKillip, Dan, 106, 108, 140, 147

McLaughlin, Brian M., 167

McPhail, Rev. Donald, 63

Madison Square Garden rally (1967), 38

Magidson, Herb, 162, 210, 212

"Magna Carta of Labor," 17

"Making Standards Matter" reports (AFT), 200

Maletta, Nick, 60

Mandela, Nelson, 213

March for Public Education (2003), 175–76

Marsh, Alice, 19

Marx, Karl, 120

Maslinoff, Martin, 83

Matarazzo, Ciro, 93, 94

Matousek, Doug, 94, 97–98, 99, 106

Matousek, Sylvia, 31

May 17, 1960 teacher's strike, 22–25, 204

Meany, George, 117, 125, 138, 139, 207

Mechanics Educational Society of America (MESA), 86

Melley, Ken, 132, 141

Mentoring program (NYSUT), 192–94

Mexican SITESABES (teachers' union), 205–7

Miller, David, 52

Miller, Nancy Barth, 178

Mills, Richard, 202

Mondale, Walter, 165
More Effective Schools (UFT program), 186–87
Morrison, Don, 119
Morrison, Robert, 63
Mosle, Sara, 185
"The Most Unbelievable Thing" (Andersen fairy tale), 145
Moyer, Abbie, 155
Moyer, Gregory, 155, 156, 177
Moyer, John, 155
Moyer, Rachel: appeal to Alan Lubin by, 158–59, 177, 179; early efforts to bring AEDs into schools, 156–57; on success of school AEDs in saving lives, 178–79; suffers loss of her son, 155
Moynihan, Daniel P., 165, 185
Museum of Natural History, 214

National Assessment of Educational Progress (NAEP), 201
National Board for Professional Teaching Standards, 202
National Coalition of Teacher Unity (NCTU), 121
National Commission on Excellence in Education, 196
National Council of Urban Education Associations (NCUEA), 121
National Labor Relations Act of 1935 (Wagner Act), 16–17, 23
national merger movement: Florida teacher's supporting, 130–32; growing interest in, 115; NEA Atlantic City (1972) discussions on, 115–20; New Business Item 10 (NEA Atlantic convention) role in, 117, 118–19, 132. See also NEA-AFT negotiations
National Teachers Association (1857), 97

"A Nation at Risk" report (1983), 196–99, 216
Nation's Report Card, 201
Nauman, Fred, 7, 8, 24, 25, 41–42, 212
Nauman, Judie, 7
NCTU (National Coalition of Teacher Unity), 121, 122–23
NCUEA (National Council of Urban Education Associations), 121
NEA-AFT negotiations: collapse of, 129–30; Selden's role during, 123–25, 126–27, 128; Shanker's comments on future of merger, 126; Shanker's role during, 128, 129. See also national merger movement
NEA (National Education Association): adoption of union tactics by, 215–16; affiliation with AFL, 11; AFL-CIO affiliation opposed by, 121; Atlantic City convention (1972) of, 115–20; attempts to muzzle pro-merger forces by, 132–33; conflict between FEA (Florida Education Association) and, 131–32; conflict and split within NYSUT and, 135–44; hostility toward New York teachers by, 118, 119–20, 123; international affiliation of, 203–4; lobbying for teaching center funding, 188; membership compared to AFT, 130; merges between local affiliates of AFT and, 115; "militant" membership supporting national merger, 121; move to establish New York State affiliate by, 139–42; "A Nation at Risk" report denounced by, 198; NCUEA group within, 121; NEA-AFT negotiations, 123–33;

negative perspective on NYSUT by, 135–37; NYSTA affiliation with, 30; NYSUT challenged by NYEA support by, 143–44, 146–49; origins of, 97; petition calling for merger with AFT, 121; prejudices afflicting, 2; TBO (Teachers Bargaining Organization) alliance created by, 26; teacher membership of, 67

Neira, Maria, 191

New Business Item 10 (NEA Atlantic convention), 117, 118–19, 132

New Compact for Learning (1991), 200

Newell, Gladys, 36

The New Republic (publication), 185

Newsday, 62, 88

Newsweek magazine, 201

New York: disruptive labor strikes (1966) in NYC, 34–35; *Education Week* on high education standards of, 200; Excellence in Teaching funding (1986) boosting salaries of, 180; NEA's move to establish affiliate in, 139–42; NYSUT's role in gubernatorial race (1974), 164–66; results of education reform in, 201. *See also* political arena

New York Board of Regents, 182, 184, 194

New York Central Labor Council, 167

New York City Board of Education: divisions among teachers encouraged by, 15; successful negotiations of UFT with, 26–27; on treatment of teacher's pregnancy, 31; UFT demands presented to, 21–22; unresolved conflict between teachers and, 7

New York City teachers: antiunionists among, 14–15; asked to leave in case of pregnancy, 31; Condon-Wadlin Act forbidding strikes by, 7–8, 22, 23, 25, 32, 33–34; early union negotiations on behalf of, 26–28; ethnic and religious differences among, 14–15; impact of Taylor law on rights of, 34–38; as inside players in New York politics, 112; interest in national merger movement by, 115, 120–21; NEA hostility toward, 118, 119–20, 123; night school, 18–19; pension reform on behalf of, 171–74; political impotence (1970s) of, 67; support of Mario Cuomo by, 165–66; TU members (1930s) among, 12. *See also* paraprofessionals; political arena; teachers; teaching profession

New York Congress of Teachers, 110

New York Herald Tribune, 43

New York Post, 144

New York School Boards Association, 159, 177

New York State Education, 53

New York state legislation: Condon-Wadlin Act, 7, 22, 23, 25, 32–34; New Compact for Learning (1991), 200; passage of anti-teacher bills (1971), 55; proposed weakening of tenure law, 50–51; requiring AEDs in schools, 177–79; Rose-Dominick Bill, 33–34; summary of NYSUT's contributions to, 179–80; 12-for-10 law (1989), 180. *See also* political arena; Taylor Law (1967)

New York State Teachers Association (NYSTA). *See* NYSTA

New York State Teachers'
Retirement System, 172
New York State United Teachers
(NYSUT) *See* NYSUT
New York Teacher (NYSUT), 132,
138, 139, 170, 184
New York Times: ad supporting UFT
in, 26; condemning Buffalo
teacher's strike, 33; on crippling
transit worker strike (1966), 35;
on "A Nation at Risk" report,
197; on NYSTA-UFT campaign
against Kingston-Jerabek bill, 55;
on NYSUT as major political
power, 163; photograph of
Shanker's good-bye kiss to wife,
39; Selden on national merger
movement, 115; Shanker on education reform efforts, 184–85;
Shanker's comments on political
influence of NYSUT in, 170;
"Teach or Wash Cars" editorial
of, 10; Where We Stand column
of, 162–63, 184–86, 195, 196
New York World Telegram & Sun, 20
night school teachers: raised wages
of, 19; strike by, 18–19
Nixon, Richard, 63
North Syracuse Central School
District, 31
NYEA (New York Educators
Association): end of challenge by,
148–49; establishment of,
143–44; recruitment from
NYSUT by, 146–48
NYSFT (New York State
Federation of Teachers), 46–47,
71
NYSTA Concord convention
(1972): anti-merger delegates
support of Barrett during, 105–8;
Barrett's speech during, 107–8;
Cole Resolution vote during,

108–9; merger discussion during,
99–105; opening of, 97, 98–99;
resolution to honor Jerabek during, 109
NYSTA Montreal convention
(1973), 111–12
NYSTA (New York State Teachers
Association): annual convention
meeting (1971) of, 72–74;
Challenger newspaper of, 46, 75,
79, 82, 84, 88, 90, 105; competition between Empire State
Federation of Teachers and,
46–47; conflict between UTNY
and, 52–53; fundraising for political campaigns by, 54, 55–57;
impact of Taylor Law on, 37–38;
lobbying coordination between
UFT and, 55; negotiations with
UTNY that led to the merger
forming NYSUT, 77–95;
NYSTA-UTNY merger
approved by membership of,
109–10; proposed merger
between UTNY and, 68–72;
research done on teacher work
conditions by, 44–45; Resolution
C. 63 by, 74; response to anti-
teacher bills (1971) by, 50–51;
response to Taylor Law by, 35–36
NYSTA-UTNY merger: chronology
of, 113; Concord convention discussions on, 99–108; creative
compromises during, 85–86; ini-
tial discussions leading to, 77–80;
jurisdictional battles during,
82–85; Montreal convention
(1973) following, 111–12; negotiating teams during, 80–82;
NYSTA board's disapproval of,
91–95; NYSTA and UTNY
membership approval of merger,
110; organized labor affiliation

roadblock to, 86–90; press conference (1972) on, 90–91. *See also* UTNY (United Teachers of New York)

NYSUT Committee of 100, 216

NYSUT (New York State United Teachers): AED bill supported by, 177–79; Buffalo Teachers Federation's vote to disaffiliate from, 142–43; CBTE reform opposed by, 183–84; Chilean teacher unions supported by, 212–13; collective bargaining right won by, 33; complaints about leadership of, 52–53; conflict and split with NEA and, 135–44; continuing internal divisions (late 1970s) within, 149–51; democracy building by, 213–14; higher professional standards pushed by, 194–96; increased membership following merger approval, 110–11; international solidarity practiced by, 203–14, 217; legacy of, 215–17; lobbying for teaching centers by, 188–89; as major political power, 163; mentoring program by, 192–94; motion preventing NYSUT officers advocating mergers, 132–33; "A Nation at Risk" report response by, 198–99; NEA's negative perspective of, 135–37; New York State's gubernatorial race (1974) and, 164–66; *New York Teacher* published by, 132, 138, 139, 170, 184; NYEA's challenge to, 143–44, 146–49; overriding governor's veto of education funds (2003), 175–77; pension system established by, 172; pension system reform pushed by, 172–74; Polish Solidarity supported by, 208; position on charter school bill by, 174–75; Reject D'Amato campaign by, 167–72; summary of educational achievements of, 201–2; summary of political victories won by, 179–80; teacher membership with, 67; teaching centers launched by, 191–92; unionist culture of, 135; the unique history of, 1–3; VOTE (Voice of Teachers for Education) committee of, 53, 54, 55, 56, 59

Ocean Hill-Brownsville conflict, 42–44, 118, 125, 158, 159, 161

O'Neil, John J., 43

Owego Elementary School, 181, 192–94

Pace, Anthony (Tony), 58, 59, 60, 62

Paliwodzinski, Robert, 122–23, 141, 144, 149

paraprofessionals: evolution into teacher training program, 162; NYSUT inclusion of, 159–60; release time with pay program for, 161–62; UFT debate over inclusion of, 160–62. *See also* New York City teachers; teachers

Parente, Roger, 18, 20

Pataki, George, 174, 175

PELA (Public Employees Legislative), 70

pension reform, 171–74, 180

Peterson, Donald, 106

Pinochet, Augusto, 211, 212, 213

Pisa, Thomas, 91, 92, 105, 143

Policemen's Benevolent Association, 71

Polish group Solidarity, 207–11

political arena: building teacher union influence in the, 162–66; CBTE

political arena *(continued)*
reform, 183–84; charter school issue in, 174–75; COLA bill pension reform, 171–74, 180; Conservative Party and Republican Party roles in, 57–59; defeat of anti-teacher bills, 63–64; early failures to pass AED bills, 156–57; education reform, 183–202; efforts to defeat Jerabek, 57–58, 62, 63–64; NYSUT's role in gubernatorial race (1974), 164–66; NYSUT's successful campaign against electing D'Amato, 167–72; NYSUT's support of AED bill, 177–79; overriding governor's veto of education funds (2003), 175–77; response to anti-teacher bills (1971) proposed in, 49–52, 54, 55–57; Shanker on importance of teachers in, 163; summary of NYSUT's political victories in the, 179–80; teacher response to anti-teacher bills (1971), 49–55; teachers as inside players in New York, 112. *See also* New York; New York City teachers; New York state legislation
Porter, Judy, 189–90
Potofsky, Jacob, 25
Presidential Order 10988, 28
Project TEACH (NYSUT), 191
"Proposal for Joint NEA-NYSTA Projects," 78–79
Prudenti, Tony, 59
Public Employees Fair Employment Act, 35
Public Employees Legislative Alliance (PELA), 70–71
Public Employment Relations Board (PERB) bill (1977), 179
Public Employment Relations Board (PERB). *See* Taylor Law (1967)

Public School 100 (Queens), 24
Public School 165 (Upper West Side), 24

"quiet revolution in teaching," 196
Quill, Mike, 39

Raccuia, Chuck, 93
Randolph, A. Philip, 26, 127, 158
Reagan, Ronald, 188, 196, 197, 208
Regents Action Plan (1984), 202
Regents Review Live, 202
Reject D'Amato campaign (NYSUT), 167–72
Republican Party: approach to help defeat Jerabek, 58–60; refusal to endorse Jerabek, 62; ties between teacher unions and, 163. *See also* Democratic Party
Resolution C. 63 (UTNY), 74
Riesel, Victor, 163
Robisch, Edwin, 75
Rockefeller, Nelson, 35, 44, 49, 57, 164
Rodgers, Ed, 75, 78, 86, 89, 93, 112, 149
Rogers, Will, 13
Rome Daily Sentinel, 38
Rome Teachers Association, 29–30, 31
Roosevelt, Eleanor, 26
Roosevelt, Franklin Delano, 40
Rose-Dominick Bill, 33–34
Rosengarten, Stanley, 45
Ruehle, Sue, 155
Rustin, Bayard, 157, 161
Ryor, John, 136, 137, 138, 142, 144

SABES program (Mexico), 204, 205
St. Nicholas Area rally, 20
salary/wage issue. *See* teacher salaries
Sanders, Dan: challenge to Hobart's presidency by, 149–50; early

union activities of, 13, 14; elected secretary-treasurer, 112; at NYSTA Syracuse convention, 73; NYSTA-UTNY merger role by, 81, 85; political party connections encouraged by, 163; preunion concerns of, 9, 10

Sanders, Elaine, 14

Sano, Joseph, 138

Sano, Josephine, 138

Santelli, Chuck, 182, 186–87, 199

Schneider, Judy, 178

School Boards Association, 159, 177

school voucher movement, 175

Schumer, Charles, 168, 169, 170, 171, 203

Schweissing, Emil, 109

Scott, Millard, 32

Seaver, Tom, 71

Selden, David: "Big Guild, Little Guild" argument by, 19; early union work of, 13, 23–24; estrangement between Shanker and, 125–26, 127–28; facing antiunionists among teachers, 14–15; focus on collective bargaining of, 17; national merger negotiation role of, 123–25; national merger strategy by, 120–21; national merger supported by, 115; NEA-AFT negotiation role of, 123–25, 126–27, 128; NYSTA-UTNY merger supported by, 91; regarding his dream of teacher merger, 130; strategies to increase Guild membership by, 16–17

Shanker, Adam, 43

Shanker, Albert: becomes national symbol of teacher militancy, 42–44; charter school movement role of, 174; on collapse of NEA-AFT negotiations, 129; on democratic principles and unionism, 207; early childhood and education of, 40–41; early union activities of, 12, 13; efforts to increase political influence of teachers by, 67–68; elected as UTNY president, 71–72; Emergency Coalition of Teacher Organizations role by, 55; estrangement between Selden and, 125–26, 127–28; found in contempt for organizing strike, 38–39; Hobart's criticism of negotiations with, 79–80; on importance of teachers involvement in political arena, 163; influence on Alan Lubin by, 157–58; on lack of respect by administrators for teachers, 182; legacy left by, 199–200, 215, 216–17; on "A Nation at Risk" report, 198–99, 216–17; NEA hostility toward, 118, 119, 135–36; NYSTA-UTNY merger negotiating role of, 81–82, 85, 86, 88, 90–95, 99, 100, 101–2, 110; Ocean Hill-Brownsville conflict role of, 42–44, 118, 125, 158, 159, 161; paraprofessional release time program promoted by, 161–62; on persecution for being Jewish, 40; physical and personal characteristics of, 39, 42; on Polish Solidarity movement, 209–10; predictions on impact of NYSTA-UTNY merger, 110–11; preunion concerns of, 9, 10; proposed UTNY-NYSTA merger by, 68–72; reaction to NEA-NYSUT conflicts, 141; response to Sanders' candidacy, 149–50; on solidarity of unionism, 204, 217; speech regarding May 17th 1960

Shanker, Albert *(continued)*
strike, 22–23; speech to
NYSUT's delegates about con-
flict with NEA (1976), 144–46;
on successful fight against
Jerabek/anti-teacher bills, 74;
suggests Hobart as president,
111–12; on teacher participation
in negotiations, 27; teaching cen-
ters promoted by, 187–88; Where
We Stand column written by,
162–63, 184–86, 195, 196
Shanker, Eadie, 39
Shanker, Mamie, 8, 9, 14, 25, 40
Sherman, David, 190
Simmons, Margaret A., 93, 95
Simonson, Rebecca, 12, 19
SITESABES (Mexican teachers'
union), 205–7
Skuse, Ray, 57, 163
Slater, Gary, 140–41
Sleeper (film), 44
Slotkin, Carol, 210, 211
Sobol, Thomas, 200
"Solidarity Forever" (labor hymn),
120
Sordid Friday (1971), 50, 53, 54
Soviet Union: Polish Solidarity
movement against, 207–10; role
of labor in fall of, 209
Sparber, Susan, 171
Spaulding, Francis, 33
Squillace, Frank, 141
Stam, John, 9
Stavisky-Goodman Bill, 179
Streiff, Dean, 36, 103
strikes. *See* teachers' strikes
SUNY, 148

Taylor, George, 35
Taylor Law (1967): Ed Koch's support of increased penalties under,
165–66; on fines for striking
teachers, 53; harsher strike penalties added (1969) to, 44; loophole
allowing school board to be final
contract arbitrator, 45; Madison
Square Garden rally (1967)
protesting, 38; passage of, 35–36;
repeal of one-year probation
penalty of, 179; significance for
teachers and schools, 36–38;
Triborough Amendment (1982)
to, 179. *See also* New York state
legislation
Teacher Education, Certification,
and Practice Board, 182, 184
The Teacher Rebellion (Selden),
120–21
teachers: appeal for revised self-
image of, 11–12; "Coffee Cup
Teachers," 75; Florida, 130–32,
136–37; historic poor working
conditions/low pay of, 9–10;
national merger movement by,
115; petition call for national
negotiations by, 122. *See also* New
York City teachers; paraprofessionals; teaching profession
teacher sabbaticals, 49
teacher salaries: anti-teacher bill
(1971) eliminating minimum,
49–50; climb from 1962 to 1973
of, 69; Excellence in Teaching
funding increase (1986), 180; historically low, 9–10, 52; increased
for night school teachers, 19;
Selden's proposal to win increase
of, 19; UFT success in raising,
26–27
"Teacher's Blues" (song), 16
Teachers Guild: "Big Guild, Little
Guild" paper, 16; collective bargaining focus of, 16–17; offices
of, 10–11; organizing get-togethers of, 16; origins of, 12, 215;

proposed merger between HSTA and, 19–21; Sheldon's strategies to build membership of, 16–17; support of Jamaica High School's strikers, 18–19

Teachers' Recognition Day proposed strike (1960), 22

teachers' strikes: Buffalo teachers' strike (1947), 32–33; Condon-Wadlin Act forbidding, 7–8, 22, 23, 25, 32, 33–34; "Guild Coffeemobiles" providing coffee at, 18; Jamaica High School (Queens), 18; November 7, 1960, 7–8, 22–25, 204; Taylor Law on fines given to teachers for, 53; teachers sent to jail (1970) for, 45; UFT September 9, 1968, 43–44; by UFT under Taylor Law, 38–39

Teachers Under Dictatorship Committee (AFT), 210

Teachers Union (TU), 11–12

teacher tenure issue, 49, 50–51

teaching centers: description of, 189–90; New York establishment of, 189; NYSUT approach to, 191–92; proposed as education reform, 187–88; UFT approach to, 190–91

teaching profession: attrition rate of, 191–92; CBTE attempt to reform teacher training, 183–84; Costello on lack of respect given to, 52; "grandmothers-and-apple-pie" respect given to, 29; international solidarity of, 203–14; lack of respect by administrators for, 182; lack of structured mentoring in, 181; NYSUT's push for higher standards for, 194–96. *See also* education reform; New York City teachers; teachers

"Teach or Wash Cars" (*New York Times* editorial), 10

Tedesco, Delores, 9

Thaler, Dick, 9

Thearle, George, 192, 194

Theobald, John J., 7, 8, 20, 21, 22, 25

Theodore Roosevelt High School (Bronx), 18

Threatt, Dan, 56

Tice, Walter, 67, 68, 69, 81, 86, 111, 116, 119, 122

Tornillo, Pat, 130

Trachtenberg, Ely, 16, 19

transit worker strike (1966), 34–35

Transport Workers' Union, 38

Triangle Shirtwaist Factory, 8

Triangle Shirtwaist Factory fire (1911), 8–9

Triborough Amendment (1982) [Taylor Law], 179

12-for-10 law (1989), 180

UFT (United Federation of Teachers): conflict between Ocean Hill-Brownsville governing board and, 42–44; debate over expanding membership to paraprofessionals, 159–61; established as voice for all NYC teachers, 26; founding of, 21, 215; increased membership (1960s) of, 32; list of contract demands presented in 1960 by, 21–22; lobbying cooperation between NYSTA and, 55; More Effective Schools program by, 186–87; NEA as rival union to, 26; need to expand influence of, 67; paraprofessionals included in membership of, 159–62; Polish Solidarity supported by, 208; proposed merger between NYSTA and, 68–72; September 9, 1968

UFT (United Federation of Teachers) *(continued)* strike by, 43–44; strike under Taylor Law by, 38–39; successful negotiations with Board of Education by, 26–27; teaching centers established by, 190–91; *The United Teacher* paper of, 23; UTNY statewide organization of, 52

unions: AFL-CIO, 125–26, 127, 164, 173, 207, 208; Amalgamated Clothing Workers Union, 8, 9, 25, 40; American Federation of State, County, and Municipal Employees (AFSCME), 38, 70–71, 121–22, 159; American labor movement and, 27–28, 207–11; Brotherhood of Sleeping Car Porters, 26, 158; CATU (Committee for Action Through Unity), 20–21; CSEA (Independent Civil Service Employees Association), 71; Fire Fighters Association, 71; International Brotherhood of Electrical Workers, 25; International Ladies Garment Workers Union (ILGWU), 25; Mechanics Educational Society of America (MESA), 86; Policemen's Benevolent Association, 71; Presidential Order 10988 allowing public employee, 28; Transport Workers' Union, 38. *See also specific teacher unions*

United Federation of Teachers, *See* UFT, 32

United Teachers of Dade, 130–31

The United Teacher (UFT paper), 23

Urbanski, Adam, 208, 210

UTNY (United Teachers of New York): conflict between NYSTA and, 52–53; merger brokered between NYSTA and, 77; NYSTA-UTNY merger approved by membership, 110; "Proposal for Joint NEA-NYSTA Projects" on, 78–79; Shanker's election to presidency of, 71–72. *See also* NYSTA-UTNY merger

UUP (United University Professionals), 148

Van Arsdale, Harry, 25

Verdugo, Oswaldo, 211–12

Vietnam War, 125

VOTE (Voice of Teachers for Education): contributions to defeat Jerabek by, 60; funds raised by, 53, 54, 55, 56, 59

wage/salary issue. *See* teacher salaries

Wagner Act (1935), 16–17, 23

Wagner, Robert F., Jr., 23, 25

Walesa, Lech, 207, 209, 211

Wellbourn, Penny, 189–90

Wenzle, Ted, 71

West Babylon Teachers Association, 56

Where We Stand column (*New York Times*): influence of Shanker's, 184–86; on national certification standards, 195, 196; on political achievements by teachers, 162–63

White, Francis J. (Frank), 57, 80–81, 90

Whitelaw, Dave, 94

Wilkomirska, Wanda, 208

Willette, Lee, 74

Wilson, Harry, 54

Wilson, Malcolm, 112

Wise, Helen, 129, 130
Wittes, David, 23
Wood, Jimmy, 75, 139, 150
World Confederation of
  Organizations of the Teaching
  Profession, 204
Wynn, Lauri, 118, 142

YFT (Yonkers Federation of
  Teachers), 67
Young People's Socialist League, 41
Yules, Herb, 178

Zogby, John, 166
Zwick, Edward, 109